Time
Basics

Jim Muncy

Few Keys
Valdosta, GA

ISBN: 978-0-9722197-1-6

Few Keys
Valdosta, GA

Table of Contents

This book is dedicated to all my students past, present, and future. You teach me more than I could ever teach you.

Everything Starts With the Basics

How legendary football coach Vince Lombardi would start out his first practice of every season has become almost as famous as he was. He would bring his team together, hold up a football, and exclaim, "Gentlemen, this is a football." He obviously didn't do that to let these seasoned football players in on a secret. In their decades of playing the game, they had figured out what a football looked like. He did so to make a point. *Everything starts with the basics.* No matter how experienced or skilled you are at something, you should never forget the basics.

What is true in athletics is even truer in academics. If you wanted to be a doctor, where would your education begin? Would you start by learning what prescriptions to write for what symptoms? No, before you would study medicine you would need to learn the basics on which medicine is based. You would first learn biology and chemistry. Only after studying the basics of science would you be truly ready to learn medicine. Or what if you wanted to be an engineer? Would you begin your education by learning how to design bridges? No, you would start by studying the basics on which engineering is based. You would first learn calculus and physics. Without a firm grasp of these basics, none of the other things you might learn in engineering would make much sense.

So whether it is football, medicine, engineering, or anything else you may want to master, it all starts with a firm grasp of the basics. That is why we are going to look at the twenty-four time basics in this book. Time is limited and everything we do takes some of it from us. Thus, time management is the one thing that we must master in order to master anything else. We will look at the basics that all those who effectively manage their time understand.

Why Don't We Study Time Management?

Most people feel like they need to do a better job managing their time. People I meet often ask me what I do for a living. When I tell them that I am a professor, the obvious follow-up question they ask is what I teach. I tell them that I teach in the College of Business and then I list out my classes. I tell them that I teach selling and I see them hiding their wallets. I tell them I teach computers in marketing and they yawn. Then I tell them that I teach time management and, almost without exception, they say "I need to take that class." When I tell them that I wrote a book on time management, they always say, "I need to read that book." So why don't they? Everyone seems to know they need to read a book on time management but so few do. Why? I think I figured it out the very first semester I taught my time management class.

I knew that different people have different time management challenges so I thought I would approach the whole semester from that perspective. The very first class period, I divided the students into four groups based on their personality types. You may be familiar with the four basic personality types that date all the way back to Hippocrates. One type is fun loving, one is demanding, one is laid-back, and one is careful. I did an exercise where students were sent to the four corners of the classroom based on their personality type. I knew what percentages to expect. If my class was anything like the general population, the smallest group would be the demanding group followed by the careful ones. The largest two groups would be the fun loving ones and laid back ones. It didn't turn out that way.

In one corner was about eighty percent of the class. They were the careful, cautious types. Hippocrates called these people "melancholies". These are the "Life is to be organized and perfection is to be demanded" people of the world. They feel best when everything in their lives is in perfect order. They love to have all their ducks in a row and quacking in unison. If you don't know who they are, go to an accounting convention. You will find plenty of melancholies. We want our accountants to be very organized and careful. The last thing I want to hear my accountant say is, "I just don't know where all the money went." The world needs some of us to be melancholies but it doesn't need us all to be so. They make up about twenty-five percent of the population. That is why it surprised me that they were the vast majority of students in that class.

In contrast, I only had two students who were what Hippocrates called sanguines. This is actually the most common personality type of the four. Sanguines are the fun-loving, life is a party types. They are more people oriented and less task oriented. As a group, they typically are too busy having fun to stay organized. Again I was surprised that there were only two fun-loving sanguines in the whole class, especially given that they are the biggest group in the general population.

So there I was trying to figure out why my numbers were all off. Had I messed up in how I helped my students identify their personality? Did I actually send people to the correct corners? What went wrong? As I looked at these students, here is what I saw. In one corner of the classroom I saw all these melancholies looking well-kept and standing in perfect order. Across the room in the other corner, I saw these two sanguines wondering when we would get done so that they could go play. It dawned on me why my portions of personality types were so different from the general population.

Who signs up for a class on time management? It's not the fun-loving sanguines. They see a class on time management, their eyes glaze over, and they think, "There's not going to be any fun there." I had two poor sanguines in the class and the only reason they were there is that they couldn't fit any other class into their schedule. But the serious, well-organized melancholies saw a time management class and thought, "Oh boy, we get class credit for organizing everything!" That's about like signing up a squirrel for a class on gathering nuts. It is what they were made to do. Organizing is woven into their very being.

A Book for Everyone

From that class, I had the epiphany experience from which this book was born. I realized why so many people want to get a handle on their time but so few actually do. I realized why everyone knows they need a book on time management but few people will actually read one. I thought back to all the books I had read on time management and they were almost all the same.

Who writes books about time management? The Perfect Paula's of the world. They love to have control over every square inch of their world. They love to think about how to organize things. Since the ultimate organization challenge is managing one's time, they write time management books. Nothing would be better for them than to share with the world all their great ideas about how to squeeze a little more order into a twenty-four hour day.

Who reads books on time management? It isn't the fun-loving sanguine types. They would put a book on how to gain order in their lives in the same category as a book on how to clean the wax out of their ears—potentially useful but not very interesting. Obviously it is the perfectionist melancholies who would buy and actually read books on time management. They would love to find a better way to categorize their business cards and organize their in-box.

So most of the time management books are written by melancholies for melancholies. That's fine for the melancholies of the world. But what about the rest of us? We also need to manage our time, just not in a melancholy sort of way. How do we get a better handle on our time? Unless you are absolutely obsessed with order, then you need a different type of book on time management than you typically can find. Hopefully this is that book. Even if you love books on how to order your life, this book has a lot to offer you. Because it does take a different approach to managing your time, it can provide something many other books do not.

Managing Your Life Not My System

This book isn't meant to simply give you a better feeling of control. It is meant to give you a better life. As I said earlier, everyone tells me that they need to take my class on time management. Not many of them say that because they want to find better ways to organize their schedule. Most of them feel as though there are some great things in life they are missing out on because of how they spend their time. If they could just get a better handle on their time, they could get to the things that matter most to them. They could spend more time with their families. Their careers would take off. They could get to that hobby or sport that they haven't had time for. They would be able to exercise and live a healthier life. They wouldn't have to feel as guilty because of the important things that never make it onto their schedule. They might even have some time to stop and smell the roses.

In this book, I won't give you a one-size-fits all time management system. Such systems violate Steven Covey's admonition to "diagnose before you prescribe." Covey gave a great example of how one-size-fits-all solutions don't work. Let's say I went to my eye doctor because things were looking a little blurry. I tell him my problem and he says, "You know, I had the same problem until I got these glasses." Then he pulls his glasses off of his face and puts them on mine. "There, you should be fine." How much do you think his glasses will solve my eye problem? There is a small chance that they will work. There is a much greater chance that his glasses would make my vision worse. Unless we just happen to have the same vision challenges, I cannot improve my eyesight by simply wearing his glasses.

Seeing Our Differences

In a similar way, my time management solutions won't fix your time management challenges. There are three reasons why not. We don't share the same personality, profession, or position in life. Let's look at these three differences between us. By doing so, we will see why the dream of a packaged time management system is an elusive one.

Personality

We have already seen the first of these reasons. We don't all have the same personalities and so we don't all have the same time challenges. A detailed system with lots of boxes to check and columns to fill might excite the melancholies of the world. It wouldn't be nearly as exciting for the rest of us. It would make a sanguine's eyes glaze over. Only a few people are really built for the complex time management systems I see being advocated in many books. Still, people of all personality types need some way to effectively manage their time. They just need an approach that fits who they are.

Profession

The second reason why my time management system probably wouldn't work for you is that you probably aren't a college professor. As a professor, I have professor time challenges. They are different than the time challenges faced by salespeople, accountants, doctors, administrative assistants, high school teachers… I don't even have the same time challenges as many other college professors. I spent much of my academic career teaching at research schools—University of Oklahoma, Texas Tech, and Clemson. I had to center all of my time around my research. After several years of doing that, I wanted to experience the applied side of business. I moved to Valdosta State which is a balanced school. I still do research but I also have more time to work on side business ventures. When I moved from research schools to a balanced school, my time challenges changed. At the first three schools where I taught, the challenge was to throw everything out that interfered with my research. Since I have been at Valdosta State, my challenge has been to balance my teaching, research, and outside engagement activities so as to not let one short-change the others.

Place in Life

The third reason my system might not work for you is that you may not be in the same place in life that I am. I actually tried teaching my time management system to my college students. That was another class activity that didn't work out like I expected. I was in the middle of raising four children and I had to fit my big family in with everything else I was doing. When I forced my students to try my system, the most common comment I received was, "I see how this would work for you but I don't see how it fits my life." I thought I could help them with what worked for me but I didn't diagnose before I prescribed.

You Need a System

Don't get me wrong. I am not against systems. There is a whole section of this book that focuses on developing a time management system. Neither am I against books that teach specific time management systems. I have read many such books and I have benefited greatly from them. They have given me a lot of good ideas for how to develop my time management system. I would strongly encourage you to read books on time management that lay out specific systems. I believe you could gain a lot from them. I am simply saying that I don't believe in one-size-fits-all time management systems. Because of different personalities, professional demands, and places in life, different systems are needed for different people. Thus, we each need to develop a system that fits our own unique needs.

Since we each need our own unique system, we need to know how to build one. How do we build a time management system? The same way we build anything. We start by building a foundation. Think of what Coach Lombardi was saying to his players when he would proclaim, "Gentlemen, this is a football." Was he saying they didn't need to learn plays? No, he was going to teach them the plays to run but he wasn't going to start there. He would start with the basics of tackling, blocking, etc. In time management, we need systems. But any good system must be built on the time basics. So we learn the time basics and from there we are ready to build a system.

Building on the Basics

In this book, we are going to lay the foundation for whatever system you employ to manage your time. We will explore the twenty-four time basics upon which all good time management is built. I assume you are reading this book because you want to get more out of life and you know that better time management will let you do so. You need to build your own personal system based on the basics presented in this book. You will never master your time until you master the time basics.

After having taught time management for many years, I know that I can't skip teaching the basics. That would be like skipping the engineering basics if I wanted to teach you how to build a bridge. I wouldn't teach you how to design bridges simply by showing you how I designed one bridge. Let's say I gave you every detail on how I designed a bridge over a two-lane interstate. If you learned all these details well enough, you too could design a bridge over a two-lane interstate. But what if you needed to design a bridge over a river, a railroad track, or a two lane road? You couldn't do it. If you wanted to learn to build bridges, you would learn the basics of civil engineering. Then you could apply them to whatever bridge you wanted to design.

In a similar way, this book will give you the twenty-four basics for managing your time not my time. They will help you face your time challenges not my time challenges. That way, you will know how to manage your time even if your personality, profession, and place in life are different than mine. You can manage the unique daily challenges you face if you manage the basics. These time basics are for everyone. They are universal. How you will apply them to your life will be totally unique to you. Nobody else is just like you. You will use the universal basics to achieve what you want in life by facing your own unique time challenges.

Structuring the Basics

There are twenty-four time basics. They are placed into four sections. The first section discusses having a vision for your life and your time. In it we look at how we can make sure we invest our time in things that really matter rather than just blow it on what catches our attention at the moment. The second section discusses how we can take that vision and focus it in on our daily activities. Here is where we discuss how we develop a time management system and get the most out of our daily schedule. The third and fourth sections cover how we can give our time management systems speed and power. We want to move faster and become more powerful in managing our time. The second half of the book will show us how to do so. Those are the four pieces of the time management puzzle—vision, focus, speed, and power. We will look at the basics of putting them into our lives to get the most out of our time.

I have structured every chapter in the same way. They are all brief. In fact, each one is just eight pages long. I could have included much more detail about each of the time basics but there is something discouraging about a sixty page chapter in a book on time management. If you are concerned about your time, you probably don't have enough of it to read a bunch of long chapters. So I have distilled the most important content for each basic down to eight pages.

In every chapter, I include lots of stories, examples, analogies, and quotes. Some may see these as fluff. They are not. I am not wasting your time. I am applying what we know about cognitive science to help you remember the basics. Research has shown us that you don't just have random ideas floating around in your head. For you to remember something, you have to hang it on something else. The stories, examples, analogies, and quotes will give you something to hang the concepts on. In fact, you will probably remember these stories, analogies, etc. more easily than you will remember the concepts they teach. That's good because I have tried to design them in such a way that you cannot remember a story, example, analogy, or quote without also remembering the point I was making with it.

How can we move beyond the basics? Visit *timebasics.com* for many tools that will help you take further steps in managing your time. You will be able to tap into several free resources that you can incorporate into your own time management system. It is also a source for time management videos, blogs, and relevant links. If you want some practical exercises on mastering the individual basics, be sure to get Living the Basics which is the workbook for *Time Basics*. It too is available at *timebasics.com* or at select bookstores.

What Is Time Management?

Before we move into studying the basics, we must answer the most basic question of them all. What is time management? We will define time management as *the matching of our current activities with our goals for the future.* Thus, by definition, our time is managed to the extent to which our current activities are moving us towards where we want to be in the future. Basketball great LeBron James knows what it is like to work towards some goal in the future. He was asked what the biggest challenge in working towards an NBA championship is. He answered, "Every single day we have to understand that we can't waste that day."

That is why we manage our time. We see what we want life to be like in the future. That future has several different aspects to it. We see the career we want to have. We see how we want our family to be. We have financial goals we want to achieve. We see how healthy we would like to be and how we want to look. There are fun things we want to be able to do. All of these aspects of our future are competing for our current time.

How can we make sure that we are pursuing them all in a balanced way? We don't want there to be a huge hole in our future when it arrives. More importantly, how can we make sure that we aren't doing things that take us away from building the future we desire? How can we make sure that, every single day, we don't waste the day? We do so by learning and applying the time basics. So let's jump in and start exploring the twenty-four time basics one by one.

Vision

The Perception Principle:

It Is Later Than You Think

The Principle of the
Excluded Alternative:

To Say "Yes" to Something Is to
Say "No" to Something Else

The Effort Principle:

You Can Do Anything but You
Cannot Do Everything

The Priority Principle:

Words Can Be Deceptive but
Behaviors Don't Lie

The Value Principle:

Poverty Awaits Those Who Spend High
Value Time Doing Low Value Things

The Distraction Principle:

The Most Appealing Path Is
Seldom the One We Are On

Part 1

Vision

I have a good friend of mine named Joe. There is so much he accomplishes with his twenty-four hours. He is incredibly enthusiastic and goal driven. He lives every day with focus and passion. He is deeply committed to his family and the business he has built has made a huge positive impact on the lives of many. The other day, a group of us were talking about how Joe keeps going year after year. We wondered how Joe could always make huge strides in his personal and professional life. My son shared something that may be the answer.

Joe has picked an age in the future as his finishing line. Though somewhat arbitrary, it is a reasonable age beyond which he will probably not be able to keep up the pace. He has a bowl of marbles on his desk and there is one marble in it for every month between now and that finishing line. At the end of each month, he reaches in, grabs one of the marbles, and throws it away.

Here is what the bowl of marbles gives Joe. It gives him vision. First, it gives him a vision of the possibilities. There are a lot of marbles in the bowl. Joe has already achieved many great things. Still, in those marbles, he sees the potential to achieve so much more. As long as there is time, there are possibilities. If he ever thinks about backing off or slowing down, he can see that there is plenty of time to make some amazing things happen in his life and in the lives of others.

At the same time, the bowl of marbles gives him a vision of the brevity of life. There are only so many marbles in the bowl. There aren't as many marbles as there once were. The bowl of marbles helps him see that, though the possibilities are limitless, time is not. The only way to make the most of the possibilities is to not let any time just slip away.

All effective time management starts with vision. We must have a clear vision of the limitless possibilities and an even clearer vision of the brevity of time. Time management is where these two visions meet. On one hand, if we just have a vision of the possibilities, we will waste so much time because we never feel the urgency to act. We live our lives in the land of "someday maybe." Months will pass us by and we won't even notice they are gone. On the other hand, if we just have a vision of how limited our time is, we won't know what to do with it. We may even get discouraged because we know that we cannot do everything we would like to do in the time we have.

Good time management begins when we develop a vision of both the brevity of time and the potential to do great things with the limited time we have. Part 1 of this book is about getting the proper vision of time. We will start by looking at an illusion that distorts our perception of time. We think that there is more of it than there really is. Then we will explore how to do the most with the limited time we have. This involves clear decisions about what we leave in and what we leave out of our lives. Following that, we will look at setting priorities and ordering our time. We finish Part 1 by addressing how to keep our vision clear, even in the midst of distractions.

The goal in discussing these first six time basics is to help you gain a clear vision of how to approach the limitless possibilities with your limited time. The biggest problem in time management is that we let so much of our time just slip away. We do so because we either feel time will go on forever or because we fail to see what we can do with such limited time. Simply developing a clearer vision of how to accomplish so many things with so little time will solve many of our time management problems.

1
Perception

The Perception Principle:
It Is Later Than You Think

There was this nice Scottish couple who inherited a vase. It was old but pretty and so they set it out in their living room. I don't know for sure but there were probably times when the dog ran by and almost sent it crashing to the ground. There might have been times when kids were playing in the house and nearly smashed it with a cricket bat. Then one day the couple visited a museum. They saw a vase that looked a lot like the one in their living room. They had their vase appraised and found out that it was worth ten million dollars. Suddenly they started treating that vase a little differently.

Let me ask you a question. If you had a ten million dollar vase, would you just plop it down somewhere in the living room where the dog would run by it and the kids would play around it? You might *if* you didn't know it was a ten million dollar vase. But my guess is that as soon as you realized that it was worth ten million dollars, you would start treating it in a totally different way. When we think something is a trinket, we treat it like a trinket. But when we find out it is a treasure, we start treating it like a treasure. The reason why most people treat their time as a trinket is because they don't understand that it is a treasure.

Scarcity Is What Gives Value

What makes this vase so valuable is that it is the only copper-red vase of the early Ming Dynasty still in perfect condition. Only a small number of the copper-red Ming vases like this one even exist and all the rest of them have some damage. It is worth so much because it is so rare. Scarcity is what gives this vase its value. Scarcity is the only thing that makes us value anything.

We don't see the brevity of time and so we don't value our time. Because we don't value our time, we treat time as if it were a trinket and not a treasure. It seems as if our time will go on forever and we act accordingly. This is the illusion of time and it isn't anything new. Over two thousand years ago, Roman philosopher Seneca figured out that people really don't comprehend just how valuable time is. He said,

> We all complain of the shortness of time, and yet have much more than we know what to do with. Our lives are either spent in doing nothing at all, or in doing nothing with a purpose, or in doing nothing that we ought to do. We are always complaining that our days are few and acting as though there would be no end of them.

We know time is short but I am not sure we really comprehend it. If we did, we would stop treating time like a trinket and start treating it like a treasure.

Michael Landon was the handsome actor who starred for twenty-eight straight years in full-hour television programs. Only Lucille Ball made the cover of *TV Guide* more times than he did. Even after he turned fifty-four years old, he was still the picture of perfect health. Working out in his home gym, he would tell visitors, "I have never felt better in my life." But before he would have turned fifty-five, cancer had quickly taken his life.

In his last few weeks Landon spoke of something that few of us really grasp before it is too late. He finally realized just how precious and valuable time is. He said,

> Someone should tell us, right at the start of our lives, that we are dying. Then we might live life to the limit, every minute of every day. Do it, I say! Whatever you want to do, do it now! There are only so many tomorrows.

We need to always be aware of the scarcity of time. Otherwise, we will waste it all away.

No matter how important something is, we will not value it unless it is scarce. The other day, I purchased a can of compressed air to clean some of my camera equipment. It cost me five dollars. Imagine that, I just paid five dollars for air. I thought I was being ripped off. Air isn't worth five dollars. Or is it? We don't place a lot of value on air because it is all around us. But just go thirty seconds without air and you will start to see how valuable it really is. To the drowning man, air is the most desired thing in the world. To the person with a breathing disorder, nothing is more valuable than air. Scarcity makes it precious to them. The rest of us know it is important but we really don't comprehend its true value. We could not live five minutes without air but we do not value it because we have it in abundance.

No matter how important something is, we won't value it unless we see it as scarce. To paraphrase Thomas Paine, only scarcity gives something its value for that which we acquire too easily, we esteem too lightly. That is precisely why we don't value our time. It is the most valuable thing we have but there is an illusion that it is never ending. Until we see how scarce time is we will never value time as we should.

It Is Always Later Than We Think

If there is anything significant we want in life, it is always later than we think. For example, I recently had a student who was reading a book on personal finances. She said that the section she had just read wasn't really relevant to her because it was about preparing for retirement. I wanted her to understand that, when it comes to saving for retirement, even at age 21 it was later than she might think. To illustrate this point, I showed her what kind of money she would have when she turned 65 if she put $500 per month away starting at age 21 (assuming a 9.25% return compounded monthly). Then I compared what would happen if she skipped saving for retirement at various stages of her life. At age 65, she would be in the same financial position if she skipped:

> 1 year at age 21
> 3 1/2 years from age 30 through age 32 1/2
> 8 years from age 40 through age 47
> 20 years from age 45 to when she turns 65.

I am not sure she understood the concept but she couldn't argue with the math. She could start saving when she turned 21 and stop when she turned 45. Or, she could wait just one year and start saving when she turned 22 and keep saving until she was 65. Both savings plans would yield the same result. That one year of savings that she didn't think mattered when she was 21 could cost her two decades of savings later in life. It is hard when you are young to grasp the time value of money. By the time we figure out that we need to start early planning for retirement, it is too late to start early. Someone needs to tell us early in our financial lives that it is later than we think.

Let me give you another example. I have a couple of friends that are in their mid-sixties. They still play two hours of full-court basketball three days every week. How do they do that? Well, if they started trying to get into shape to do so at age 65, it would be tough. However, their whole lives have been spent staying in shape so that they could still be strong and vibrant well into their later years of life. Again, the point is that you cannot wait until the last third of your life to begin preparing physically for the last third of your life. You don't want to be like the eighty year old man who told me, "If I had known that I was going to live this long, I would have taken better care of myself." You cannot wait until the aches and pains arrive to start fighting off the aches and pains. In terms of taking care of our bodies, it is way later than we think.

This doesn't just apply to preparing for our later years in life. Every semester, my students are amazed at how quickly the end-of-semester projects sneak up on them. The semester starts and fifteen weeks seems like forever before those things are due. It still seems like the semester is just getting under way when midterms hit. Then, it is off to Fall or Spring break and there is almost no time, so it seems, before everything comes due. Pick any random week in a fifteen week semester and I guarantee you that it is later than the students think.

If college isn't early enough to see that things are later than we think, let's go all the way back to infancy. Researchers have concluded that there are crucial stages that a child goes through in its intellectual development. The way this development occurs is through mental stimulation. We tend to think that the most important years of a person's intellectual development occur in school. Not so. The amount of growth that happens in this area in the first few years of life is astronomical when compared to any other stage in life. If we think that we wait until a kid goes to school to have him or her start learning, we are waiting too long. Now I am not saying here that we start forcing math on our two year old but I am saying that the environment for learning and exploration must be built in the home at a very young age. If it is not, those crucial developmental years are gone. When it comes to learning the skills we need in life, even for a baby, it is later than we think.

So when is it later than you think? It is always later than you think! There is a reason I am starting this book talking about the need to understand just how valuable time is. I didn't really want to start here. It seems so negative to talk about how quickly time is running out. However, we shouldn't take it that way. It isn't as if there is not enough time. There is enough time to do everything we need to do. There is plenty of time to live a wonderful life, have a lot of fun, accomplish a lot of things, and fulfill our purpose in life.

Think about this. Orville Wright was 32 years old and his brother Wilbur was 36 on that cold December morning when the Wright Flyer made its first flight. Thomas Edison was only 32 when he turned on the first light switch. Before Martin Luther King turned 28 he had successfully led the movement that ended segregation on the Montgomery public buses. This was the spark that ignited the whole civil rights movement. He was 34 when he gave his famous, "I Have a Dream" speech. This was the philosophy that guided the movement. Albert Einstein was 26 when he published four papers that provided much of the foundation for modern physics and changed the way scientists view space, time, and matter. Mozart composed over 600 works, many which endure to this day, and yet he died before he turned 36 years old. Alexander the Great conquered most of the known world and never saw his 33rd birthday. Alexander Graham Bell was 29 years old when he placed the first telephone call to Thomas Watson.

We have just looked at the beginning of human flight, the lighting up of the world, the starting of the civil rights movement, the changing of the way science views the universe, the writing of many of the most loved pieces of classical music, and the conquering of the known world. All of the people behind these accomplishments were in their twenties or thirties when they made them happen. Though none of us are guaranteed tomorrow, our life expectancy is in the seventies or even into the eighties. The nineties aren't uncommon and 100 years of age is not out of the question. If people like Edison, Einstein, King, and Mozart can accomplish so much in a few decades, imagine how much we could accomplish in eight or nine decades. And even if we already have most of those decades behind us, there is still plenty of time to accomplish some incredible things.

So why don't we? Maybe it is the same reason the nice Scottish couple didn't keep their ten million dollar vase in a safe place. Maybe we don't realize what we have. Let's be honest. You probably don't value time as you should. I know I don't. It is only when we contemplate the shortness of time and the immense potential of what we can accomplish with it that we begin to gain perspective on just how valuable time really is.

The Illusion of Time

The problem is that time has so many ways of faking us out. Time gives us a brief abundance. We have all the time there is until one day we have no more. There are 24 hours in a day. Each and every one of us is given those 24 hours. When they are gone, we have another fresh 24 hours simply given to us. They just keep coming and coming. We have all the time there is and then, one day, we are given no more. It is all gone.

The abundance of time we have today makes us never consider that this abundance will be gone and we will have none left. We have all heard of people who are told that they only have a few months to live. My guess is that, when hospice is called and the reality actually hits that our abundance of time is indeed coming to an end, we change how we view time. Wouldn't it be nice if we could figure out the value of time at the beginning of our lives rather than at the end?

Even in the abundance of time, there is scarcity. From a practical perspective, it is the only thing that there is a limited amount of. There is a limited amount of food but I am not going to eat it all. There is a limited amount of water but I am not going to drink it all. There is a limited amount of air but I am not going to breathe it all. However, every day, there is a limited amount of time and I am going to use it all up. By the end of the day, I will have used every bit of time that the day had to offer. At year's end, I will have used every single second that year made available to anyone.

Time also fakes us out because it drags by so fast. The days are long and the years are short. It seems to defy the laws of mathematics. If you multiply 1 times 365, you get 365. But if you look back at how quickly the year zipped by, it seems a lot less than 365 times how slowly some days went by. In fact, the year probably seems even shorter than how slowly 52 Mondays dragged by.

The other illusion of time is that it gives us precious bad times. We may wish to hold on to the good times and let go of the bad times. Even if we could, we wouldn't want to do that. Both are to be prized. Hard times are to be valued too. In his *Book of Virtues*, William Bennett shares a French fable called "The Magic Thread." A boy named Peter was given a special ball of twine. Any time he wished, he could pull the twine and fast forward his life. It was his opportunity to skip the dull, mundane, boring, and miserable times. He only had to live the good times. The first time he used it was at school to skip to the end of a boring day of classes. He thought it was great so he started pulling the string every day. Every day he would enjoy the good times and skip right over the bad.

Pulling the twine, his life quickly sped by. The last years of his life arrived so fast and, when they did, Peter realized his folly. He regretted having ever pulled the twine. He wished he had experienced all of life–both the good and the bad. The moral of the story was that even the bad times add to the richness of our life. Fortunately for Peter, he got a second chance. At the end of the fable, he wakes up to discover it was only a dream. Peter learned the lesson that all time is to be valued. It is an illusion to think that only the good times are precious. If we only experienced the good times, we would live short and shallow lives.

Molding Our Lives

We only have so much time and it is up to us to decide what to do with it. Time is like the potter's clay. We can mold it however we wish to form whatever life we want. That is exactly what Benjamin Franklin said. "Dost thou love life?" he asked. "Then do not squander time, for time is the stuff life is made of." Franklin was right. We take time and, however we mold it, that is what our lives become.

A few people are like the potter who took some clay and molded the Ming dynasty vase mentioned at the beginning of this chapter. Obviously, no one knows who that potter was but can you imagine the care he or she put into molding a vase that would be so highly valued several hundred years later. What if we took the care and molded our time like that potter molded the clay? What kind of life could we create? Unfortunately, most people take the very stuff that life is made of, plop it on the wheel and hope a treasure will emerge. Then they wonder why all they get is a glob.

Jim Rohn tells of the most perplexing discovery he made one day. He discovered that rich people have 24 hours in their days and poor people have 24 hours in their days. He said that it started to drive him nuts wondering why one person got rich with 24 hours and another person barely got by. Then he figured it out. He realized that they do different things with their 24 hours. One person takes time and molds a fortune. The other takes the same time and molds poverty.

When I heard him say that, I couldn't help but think of Bill Gates. He and I were born less than two months apart. We started making money at about the same time. He did get a two month head start on me but that's all. Since then, he has had 24 hours every day and so have I. Now when it comes to molding our time into money, he has done a much better job than me. We had the same time but we got different results. Why? Because he did different things with his time than I did with mine.

I am not saying that I want to trade places with Bill Gates but I would definitely trade bank accounts with him. Certainly there is more to life than making money. But that raises an important question. What is there to life? When we mold our life, what do we want it to look like? Though I want it to be more than money, I do have to admit that I would like my final creation to at least have a green tint to it.

We need to start by figuring out what we want to do with our time. Actress Lily Tomlin once quipped, "I always wanted to be somebody, but now I realize I should have been more specific." I sometimes feel that is the way it is with time. We all want to do something with our lives. Actually, we all are doing something with our lives. We are molding something with our time. Perhaps we should be more specific about what we want the end product to be.

Peter Drucker was probably the greatest management author, consultant, theorist, and spokesperson of his time. He is to modern management what Einstein or Newton is to physics. He knew management like no one else has ever known management. Here is what else Peter Drucker knew. It all starts with managing our time. He said, until we manage our time, we cannot manage anything else.

We go through our day managing our money, planning the route we will take to work, managing our careers, planning our dinner, managing the office fantasy football league, planning the summer vacation, managing what we will let entertain us... Somewhere in there, we need to spend some time planning and managing the one thing we cannot replace—time.

Don't Blink

I really enjoy the incredible wisdom expressed in certain country and western songs. That is why I like playing them for my college students. I'm pretty sure they don't like hearing them as much as I like playing them but I hope they get the message. My favorite song to play for my time management class is one by Kenny Chesney. An old man was interviewed on television on the day he turned 102 years old. The reporter asked him if he had any advice. All this old man could think of was, "Don't blink, a hundred years goes faster than you think." I am sure if we make it to that age, we will still be perplexed by the illusion of time. No matter what our age is, it is later than we think.

The Perception Challenge:
Resolve to treat time like a treasure and not
like a trinket.

2
The Excluded Alternative

The Principle of the Excluded Alternative:
To Say "Yes" to Something Is to Say "No" to Something Else

Since it is later than we think, we must be careful not to waste precious time. Of course none of us wake up in the morning thinking, "How much time can I waste today?" We don't mean to waste any of our time. It just happens. We do things which crowd out more important things. It isn't that we are doing bad things. We may actually be doing good things. We just aren't doing the most important things and so we lose the opportunity to get the most out of our time. That is exactly what happened to me a number of years ago when I owned a publishing company.

I had developed several contacts among those who published academic periodicals. So I started a company which would take care of the production process for them. Because I subcontracted out every step in the process from typesetting all the way to the distribution of the final product, it didn't take much of my time. I could focus my efforts on growing the business. Before long, I had a rapidly growing company that was becoming very profitable.

Then I made a huge mistake. I added up how much more profit we could make if we did the production for all these publications in-house. I realized that, in just a matter of weeks, I could quadruple our profits if we started doing the production ourselves. So we purchased all the equipment we needed and we built a complete production facility. Indeed, our profits did take a dramatic jump in a very short time. Here was the problem. The company plateaued at that new level. We were never again able to get into the growth mode. Eventually, I sold the company to someone who was simply looking for a steady source of income.

What I realize now is that I fell victim to the Principle of the Excluded Alternative. By saying "yes" to production, I was saying "no" to marketing. I could do production or I could do marketing. I had the ability to do either. But given my other commitments in life, I didn't have enough time to do both. There weren't enough hours in the day. When we were having other companies take care of our production for us, most of my time was spent on marketing and sales. However, when we decided to bring production in-house, all my time was spent overseeing the production process. I no longer had time to market the business. Here was the problem. I said "yes" to a job that anyone could do thus saying "no" to the one thing that only I could do. It was easy to find people and companies to do the production side of our business. However, it was much harder to find someone who had the connections and knowledge of our industry that I did. We really couldn't find anyone other than me to do the marketing for us. I chose to say "yes" to something that gave us immediate profit rather than "yes" to the one thing that would give us long term growth. I never deliberately said "no" to marketing. I just made it the excluded alternative. In doing so, I turned a gold mine into merely a cash cow.

Making Choices

That was poor time management. Effective time management comes when we make good choices with our limited time. However, it doesn't necessarily follow that poor time management comes from making bad choices about our time. Some of the worst time management occurs when we don't make choices at all. We just let things happen. That is what happened with my company. I didn't choose to kill the growth by halting my marketing efforts. Marketing just fell off of my calendar when I chose to bring the production in house.

Good time management doesn't happen when we just let things drop off our schedule. It happens when we carefully consider what must go so as to make time for what should stay. I enjoy playing golf. I love being outside on a beautiful golf course. I like the challenge of each hole. However, for the past twenty years, I haven't picked up a golf club. For the last twenty years, my wife and I have been raising our children. When our kids were just being born, I played a lot of golf but then I realized that saying "yes" to eighteen holes of golf meant saying "no" to four hours with my family. Even though golf is a good thing, I decided to say "no" to it because I would rather do that than say "no" to my family for four hours.

In contrast, I sometimes say yes to computer programming. I actually enjoy doing a little computer programming now and then. I realize that when I sit down to do some programming, I am saying "no" to a lot of other things. You might find it bizarre that I would say "yes" to computer programming and "no" to golf. But for me, the combination of the fun it provides and the usefulness of the programs I write justifies the time I take away from other things.

Notice the two things I considered when I decided to say "yes" to computer programming and "no" to golf. I looked at whether it was important and whether it was fun. The computer programming is useful and it is fun (at least for me). For most people, it would be neither useful nor fun and so just the thought of spending some time doing computer programming seems totally out of the question. On the other hand, many people continue to play golf even though they have very busy schedules. Because of the benefits it provides they see it as important. It is good exercise. It relieves stress. It is a good chance to spend time with important people. Throw in the fact that it is also fun and you can quickly see how that, for some people, it is well worth the amount of time it takes.

When we say "yes" to something, these are the two things we need to make sure we are taking into consideration. We need to consider if it is fun and/or if it is important. What I may see as fun and important can be quite different from what you see as fun and important. That's OK. Here is what is not OK. It is not OK to spend our lives saying "yes" to a bunch of things that are neither fun nor important. That will ensure that we say "no" to living a fun and meaningful life. We can look at it this way. Everything we do is either fun or it is not fun. Everything we do is either important or it is not important. That means everything we do falls into one of four categories. Let's explore each of these types of time individually.

Our Best Time

The best time in our life is spent doing important things and having fun doing them. I am convinced that the people who have the biggest impact on the world are the ones who find a way to combine their passion with the ability to make an impact. Having read a lot of biographies, I've noticed that people who have accomplished great things all enjoyed what they did. The trick in life is to find a way that you can make an impact doing the things you like to do.

I'm sure you have heard it said that, if we make a living doing something we love, we won't have to work a day in our life. That should be our goal. When we make our living doing something that we love, we spend most of our careers in the "best time category." We have to make this happen though. It is hard to find well-paying jobs that are fun. A few years ago, I had a student who loved art. He was very good at it. So, when he went to college, everyone just assumed he would major in art. Instead, he chose to major in business and take all the art classes he could while he was getting his marketing degree. He told me he wanted to be an "artist," not a "starving artist." By the time he graduated, he had made more money selling his art than most art majors make selling their work in a whole lifetime. He is spending his life doing the thing he enjoys and he is being rewarded in the marketplace for it. But he made it happen. He didn't just have fun doing his art with the hopes that someone would pay him for it.

We have a potential problem when things are both important and fun. We have to be careful not to let them make our lives unbalanced. Remember, to say "yes" to something means to say "no" to something else. Life isn't about achieving great things in one area of our life at the expense of everything else. If we find one great thing that we love doing and we focus only on it, we run the risk of being a huge success in one area of our life and a failure in everything else. J. Paul Getty loved being a businessman and he became the richest person in the world. Yet he said he would have traded it all for one successful marriage. Yes, Getty spent his life saying "yes" to things that were both fun and important. However, in doing so, he said "no" to the things that would give him what he really wanted in life.

Our Fun Time

Everyone should do things just for fun. We don't need to spend all our time every day doing things that are important. In fact, we all need to have some time that we spend just having fun. Some people grow up and forget how to have fun. Remember as a kid doing things like running through the sprinklers? Now that's not an important thing to do but remember how much fun it was. When was the last time you ran through the sprinklers? OK, maybe we don't need to literally run through the sprinklers but we do need to have an adult version. Do you have something that you do just for fun? If not, you need to find something. Always remember that part of success in life is having fun. If we are living a highly productive life but we have lost the ability to just have fun, our best days are behind us.

Here is the challenge with our fun time. We must be sure we don't try to make all of life nothing but one big party. All work and no play makes Jack a dull boy. On the other hand, all play and no work makes Jack a lazy bum. Our fun time comes at a cost. It is what economists call "opportunity costs." One time, noted author Jim Rohn asked a friend how much his television cost him. His friend replied that it cost him $800. Jim Rohn said that it cost him $800 to buy it. But that isn't what it costs him. If he considered the money he could make with all the time he spends in front of the television, then he could see that the television that cost him $800 to buy is costing him tens of thousands of dollars every year to watch.

Whether it is television, video games, golf, or a host of other things that we may enjoy doing, when we say "yes" to them we are saying "no" to something. Ironically, what we are saying "no" to might be a lot more fun in the long run. I can watch the vacation channel or I can turn off the television and take that time to make the money to actually go on those vacations. What is more fun, watching other people going on exotic vacations or going on them myself? If I am saying "yes" to the vacation channel, I may be saying "no" to the vacation.

Our Sacrifice Time

Sometimes we have to say "yes" to something that isn't fun because it is important. We don't all enjoy our vocation but our jobs may be important because we need the money. We don't all enjoy exercising but it may be important because it will make us healthier. We may love our college major but we don't enjoy every class we take to get our degree. Not all the important things in our life are fun.

Stephen Covey talks about this in 7 Habits. He says that successful people do the things unsuccessful people don't like to do. And what are the things that unsuccessful people don't like to do? They are the very same things that successful people don't like to do. Even though they both don't like to do these things, successful people go ahead and do them anyway. That's how they become successful. If we are always thinking fun and never thinking important, life doesn't have many rewards in store for us.

Sometimes we need to sacrifice fun for significance. I work in the church nursery. I would rather be in the worship service. But I remember people sacrificing for us when we had small children and so I think I need to do the same for people who are where we were back then. I see a lot of good that came in our lives from the people who made these sacrifices when our children were young and so I certainly am willing to do the same for others now that I am able.

Sometimes we sacrifice fun for our future. Sometimes people tell me that they would love to be a college professor too. I tell them that, as far as jobs go, being a professor is great. A college campus is a great place to work. It is wonderful to feel like you have impacted some student's lives. And just being in the classroom is fun. Then I tell them that, if they want to teach college, they need to get a Ph.D. They usually respond with, "I don't want to go through a Ph.D. program." I agree with them. Nobody in their right mind wants to do the work a Ph.D. requires. I tell them that a Ph.D. program is academic hazing. You don't do the work of a Ph.D. program because you want to do the work of a Ph.D. program. You do the work of a Ph.D. program because you want the results of a Ph.D. program. You sacrifice now for the benefits you will receive in the future.

Our Wasted Time

Finally, we sometimes find ourselves in a situation like the unfortunate college student who answered an advertisement for a summer job. The ad promised a summer "cruising the Caribbean." He quickly ran down to the address on the advertisement. As soon as he walked in the door, he was knocked over the head. When he woke up, he was chained to another guy in the hull of a ship with a big oar in front of them. All summer long they were forced to row this boat around the Caribbean. There was a guy beating a drum. Every time he hit the drum and yelled "stroke," they had to row the boat. His whole summer was spent in that dark and dingy hull oaring to the beat of the drum. At the end of the summer, as he was getting off the boat, he asked the guy who he had been chained to if they were supposed to tip the drummer like they tipped the bands that played back at school. His companion answered, "I don't think so. We didn't tip him last year."

Two guys spent the summer doing something that was neither fun nor important. Here was the difference. The first year guy did so out of ignorance. The second year guy should have known better. Sometimes we have no choice but to do some unimportant thing that we don't like doing. That is understandable. It happens to us all. But what if we have a choice? What's our excuse then? Sometimes we are like the second year guy. We should know better. If we ever ask ourselves, "why am I doing this?" and the answer is neither "because it is important" nor "because it is fun," then we need to get better at saying "no."

Why do we say "Yes"

So why do we say "yes" when we really want to say "no"? There are two reasons.

We Say "Yes" Because We Can't Say "No"

Sometimes saying "no" isn't a real option. If our boss plops something on our desk and tells us to have it back to him by Friday, saying "no" to him could mean saying "yes" to the unemployment line. But, because of the Principle of the Excluded Alternative, saying "yes" to the newly plopped papers means saying "no" to something else.

Recently I had a student share with the class a challenge she was having at work. Her boss was always giving her more work than she could possibly get done. She couldn't say "no" to him but she also couldn't get done all he was asking her to do. She was falling victim to the Principle of the Excluded Alternative. She asked me what she should do. How should she decide which projects to work on and which ones to send to the bottom of the pile? I told her that she shouldn't make that decision. She should let her boss make the call. She just needed to give him the information he needs to make that decision. I told her to keep a quick list of all the things she is working on and, whenever he gives her something else to do, show him the list. I told her to be extremely tactful and respectful but to ask him where the new project should fall on her list.

A couple weeks later, she said that she started doing as I suggested and her boss was actually quite appreciative of it. In fact, he didn't realize how much stuff she had on her plate and how productive she was being. Often, he would drop something off for her to do and, when she asked him to help her prioritize it, he would say that it wasn't as important as anything else she was doing. As a result, she was always doing exactly what was most important to her boss and he was always aware of how much she was actually getting done.

Here is the point. We aren't trained to think in terms of the Principle of the Excluded Alternative and neither are the people who tell us to do things. For many people in authority, that is a blind spot for them. With a little tact and diplomacy, we can help them become better stewards of our time that we entrust to them.

We Say "Yes" Because We Won't Say "No"

Sometimes, when we are asked to do something, inside we are screaming "no" yet our mouths end up saying "yes." When it comes to saying "yes" or "no", we need to get our mouths to start listening to our brains. Remember, "no" is the most important word in our time management vocabulary and we need to learn how to say it. There are many reasons why we have a hard time saying "no." We may feel guilty.

We may not want to hurt someone's feelings. We may be afraid that we won't be asked when it is something we actually do want to do. We may fear that the person may never invite us to anything again. All of these feelings make it hard to say "no."

Stephen Covey talked about the "guilt-free no." He said that the only way to feel good about saying "no" is to have a burning "yes." The more I have a burning passion about what I am doing, the easier it is to say "no." Let's say I am on the internet wasting my time on some marshmallow-of-the-mind site and my wife comes home from the store. She asks me to help her bring the groceries in from the car. If I say "no" I feel like a real jerk. It would be hard to say "no" to her so that I could say "yes" to something totally insignificant. But what if the situation were different and I was about to rush one of the kids to the doctor because she had just fallen and probably broken her arm? I would have zero problem telling my wife that I couldn't help her with the groceries. I don't feel guilty saying "no" to my wife in that situation because I have a very important "yes" in my life. The only way we get to where we can feel OK about saying "no" is to find a way to remember our burning "yes."

Being Careful with Our "Yes"

Every year, I see so many eighteen-year-olds arrive on our college campus with great intentions to study and make good grades. The problem is that there are so many cool things for a college freshman to say "yes" to. It is not possible to say "yes" to every cool thing that a freshman could do on a college campus and still have time to study. The students who survive to see their sophomore year are the ones who don't make studying the excluded alternative. Things don't change once we leave college. There will always be a bunch of stuff we want to say "yes" to. Before we say "yes," we must learn to stop and ask, "By saying 'yes' to this, what am I saying 'no' to?" If we are careful with how we use the word "yes," then the most important things in our life won't fall victim to being the excluded alternative.

The Challenge of the Excluded Alternative:
Resolve to say "no" by decision and not by default.

3
Effort

The Effort Principle:
You Can Do Anything but
You Cannot Do Everything

The Principle of the Excluded alternative forces us to recognize that we only have so much time. If we use our time for one thing, we cannot use it for something else. A closely related basic is the Effort Principle. It says that we only have so much effort we can exert. We can spread it out, reacting to anything or everything that comes our way, or we can save it for the things that really matter. Most people spread their effort very thin by giving it to whatever happens to show up. Effective people take the same effort and strategically place it where they need it the most.

David Allen described most people's typical day when he said, "Much of our life and work just shows up in the moment and it usually becomes our priority when it does." We struggle to manage our time when we react to whatever just shows up in the moment. People who effectively manage their time don't operate that way. They accomplish great things by narrowing in on the limited number of things they really want to accomplish. Just because something shows up in the moment, that doesn't mean it deserves our effort.

Truett Cathy, the founder of Chick-Fil-A, was one of the most successful business leaders to ever come from the state where I live. When he was alive, I got a chance to meet him in his office. When I was escorted into his office, I noticed that it was elegant but simple and nicely kept. What I remember most about my visit was something I saw in that neat, clean, and well organized office. It was his inbox. Truett Cathy's inbox was stuffed to overflowing. The pile of things in his inbox must have been at least a foot high.

I don't know if Mr. Cathy's inbox was always filled to overflowing but that day it was. It really caught my attention because it wasn't what I expected at all. I guess I thought that this man who was running a multi-billion dollar corporation had nothing better to do each day than sit in his office and clean out whatever happened to find its way into his inbox. Perhaps it didn't occur to me that he might not have the time to sit around all day taking care of anything and everything that people might pile on him. When I realized how little sense it made to think that way, it totally changed my perspective on my own inbox.

Before I visited Truett Cathy's office, my inbox was the most depressing thing in my life. It always seemed to fill faster than I could possibly empty it. If something came my way that I thought I might eventually want to get to, I would throw it in that inbox. Then, when I would have a break in my schedule, I would go to work trying to empty my inbox. Even when I would attack my inbox with a vengeance, throwing things out right and left, I never saw it empty.

Seeing Mr. Cathy's inbox was almost therapeutic. It helped me come to grips with the fact that my inbox would never be empty. No matter how hard I tried, I would never see the bottom of my inbox. I realize now that, when I die, my inbox will be full. That's OK. When God sees me on the other side, he won't smack me down because I left behind a pile of stuff in my inbox. As I write this, I can glance over at that overstuffed inbox and not feel the slightest pang of guilt. A full inbox bothers me no more.

We all have a figurative inbox in our lives. It is the place where we find all those things that just show up in the moment. We can try to spread our effort across everything in the inbox or we can spend it on the few things that matter most. Either way, we probably won't get all the way through the inbox. If we spread our effort out, we may get to more things but we still won't get to everything. If we take the same amount of effort and use it on the few things that are most important, we will accomplish greater things. Either way, at the end of the day, all our effort will be spent and there will still be stuff sitting in our inbox. We threw all the effort we had at the day. The question is whether we knocked over a few big things or just made dents in a lot of little stuff.

How to Deal With Your Inbox

When I teach time management, I love to approach it from the perspective of the figurative inbox. Remember, your inbox is *your* inbox and so you choose what to do with it. If you want to spend your life trying to clear it out, you can do that. On the other hand, you don't have to approach your figurative inbox that way. You can choose only those items that are most important to you. You can select any item you want and go to work on it. Always remember, you will never get to everything in your figurative inbox. When the day is over, chances are you won't have done everything you wanted to do today. When this year ends, you probably will not have accomplished everything you wanted to accomplish. Even when your life is over, there will likely still be stuff on your bucket list.

Living a great life happens when we see the many possibilities and then invest our effort only on the ones that best fit who we are. It shouldn't discourage us when so many things find their way into our figurative inbox. That gives us options. The problem comes when we aren't particular about which options we choose. With effective time management, you select only those items in your figurative inbox that are best for you. That doesn't mean having an empty figurative inbox. It means having a full figurative inbox but knowing which items to select and which ones to let go. How do we do this? It is a three step process.

Order the Inbox

First, we need to order our inbox. There are an almost infinite number of things that can somehow find their way into our inboxes. Sometimes I look at my inbox in amazement at how quickly it grows. But just because two things make it into the inbox, that doesn't mean they are of equal importance. I went to pick up my mail today and there were some nice promotional pieces from direct marketers and there was a check from someone who bought a few cases of one of my books. I brought in the stack and threw it into my inbox. I may want to look at a couple of the advertisements but they aren't nearly as important to me as the check for the books. An advertisement and a check are both in my inbox but they are certainly not of equal importance sitting in there.

So how does ordering our inbox work? I recently had dinner with someone who worked in corporate communications for the Coca-Cola Corporation. In a sense, his inbox was ordered for him every morning. He would arrive at work and there would be three folders on his desk. One was red. He knew that whatever was in that folder, he had to get to it immediately. He said that if you didn't get to whatever was in the red folder immediately, the HR people would be visiting you with a box to help you pack your belongings as you made your last trip out the door. No matter what it took, you had to get through the red folder. All of the other unimportant things in life like eating and sleeping had to wait if there was anything in your red folder. People who couldn't get through their red folders were quickly replaced by people who could. It was just that brutal.

Then there was a yellow folder. Those were the things that needed to be handled soon. They weren't drop-dead important right now but they could quickly become so. He said that you had better be good at cleaning out the yellow folder or else your only future with Coke would be at vending machines.

Then there were the green folders. These were the things that helped you really seal the deal as a good Coke employee. You had to quickly clear the red folder or you were immediately gone. Clearing your yellow folder didn't differentiate you from the other employees. It differentiated you from the unemployment line. But the green folders were where you really had the potential to shine. If you could do a great job on the stuff in the green folders, you didn't just have a job with Coke. You had a bright career.

When he shared that with me, I loved the idea. What if I could order my life around three folders? There are some things where you drop the dishes and run as fast as you can to take care of them. They may not necessarily be the things that will help you most in the long run but you had better take care of them quickly. They need to be sitting at the top of our figurative inbox in a bright red folder. Next, you have things which have an urgency to them and they deserve your attention right after you clean out the red folder. They need to be sitting in a yellow folder right underneath the red one in your figurative inbox.

Most of us get to the red folder stuff in our lives. We are also pretty good at finding our way through our yellow folders. It is the green folders that give us the biggest problems. And yet how we deal with the green folder determines to a large extent how successful we are in life. The problem with our green folders is that it will grow much faster than we can possibly clear it out. If we aren't careful, it can quickly morph from a green folder to a green binder to a green box to a green room. The bigger that folder is, the harder it is to figure out exactly what we should go to work on next. A huge part of your effectiveness in life will be determined by your ability to order your green folder. Throughout this book, we will present many ideas about how to get the most out of your green folder. Usually the red and yellow items aren't the problem because they are screaming at us. We just can't let our green folder sit there unattended because it speaks to us in a quiet whisper.

Always Pull from the Top

So we have our inbox ordered. Now here comes the big challenge. We need to be sure that we are always pulling from the top. If your inbox is figurative, think of it as holding everything you would like to do with your life on various sheets of paper. Each thing you can do would be on a separate sheet of paper, and those sheets are sitting in your inbox.

Every time you go to do something, it is like you are going to your inbox and picking up a sheet of paper and doing whatever that sheet of paper represents. If you pick up a grocery list, you go shopping. If you pick up a bill, you work on your finances. If you pick up a picture, you call a friend. Whatever you pick up is what you do.

We are actually doing this all day long every day. The inbox may be figurative and the pieces of paper may actually be just thoughts stored in our mind but everyone walks through their days picking up one thing after another and then doing them in some order. What we really need to consider is the order with which we are picking up the pieces of paper. Hopefully we stacked our inbox the way we laid out earlier in this chapter. We have the drop-the-dishes stuff on top (red folder tasks). Next, we have the stuff we must get to soon (yellow folder tasks). Before we can get to a lot of the really important things that will make a huge difference in lives, we have to knock out all of the tasks in our red and yellow folders.

What can be a huge problem is if at the end of the day, we never get past the red and yellow folder tasks. That can happen when we have so many items in our red and yellow folders that we never can get past them. Our green folders never make their way to the top. If so, we are like the person who is so busy mopping up the water on the floor that he doesn't have time to fix the busted pipe. If we ever want a dry floor, at some point we have to stop mopping long enough to fix the plumbing.

Another reason why we may never pull from the green folder is that, by the time we get to it, we are just too physically or mentally spent that we cannot face the first green item. So we stop to take a breather or we just start looking down the pile for something that is fast (we can do quickly), fun (we enjoy doing), or frivolous (it is easy to do but not that important). While we are either taking a rest or working on the fast, fun, or frivolous green folder items, the red and yellow items begin to pile up again.

Seldom do the things at the top of our figurative inbox have the greatest pull. That's because the most interesting things to do are seldom the most important. If we reordered our inbox based on what we would enjoy doing, my guess is that it would look quite different than it did when we ordered it based on what we should be doing. We all want to pick from the middle or even the bottom of the pile. That's probably where the most fun things are.

What is interesting about highly successful people is that there are things down there in the pile that they would rather be doing. When it comes to the temptation to pick from down in the pile, the most successful people are no different from the rest of us. They too want to pick from the middle of the pile. What makes them highly successful is that they resist that temptation. When their hand reaches for the middle of the pile, something grabs it and moves it back up to the top. What is it that grabs the hand? It is their view of the future. Highly successful people have places they want to be in the future and they know the things that will get them there are on top of the pile. It is that clear picture of the long term benefits of completing the most important things that keeps the most effective people grabbing from the top.

Occasionally, Clean It Out

There is a third thing we need to do with our figurative inbox. Occasionally we just need to clean it out. And I don't mean we need to pick through it and toss a few things away. We need to clean our inbox like General Sherman cleaned Atlanta. On one hand, the stuff at the bottom shouldn't bother us because we will never get to it. On the other hand, it is there staring at us and it does have the potential to get us off track from what we really need to be doing.

One of the better books I have ever read on managing your time and priorities was *The ONE Thing* by Gary Keller. Keller was a very successful businessman and he attributed his success to his ability to always narrow everything down to one single thing. He said that he could always figure out what was the one thing he needed to be doing with his life. The book was a huge best-seller because it really spoke to the desires in all of us to simplify our lives. When we look at our to-do list and there are fifty things on it, we can get more than just a little discouraged. But how wonderful would it be to wake up in the morning knowing that we only had one single really important thing that we needed to accomplish that day. Now that's exciting.

I am not sure many of us can actually narrow everything we do down to one thing like Keller suggests. As a professor, there are always going to be at least two different things that I need to do. I have to teach my classes or there is no reason for me to be on campus. Also, I have to keep up my research or I won't be academically qualified to teach my classes. So the idea of ONE thing doesn't really work for me. On the other hand, those are the two main things that matter most to my academic career. I need to concentrate on them and not waste my effort on the many other things that just show up in the moment.

I remember hearing best-selling author and speaker John Maxwell say that he has narrowed his list down to five things. He speaks, he networks, he writes, he mentors, and he leads. That's it. He doesn't do anything else. Everything else is off of his plate. Everything! Through giving those five things all of his effort, he has spread his message to millions around the world. Had he spread his effort across anything that just happens to show up in the moment, his message would have gone nowhere. He is very talented but his talent is wasted any time he is drawn away from the five major things he should do with his time.

The point is not that we have a set number of things that truly matter in our inbox. It might be one, two, five, or some other number. The point is that we should not let the number of figurative inbox items get so large that we lose control. Seeing all the possibilities is nice but, at some point, we need to realistically assess whether we will ever get to some of them. If not, then it is best to let them go, not because they are bad but because they can be distracting.

Almost Anything

The Effort Principle states that we can do anything but we cannot do everything. We can pick out anything we would like to achieve and give it our best shot. No matter how great or small that something is, if we give it our best effort, we can make it happen. That only works, however, if we don't try to do everything. We must live with the fact that there will always be more things that we would like to do than there is time to do them. If we try to do everything, we will succeed at doing nothing. But if we will concentrate our efforts, we can accomplish anything.

Now obviously there is a bit of hyperbole in the Effort Principle. We cannot literally do anything. A young girl came home from school after a nurse had spoken in her class. This girl told her mother that she wanted to be a nurse. Her mother said, "Honey, that's great." Wanting to broaden her daughter's horizons to all the possibilities she said, "You can be anything. If you want, you can be a doctor. You can be a businessperson. You can be a lawyer. You can even be President if that's what you really want to be. You can be anything you want to be."

"I can!" the girl responded with great excitement. "I want to be a pony."

Obviously there are some things we cannot do. I am 6'5" tall and I have wide shoulders on a big frame. No amount of effort would make me the winning race horse jockey in the Kentucky Derby. There are a few things I could never do. There are a few things that you could never do. No person could literally do "anything." But the number of things we can't do is very small compared to the number of things we can do.

The things that I can't do shouldn't really matter anyway. I figure I can live an incredible life even if I never am a race horse jockey. We shouldn't worry about the few things we can't do. Here is what we should worry about. We should be concerned about the few important things that we aren't doing because we never give them our full effort. We should worry that we may never do a few really big things because we waste all of our effort on too many small things.

The Effort Challenge:
Resolve to spend your effort on the most important things and not the moment's important things.

4
Priorities

The Priority Principle:
Words Can Be Deceptive But Behaviors
Don't Lie

Andrew Carnegie became one of the wealthiest people in the world. He did so in the steel industry but he openly admitted that there were a lot of people who knew more about steel than he did. He said that the secret to his success was not in how he learned to make steel but in how he learned to deal with people. One of the most important things he learned was that words can be deceptive but behaviors don't lie. "As I grow older," he once said, "I pay less attention to what men say. I just watch what they do." If you listen to what people say, they will tell you what they value but if you watch what they do you will see what their true priorities are. This works with the person in the mirror too.

As we have seen in the previous two chapters, we cannot do everything so some things must fall off of our schedule. There is a thin line between what makes it onto our schedule and what drops off. That line can be seen as the truest measure of our priorities. That is also the dividing line between those who manage their time and those who don't. Managing our time and managing our priorities are so closely intertwined that some people see them as one in the same.

One time I was speaking to an audience of salespeople in Orlando on the topic of time management. I was backstage about to be introduced by a friend named Tommy. Right before he went on stage to make the introduction he said, "Jim, I never thought there was such a thing as time management. How do you manage time? It just is. I always thought that you manage your priorities not your time." With those words he climbed the stairs up to the stage to introduce me and a couple minutes later I was speaking to a few hundred salespeople about how to manage their time.

That is an interesting question to ponder. Is there really such a thing as time management? However, the time to ponder that question is not while you are on stage talking to a few hundred people about time management. There I was talking about time management with one part of my brain and another part of my brain kept interrupting me going, "Now is that right? Does time management even exist? Shouldn't you qualify that statement?" Do you know how hard it is to give an intelligent sounding speech when your brain is in the middle of an argument?

Well, I have pondered that question for many years and here is what I have concluded. There is such a thing as time management. The fact that time is fixed is the exact reason why you must manage it. Let me give you an example of what I mean. Back when I was in graduate school, I did what I affectionately called my summer internship in logistics. The place where I worked had a warehouse full of boxes and a yard full of trucks. Our job was to shuffle all the merchandise around, getting it into the right trucks. They would give us a set amount of merchandise and we had to make sure we fit it into the truck. That's where our management skills were needed. If our trucks had been the size of a football stadium, our task would have been easy. We would have just tossed the merchandise anywhere and been done with it. But they weren't. We had to load one truck-load of freight into one truck. We barely had enough room to put everything into the truck. We had to be very careful not to waste any space or else everything would not fit. Because our space was fixed, we had to be careful how we managed it.

What We Put into Our Twenty-Four Hour Box

In a sense, that is what we do in time management. We have a container. We will call it our "box." It is our time. It has an exact size—twenty-four hours. We can't stretch it. The size of our box is totally beyond our control. In contrast, we have complete control over what we would like to put into the box. What we care about and what we want to do with our lives is totally unique to each of us. No two people value the same things in life. We are totally free to decide what is important to us and what is not. It is the ultimate in free choice. If we want to place a high value on money and a low value on exercise, that is up to us. If we want to value our families and not value the television, we can do that. The exact value we place on the various things that compete for space in our box is totally up to us.

So it is as if we have a warehouse full of things we could value and a twenty-four hour sized box to put some of them in. Everything is not going to fit. Our priorities represent the top of the box. That is the defining line between what we put in the box and what we leave out of the box. We are effectively managing our priorities to the extent to which the top of the box matches our values. We may value our families but if they never make it into our 24 hour box, then we are not effectively managing our time. A family is only a priority when it makes it into the box. We may really desire to be healthy but if exercise never makes it into the box, we aren't making exercise a priority. For exercise to truly be a priority, it must make it into the box. If we want more money so as to provide a better life for ourselves and our families, we have to put something in the box that will make us more money. Life will decide what to give us based solely on what we put in the box. If we value something but we don't put it in the box, our priorities are messed up and so we aren't properly managing our time.

Let's do a little exercise to see how effectively we are managing our time. Pretend for a moment that the spinning of the world just suddenly slowed down. Instead of taking 24 hours to go full circle, it now takes 25 hours. Days are no longer 24 hours long but rather they are 25 hours long. Your box has just grown from 24 hours to 25 hours. What would you do with your extra hour? What is that one more thing you would put in the box? OK, I know you are thinking, "Halleluiah, one more hour of sleep." But let's say that wasn't an option. You have to do something with that extra hour other than sleep. What would you do? Before you read any further, make sure you know what you would do with your extra hour.

Here is what you have just identified. You have discovered what the most important thing is to you that you are leaving out of your box. Now think about what is in your box. Think about what you do on a daily basis. Is everything in your box more important than the most important thing you are leaving out of your box? So for example, let's say you decided that if you had an extra hour, you would use it to get some exercise. Well, think about this. Is everything in your box more important than exercise? Next time you are on Facebook, playing some video game, or just watching that extra television program, ask yourself if that is more important than exercise. Or let's say that there is a project at work that you would really like to get to but you haven't had the time. Well, next time you are hanging out at the water fountain or surfing the internet from work, ask yourself a simple question. Are these things more important than that project?

If everything in your box is more important than the most important thing you are leaving out of your box, then your priorities are straight and you are in the top 1% of the world at managing your time. But if you are like the 99+% of us who have more important things out of the box than we are putting in the box, then it may be time to reevaluate how we are packing our twenty-four hour box.

Priorities Made Simple

Setting your priorities is simply a matter of deciding what to put in the box and what to leave out. Perhaps the reason why so many people have such a hard time setting their priorities is that they make it more complex than it needs to be. Some people get confused into thinking that, when I set my priorities, I have to decide what is the #1 most important thing, what is the #2 most important thing, what is the #3 most important thing… That can lead to some very difficult choices. Some things in life are essential and so it makes no sense trying to figure out which one is more important. That is like trying to figure out whether breathing in or breathing out is more important. We really should do both.

So, for example, why agonize over whether our family or our career is more important. I don't want to leave either of these out of the box. Is it more important to spend time with the family or to go to work and make money? Which is a higher priority? That is a silly question. Quit your job so that you can spend all your time with Junior. After Junior goes without food for a few days, he will be begging you to go back to work. On the other hand, if you spend so much time at work that you never get to see Junior, he may be asking some serious questions about whether or not you even love him. Which is worse, starving the kid for love or starving the kid for food? Neither is acceptable and so we don't have to rank them. We just need to make sure that both spending time with our family and making money are in the box. As long as they are both in the box, we are managing our priorities. Leave either one of them out of the box and our priorities are messed up.

What If I Must Make a Choice?

OK, but what if it comes down to making a choice between taking an important business trip or attending an important family event? Don't you have to prioritize them to decide which one to do? Hopefully not. The decision isn't a simple #1 priority versus #2 priority question. There are a lot of things to consider in making such a choice. When I was Executive Director of a large consumer research association, I had to make the Board Meetings regardless of what was going on with the family. That didn't mean that my career was more important than my family. Actually the main reason I took my career in that direction is because it had great benefits for both my career and my family. That was one situation where, all things considered, taking the business trip was more important than staying home. On the other hand, there was a different time in my life when my kids were young and I found myself on the road too much. At that point, I decided to take my career in a direction that required less travel. That didn't mean I abandoned my career for my family. I just found ways to keep them both in the box.

When we make everything a priority issue, we set up an artificial win-lose situation. If I have a conflict between something I want to do with my family and something I need to do at work, I am setting my work against my family. That may not be the case at all. When we put more than one thing in the box there will come a time when we will have multiple things competing for our time. If I always favor my career in such situations, then I am marginalizing my family. If I always favor my family, I am marginalizing my career. If I take everything into consideration and work to best accommodate both family and career, then I can keep them both in the box.

I recently heard of a very successful executive who was making tens of millions of dollars per year at his job. One day his daughter handed him a list. She had written down all of the significant events that had happened in her life over the last two years. There were twenty items on the list. He had missed all twenty events. He told her how much he loved her but the list didn't lie. He could explain why each of those missed events represented something very important in his career. At the end of the day, however, he had to admit that his career was a priority and his daughter was not. His career was always in the box. The important events in his daughter's life were not. He quit his mega-million dollar job so that he could make his daughter a priority. That didn't mean that he quit working all together. He just redirected his career so that he could make both his job and his daughter fit in the box. He wanted them both to be priorities.

Which Comes First?

There is also the issue of how we order our life. Shouldn't we always "put first things first?" As a general rule, that's a good idea but there are so many other considerations when deciding where to place things in our day, week, or month. Even if something is the most important thing for me to do today, that doesn't mean it will necessarily be the first thing I do. Think back to the cargo I was loading onto trucks. It didn't really make much difference if we put a piece of cargo in the front or the back of the truck. As long as it made it into the truck, it would find its way to its destination. So we made the decision about where to place the cargo into the truck based on how the boxes fit not based on how important each individual box was.

In a similar way, the real question at the end of the day is what made it into the box and what did not. If something made it into the box, it usually didn't matter when we did it. Just because something comes first in our day, that doesn't mean it is the most important or our highest priority. Your family isn't somehow less important than your job just because you spend most of your time with them in the evening after you get home from work. As long as they both get adequate time, you are prioritizing them both. There are many factors to consider when deciding where something should fit in the box. In the next chapter when we discuss the Value Principle, we will cover these factors in much greater detail.

Prioritizing With Three Simple Categories

Please note that I am not advocating that we abandon looking at how important something is as we manage our time. Throughout this whole book we will talk about how we can focus in on what's most important. We just need to keep in mind that the goal of prioritizing our time is to make sure that we get done what must be done. With that in mind, let's look at a simple way to prioritize our life that doesn't get us caught up in how important everything is relative to everything else. This approach only considers three things in setting our priorities.

What Must Go Into the Box

We can't fit everything that we might like to do into the box. At the most basic level, we must ask a simple question. What do we definitely want in our box? We must be sure to keep that at a reasonable level. If we try to cram too much into our box, there is a big chance we will break something. We have to be very careful when we decide that something is definitely in the box. I love basketball but I rarely will play league ball. If I agree to play in a league, then all the games are in the box. Back before my wife and I had children, that wasn't a problem. However, when my kids were young and my career was demanding I quit agreeing to that commitment. I could still play pick-up ball when I had time but I didn't want league ball to crowd my box. It is best to have too few things that must be in the box than to have too many. When planning your week, you want to see some space at the top of the box.

What Should Stay Out of the Box

Here is something we just have to come to grips with. Some things we want to do will be left out of the box. I am your basic American guy and so I would love to build my life around ESPN. I would love to know everything there is to know about all the major sports on every level. However, I have made a conscious effort to kick almost all of it out of the box. I give myself the luxury of following one sport on one level. I follow the NBA and that's it. I don't follow college basketball. I don't follow football, baseball, soccer, or ice hockey at all. I just follow the NBA. That's all the sports I let in my box lest I risk filling it too full. Notice that I haven't kicked all sports out of my box. We must put some fun things in our box. The challenge is to make sure we don't fill up our box with the fun things leaving no room for more important things of lasting significance. It is OK to play golf, watch TV, play video games, go fishing, follow sports, etc. Put some of that in the box. However, we must limit the room they take up or we risk running out of room for things that will leave a lasting impact on our lives and the lives of the people we love.

What Is on the Margin

We don't want to totally fill up our box with things that must be done every day. On the other hand, we don't want to waste time by leaving part of our box empty. So what do we do? We make sure we have some things that will go in our box if there is room. If there is not room, we can afford to leave them out. These are things that are on the margin. For example, I generally plan so that I have an hour or so left over at the end of the day. It is that time when I can be flexible. Literally, I use that time to stretch and listen to music. It relaxes me and keeps me from getting stiff as I age. My daughter says I am doing yoga. I tell her that big guys don't do yoga. We stretch. She says I may stretch but it looks an awful lot like yoga to her. Whatever we call it, I can benefit greatly from doing it regularly. But if I miss it one day, I don't suddenly just stiffen up. So I put stretching (or yoga) on the margin. When it fits, I put it in the box. When it doesn't, I just leave it out of the box.

Because we don't know exactly how much time everything will require, we need to keep a good number of things on the margin. Here is where knowing what is more important can be very valuable. We don't have to rank order the things that must go in or must stay out of our box. But if things are on the margin, we need to know their importance relative to each other.

If two things must go in the box, then it doesn't matter which one is more important. The same is true if two things should be left out of the box. But if two things are on the margin, then it really does matter which one is more important. That's because there is a good chance one will make it into the box and one will not. When we do have time to work on an item that is on the margin, we will have to choose which one to put into the box. It is best to pick the most important item.

Making It Fit

When I worked on loading trucks that summer, there would be times we would get to the end of our trailer and we would still have a few boxes left over. That meant we had to either repack the truck or go to the head boss and tell him that everything won't fit. Neither of these were something we wanted to do. So on more than one occasion, the forklift driver (never me) would take a third alternative. He would place a pallet on the forklift and start using it as a battering ram. He used the power of a forklift to smash that pallet into the boxes inside the trailer a few times and we had more than enough room for a few more boxes. This made me feel quite uneasy but if you saw how tough and surly those seasoned dock workers were, you would know better than to ask questions. I guess my container manager was thinking that he just solved his problem even if it did create a huge problem for the person receiving the merchandise.

That is the approach I see so many people taking to time management. They are pushing and shoving trying to get one more thing into their box. And they wonder why things are breaking. If we try to overstuff our box, something will break. We must respect the line between what is in our box and what is not. Our priorities are straight when we make sure that the things we value most are the things that make it in the box. That is how we manage our limited time.

The Priority Challenge:
Resolve to be careful what you put into your
twenty-four hour box.

5
Value

The Value Principle:
Poverty Awaits Those Who Spend High Value
Time Doing Low Value Things

Learning to prioritize our time is crucial to helping us understand what to put on our schedule and what to keep off. Prioritization is less helpful in telling us when to do those things. Though "put first things first" is a good general rule to follow, there are definitely times when it does not apply. We may have good reasons for moving the most important things away from the start of our day. For example, some of my buddies and I get together three days a week at 6:00 AM to play basketball. My wife is a lot more important to me than these basketball buddies. She is first in my life and my basketball buddies are way down the list. Though Lisa is an extremely high priority in my life, I don't always put her first in my day. In fact, she has no desire whatsoever to be the first person I spend time with on my basketball days. If I am going to get up that early in the morning, Lisa wants me to find something lower on my priority list than her to occupy my time.

When it comes to spending our time, we must realize that it is a matching process. Why do my basketball buddies and I play basketball at 6:00 AM? Because it is the time we can find a gym and because we are working professionals. That time best fits our work and family commitments. It isn't because basketball is more important to us than our families and our careers. We do it at 6:00 AM so we can make time for our families and our careers. The higher priority things in our lives are the very reasons why we put basketball first in our days.

Understanding Value

Effective time management doesn't just involve throwing everything we may want to do onto a sheet of paper and striking through items when we happen to finish them. That may be a good place to start. It can be useful to order the things we want to do from most to least important. But by itself importance does not necessarily dictate *when* we do things. Time management involves giving careful consideration to our day and deciding when is the best time to do what needs to be done. This all starts with an understanding of value. Time is valuable much like money is valuable. People who effectively manage their money do so because they understand the value of money.

On any given day, I will have some pictures of George Washington and some pictures of Andrew Jackson in my wallet. Now in terms of my favorite presidents, Washington is towards the top of the list and Jackson is towards the bottom. However, I value those pictures of Jackson more than I value the pictures of Washington. That's because the pictures of Washington are on $1.00 bills and the pictures of Jackson are on $20.00 bills. My understanding of value and not my opinion of history determines which pictures I like best.

Our understanding of value is something we must develop. If you give a child a choice between a dime and a nickel, which one will he choose? If the child is very young, he will choose the nickel because the nickel is larger than the dime. As the child matures, he will learn the concept of value. He will comprehend that a dime is more valuable than a nickel and so he will choose the dime. The child makes better financial decisions when he starts to understand the value of money.

Most adults know to choose a dime over a nickel or a $20.00 bill over a $1.00 bill. We are usually pretty young when we begin to understand the value of money. A major theme that we started in the first chapter and will carry on throughout this whole book is that time is more valuable than money. How is it then that we learn the value of money early in life but we seem quite slow to learn the value of time? To effectively manage our time, we must learn how to value our time.

A billionaire was near the end of his life when someone asked him if he would have done anything differently. He said that, if he could live his life over, he would do more big things because it takes just as long to do something small as it does to do something big. If it takes just as much time to do something of little value as it does to do something of great value, then why would we ever choose to do things of little value? Is it that our thinking about time has not developed any more than the young child's thinking about money? Just as the young child chooses the nickel over the dime because he doesn't understand the value of money, we may choose to spend our days doing trivial things rather than important things because we don't understand the value of time.

How Do We Value Our Time?

All money is valuable but a $20 bill is more valuable than a $1 bill. That is because we can do more things with $20 than we can with $1. In a similar way, all time is valuable. As Zig Ziglar says, every day is a great day and if you don't believe that, miss just one. On the other hand some time is more valuable because we can do more with it. Let's look at what makes some of our time "high value time."

Circadian Rhythm

Early this evening I walked by the kitchen and saw my daughter in there with her best friend. These two energetic young ladies were gleefully baking a cake—all full of energy, laughing, smiling, and having a great time. That is quite a contrast from what I saw a mere twelve hours ago. This same daughter had to get up very early and do something at the university. I bumped into her on campus and she didn't seem nearly as chipper at 7:00 AM as she did when I saw her baking a cake at 7:00 PM. It seems like I have a different daughter early in the morning than I do early in the evening. There is a reason for this.

Our bodies and our minds operate on a twenty-four hour clock. When it comes to physical energy and mental alertness, sometimes we are up and sometimes we are down. These ups and downs come at about the same time every day. This regular pattern of ups and downs in our energy level is called our "circadian rhythm." We don't all have the same circadian rhythm. For me, I am very much an early morning person. I like to start my day very early in the morning. In fact, I like to start my day so early that most people wouldn't even call it morning. Most people would call the time I like to get up "the middle of the night." By the time I walk in to teach an 8:00 AM class I have been up for hours. I come bouncing in and I am quickly hit with the stark reality that my circadian rhythm is different from about 95% of all college students. There I stand all full of energy looking at a classroom full of students who are thinking, "Does this guy come with a snooze button?"

Our high value time is the time of the day when we have the most mental and physical energy to throw at our work. If possible, we need to do our most important things during those times. But what if our circadian rhythm doesn't match what our schedule requires? If that is the case, we need to change it. Part of our circadian rhythm is just natural to us but part of it comes from conditioning. Back when I was in college, most of the jobs I had were at night. So even though I would prefer to get up early, I trained my body to stay up late. Once I graduated, I could go back to my natural circadian rhythm and start getting up early again. So we have two choices when it comes to our circadian rhythm. We can change our schedule to fit our rhythm or we can change our rhythm to fit our schedule. The point is that we want our schedule and our circadian rhythm to match so that we are spending our high energy time on our most valuable tasks.

Prime Time

In our professions, we need to be aware of what our "prime time" is and value that time above all else. Prime time could be a time of the day or it could be a season of the year. Whenever it is, we need to make sure we don't waste it doing low value things.

All successful salespeople know that there is something called "prime selling time." If I am in sales, my highest value time is when I can get in touch with the most buyers. In direct selling, it is in the evening when most people are home. If I am selling to small businesses, it is early in the morning when the boss is in but no one else has started grabbing his time yet. If I sell to restaurants, prime time is before the lunch rush begins and after it ends.

Accountants have a different view of prime time. In public accounting, prime time isn't a certain time of the day but a certain time of the year—during tax season. An accountant friend of mine just paid cash for a swimming pool with the money he made this past tax season. My prime time as a professor is at the very start and the very end of the semester. Retailers have a season of prime time too. It is during the Christmas buying season. Poverty awaits the retailer who decides to shut the store and take a vacation the day after Thanksgiving.

Life-Cycle of Career and Family

Our careers and our families have high value time too. Anytime we embark on a new career, we need to set aside more quality time for it. I tell my students that, when they graduate and start their first job, that isn't the time to rest. The earlier they establish themselves in their careers, the quicker they will be able to have time to relax and still do well financially. If someone is starting a new business, they need to invest more quality time in it up front. Eventually, if they structure the business right, it will take very little of their time. But at the start they have to pay the price.

Our families also go through stages where they require more attention. My wife and I had all four of our children fairly close together. Our oldest child was five years old when our youngest was born. In those early years, I had to invest a lot into the family. But those years didn't last forever. Every year, it seemed like the children demanded less and less of our time.

Now, in a perfect world, we won't have the most time intensive part of our career collide with the most time intensive period of our family. Unfortunately we don't live in a perfect world. So what happens if we are at the stage in life where both our careers and our families are pulling hard at us? This is when some serious sacrifice is needed. I have a good friend named Eric who had five little children when he was in medical school. Back then, only two things got any of his attention--his family and his medical training. He didn't play golf. He didn't watch sports. He didn't hang out with the guys. He didn't play in the softball league. It was family and medical school and that was it. Because Eric made those sacrifices then, today he can enjoy a great life. Since he didn't ignore his wife and kids, he still has a very close-knit family. They all made some sacrifices and now they have the money to really enjoy their time together. He had to sacrifice everything except his family and his career for those few years.

Here is a key phrase that we will return to over and over in this book: "For a reason and for a season." Eric and his family were willing to make big sacrifices for a season (a limited time) because he knew they were doing so for a reason (something that would benefit them all). If year after year after year our family must sacrifice while we pursue our own personal fame and fortune, something is wrong. On the other hand, there is nothing wrong with a family that will come together with a goal in mind. Time together is sacrificed to achieve the goal knowing that once the goal is achieved, the season for sacrifice is over and everyone is better for the sacrifices that were made.

How To Value What We Do?

So what do we do with high value time? There is only so much of it so obviously we need to make sure that we spend it doing high value things. At any given moment, there are millions of things we could be doing. Not all of these are of the same value. How do we know what is of high value and what is not? Let's look at five things to consider when determining the real value of those things that are competing for our time.

Roads Have Destinations

My favorite line in all of children's literature comes from *Alice in Wonderland*. Alice comes to a fork in the road and asks Cheshire Cat which road she should take. He asks her where she is going. She replies that she does not know. He then tells her that it doesn't matter. All roads lead somewhere and, if we don't have a destination, it doesn't matter which one we take. If we don't have a clear picture in our minds about what we want from life, then it doesn't matter how we spend our high value time. But once we decide what is most important to us, then we value those activities that will give it to us. We will discuss this in greater depth throughout this book, particularly when we get to the Perception Principle.

Choices Have Consequences

All choices have consequences. Sometimes we must choose between positive and negative consequences. These are the easy choices to make. If my choice is between going to church and doing drugs, the decision is easy. I am going to church. Managing our time would be a lot easier if the choice was always between good and bad. I just received an email from a publisher who was sending me some money for a foreign translation of a book I wrote. It wasn't much but, in his words, "it is better than a stick in the eye." Given the choice between a few hundred dollars and a stick in the eye, I will always take the money. Life would be a lot easier if all decisions were this easy.

Life is not that simple. Usually the choice isn't between good and bad but between good and better. Some of the things we do provide only a small benefit and some provide a big benefit. I could exercise and enjoy the benefits of good health and more energy. Those are great benefits. Or I could take the same time and watch TV. That would give me the benefit of being entertained. That's good. We don't need to throw good out of our life. We just need to avoid spending our high value time on it. We need to throw our high value time at great and give our low value time to good.

Acorns Become Oak Trees

I heard a successful government official say that he deals with acorns so he doesn't have to deal with oak trees. Little problems not taken care of can turn in to big problems down the road. So he likes to deal with small problems while they are still small. I learned this lesson the hard way a few years ago.

The tube that drained the condensation from our air conditioner stopped up. It wasn't that big of a deal. I knew I needed to take the time to fix it but I just never got around to it. The condensation that had not been draining properly made its way into the wood subflooring of the hall. One day, my oldest son started down the hall. I say started because he never finished. The floor gave way and the next thing we knew, my son along with the hall carpet were sinking into the crawl space underneath the house. He was OK but the hall wasn't. We had to completely replace all the flooring. I had made an absolutely terrible time and money management choice. I chose to ignore the air conditioner drain hose. That was easy to do. But I couldn't ignore the gaping hole in the hall. It would have taken me very little time and no money to clear the drain hose. It took me lots of time and money to replace the hall floor.

Growing problems seldom go away on their own. They just keep growing into bigger and bigger problems. If we invest a little of our valuable time dealing with the acorns in our garden, we won't have to spend large amounts of our valuable time cutting down oak trees.

Commitments Must Be Kept

Sometimes we make commitments to low value tasks. I think we are all guilty of, at one time or another, saying yes to things that add little value to our lives or the lives of those around us. In a moment of weakness, we say yes when we should have said no. Now we have this low value task on our schedule. What do we do? Do we just drop it? Or do we go ahead and give our high value time to it even if it is a low value task? Well there is something that is of much greater value than our time. It is our integrity. It is our word. It is the trust that we build when people know that they can believe what we say. So when we have committed to low value tasks, we must keep those commitments even when it requires us to spend our high value time on them. The value is not in completing the task. The value is in being a person that people know they can trust.

Life Should Be Fun

Sometimes we should take our high value time and give it to things that have no value whatsoever beyond the fact that they are simply fun to do. That was a key point we introduced when we discussed the Principle of the Excluded Alternative. We will carry that theme through the whole book. Fun needs to be part of our time management strategy. Sure, there is more to life than fun. We don't make all of our choices based on how much fun we can have. Show me a person who always chooses the fun road and I will show you a person whose life is not much fun. Life has a way of beating up people who never learn to make short term sacrifices for long term rewards. On the other hand, show me a person who doesn't know how to have fun and I will show you a person who has a life that is out of balance.

Investing Versus Spending Our Time

Most people spend their money. Wealthy people invest their money. That is how they become wealthy. Professor Thomas Stanley has made a career studying millionaires. He went into this thinking that millionaires would be extravagant spenders. He found that such wasn't the case. He discovered that most millionaires were very hesitant to part with their money. They would spend a little here and a little there but they wanted to save their high value money so they could invest it. They would spend the small stuff and invest the big money. That is how they became millionaires. Most millionaires live in normal houses, not mansions. Most millionaires drive normal cars or pick-up trucks, not extravagant sports cars. They have become wealthy because they have learned to invest their high value money.

When we spend our money, we benefit from it in the moment. When we invest our money, we can benefit from it for years to come. That is what wealthy people have discovered. The same principle applies to our time. We can spend our time and enjoy the moment or we can invest our time and enjoy the future. Now obviously we don't want all of our time to go towards our future. Some of it should be spent with no thought for the future whatsoever. What we want to be sure to do is to take our high value time and invest it. Invest it in our families. Invest it in our careers. Invest it in our personal development. Invest it in helping others. We don't want to spend all of our high value time doing low value things which will give us little in return. Save those low value things for our low value time. We want to take our high value time and invest it. That's what the most successful people in any field do.

The Value Challenge:
Resolve to spend low value time and invest
high value time.

6
Distractions

The Distraction Principle:
The Most Appealing Path Is Seldom the
One We Are On

As we finish this first section of the book, we need to explore one more basic principle about our time. This basic is less about managing our time and more about mismanaging it. We could be perfect at valuing our time, saying yes and saying no, setting proper priorities, and laying out our schedule. But what good is all of this if we are constantly chasing rabbits down the wrong trail? It is extremely important that we stick to the path that will take us where we want to go.

Taking the Wrong Path

I learned this lesson the hard way one summer back in college when I worked at a camp in the Rocky Mountains. The camp was situated in a picturesque valley in the shadow of a beautiful mountain. All summer long, a few of my buddies and I would look at that mountain knowing that the reason God put it there was so that the four of us could climb it. About midway through the summer all four of us had the same day off and so we decided that it was time to tackle the mountain that had been staring us in the face.

Now when I say this was a mountain, I don't mean it was a mountain climber's mountain. It was more of a hiker's mountain. There were several trails and it wouldn't take long to make it to the top. Our hike up the mountain took us about four hours and it was well worth it. We were above the tree line and so we could see for miles around in every direction. The mountain top wasn't just the one peak. It was actually spread out across a few acres. I wanted to make sure that I got a view from every direction.

After wandering around the top of that mountain for a while, I realized that I was separated from my friends. That didn't really concern me because, as I said, this wasn't like we were on a mountain climbing expedition. We were on a hike. However, I didn't want to be hiking after dark and so I decided to take the trail down the mountain by myself.

Right before sunset, I made it to my destination – or so I thought. Nothing around me looked familiar. Then I noticed something. The sun was setting in the wrong end of the valley. It took me a little while to figure out what was wrong but eventually I realized why the sun was setting in the east. It was because what I thought was east wasn't east at all. It was actually west. Well, if what I thought was east was actually west then what I thought was north must actually be south. I looked up and realized that I was staring at the wrong side of the mountain. Yes, I found a great trail but unfortunately it did not take me to where I wanted to go. I was in the valley that was on the other side of the mountain from our camp.

Three Problems With the Wrong Path

I learned an important lesson that day. If you want to get to your destination, you really need to take the right path. I made good time coming down the mountain. I loved the trail I was on. It was a beautiful hike. Everything about that trail was wonderful except for one thing. It didn't take me where I wanted to go. In life distractions come when we take the wrong path. No matter how much we love what we are doing, if it isn't taking us to where we want to be, we are distracted. As soon as I started down the wrong trail, I had a big problem. Actually I had three problems and they are the exact same three problems that we have whenever we allow distractions to put us on the wrong path.

We Waste Time

The first problem that I created for myself by going down the back side of the mountain is that I wasted precious time. Remember that I headed down the mountain because I only had a limited amount of time to make my destination before it was dark. If I had not taken the wrong trail, I would have made it to my destination just fine. However, when I took the wrong trail, I used up all the time that I needed to get where I wanted to go. The deadline I gave myself was quickly approaching and I was nowhere near where I wanted to be. That is what distractions do. We all have a limited amount of time to accomplish what it is we want to do. We only have so many hours in a day. We only have so many years with our kids. We only have so much time on this earth. In every way, life gives us only so much time. Sunset is coming and if we don't spend the time between now and then on the right path, we won't get where we want to go. Distractions waste what little time we have to reach our goals.

We End Up Further Away

However, it wasn't that I just wasted the time I spent on that trail. My second problem was that, when I finished going down the wrong trail, I was further away from my destination than I was when I started. My one small decision put me on a path that would eventually lead me many miles away from where I wanted to be. What's ironic is that it took about as much effort and energy to go down the wrong trail as it would have taken to go down the right one. My little distraction didn't save me anything. It actually cost me a lot because once I did all the work to get down the mountain, I still had work to do. I still had to get back to camp.

We must avoid thinking that the little distractions are just wasting the time we spend on them. Not so! The opposite of being distracted is being focused. To succeed at anything, we have to be able to focus on it for an extended period of time. But it takes time to get focused. When we are focused and clear about what we are doing, we can make great progress towards our goals. When we lose focus, we slow down. When we finally get past our distraction and start back on the right trail, we have to regain our focus. That will always take some time. It may take a lot of time. We explore this in much greater depth later when we discuss The Clarity Principle. The important point to understand is this. When you get distracted, you aren't just standing still. You are moving further away from where you need to be.

We Think We Are Making Progress

Finally, I had a third problem when I took the wrong trail. The wrong trail gave me the illusion that I was on the right trail. I thought I was making great time. It felt like I was moving toward my goal. Everything seemed OK. The trees looked the same. The squirrels weren't any different. I had to step over what appeared to be the same logs. Nothing made me feel like I was on the wrong side of the mountain. It wasn't until it was too late that I realized just how misguided my efforts were.

Distractions have a way of distorting our reality. In fact, that is often one reason why we let ourselves get distracted. We feel just as good, or maybe even better, going down the wrong trail as we do going down the right one. We will explore this idea in much greater depth when we discuss The Discernment Principle. We need to be constantly aware of the fact that we may be on the wrong trail. Usually we stay distracted because we are oblivious to the signs that something is wrong. If I would have noticed early on that the sun was on the wrong side of the sky, I could have prevented my whole trek down the wrong side of the mountain. That is why we must vigilantly guard against distractions and not just vaguely hope we are on the right trail. One thing that can help us do this is understanding why we get distracted.

Why We Get Distracted

There are three major reasons why we allow ourselves to get distracted. If we want to effectively manage our time, it is imperative that we guard against all three.

We Are Wired to Get Distracted

We are made to be easily distracted. It is in our DNA. Our very survival depends on our ability to refocus our attention at a moment's notice. There are few tasks that are so important that they deserve our total 100% undivided attention. Things can happen around us that need to distract us. When we are walking down the street, we had better not be so focused on where we are going that we don't see the truck that is about to hit us if we step off of the curb.

Being too distracted is a bad thing but the opposite of it isn't much better. We cannot be totally oblivious to everything that goes on around us. We don't want to be like the absent minded professor stereotype so often associated with Einstein. He was so focused on his world of theoretical physics that he was oblivious to everything else. Of course Einstein could get away with it. Reinvent physics and people will give you a break if your feet aren't always planted on solid ground. However, few of us have something that major on our list of accomplishments. We live in a world where the ability to refocus is a desirable trait. Actually in some professions it is essential.

One thing that always strikes me about the most successful outside salespeople is just how many of them appear to have attention deficit disorder (ADD). I have sometimes joked that if you want to see if someone would be good in outside sales, call the person's elementary school teacher. If your candidate drove the teachers crazy, then you may have the right person. I tell my friends who are doing very well in sales but not so well in staying focused to not worry about it. They don't have a deficit disorder. They have a special skill. They have the gift of rapid refocus. In school it may have really annoyed their teachers but in the world of outside sales it is incredibly useful. The demands on their attention are constantly changing and so they actually need to be easily distracted.

So we don't necessarily need to think that being distracted is always a bad thing. We just need to know when to be distracted and when to be focused. The father of American Psychology William James said, "Wisdom is the art of knowing what to overlook." Distraction is like so many other aspects of human nature. We need it but we also need to be able to manage it. If it helps us stay aware of the world around us, it is a good thing. It's the distractions that take us wandering down the wrong paths that we need to avoid.

We Want to Be Distracted

It is so tempting to let *what is fun* distract us from what we should do. Hall of Fame Golfer Tim Kite once said that you can always find a distraction if you are looking for one. Now it is easier than ever to find fun things to distract us. Just open up your web browser and start to surf. I have often heard the internet being described as a weapon of mass distraction. How much time does the average knowledge worker waste every work day surfing social media sites? The estimates are as high as one hour per day. It is said that social media sites are costing American companies tens of billions of dollars per year on lost productivity. Why do we let the internet so easily distract us? Well, look at all the boring stuff on our to-do lists. Compare that with all the interesting things on the internet. What would you really rather be doing? Many of our distractions are a lot more interesting and a lot more fun than the things which they are distracting us from.

It is also tempting to let *what is easy* distract us from what we should do. An ancient writer said that it isn't obstacles that keep us from our goals. It is a clear path to a lesser goal. If I am walking down a trail and I see a big boulder in my way, my first thought isn't, "How do I move the boulder?" No, I just naturally start looking for a clear path around the boulder. I am only going to start thinking about moving the boulder if there is no other way around it and if I really want to get where I am going. The problem is that in life, clear paths seldom take us anywhere we want to go. If we always take the clear paths to our lesser goals, then all we ever achieve are lesser goals.

That is why we so often end up on the wrong trail. A lot of the time we are looking for it either because it is more fun or because it is easier. I am all for fun and there is nothing wrong with looking for an easier way to do something. But when we find alternate paths, we must ask if they will take us where we want to go.

We Are Enticed into Being Distracted

There are people who make tremendous amounts of money because they are so good at enticing you into their distractions. I am not saying that we should blame them for us being distracted. We have to take responsibility for our own lives. On the other hand, we do have to know what we are up against. We are amateurs at staying focused. They are professionals at getting us distracted.

We can sit down to watch one television show and end up being there all night. Do you think that happens by accident? No, there were people working hard to keep you there staring at their programs. All night long, they are trying to distract you from what you should be doing. They aren't evil people sent to earth for the express purpose of crushing your schedule. They are people who have a job to do and they do it well. If they don't keep you hooked on the next program and then the next, the networks would take their job away from them and give it to someone else. Their very livelihood depends on their ability to keep you distracted and they become very good at doing so. Usually they are a lot better at distracting us than we are at not being distracted.

Weapons Against Distractions

So our very human nature is to be distracted. We want to be distracted. Not only that, there are very sharp people out there who think day and night about how to keep us distracted. This puts the challenge we face to stay focused in perspective. It isn't some little kids' battle we fight with a squirt gun. If we want to win the battle against distractions, we have to bring out the big guns. What weapons do we have to defeat distraction? Here are the five big ones.

Commitment: Henry Ford said "Obstacles are those frightful things you see when you take your eyes off your goal." The more we are committed to our goal, the less likely we are to get distracted. I tell my students that they could make A's in any and every class they wanted to. They usually give me a very skeptical look when I tell them that. I then go on to set up a hypothetical situation where the life of the person they love most is on the line and they have to make an A in a certain class to save it. I contrast that with a situation where I would just give them $25 to make an A in the same class. Then I put them in the following situation. It is the night before the final exam. You think you are ready but you are not sure. If it is for $25 you might get distracted from studying when a group of friends invite you to go get pizza with them. But how distracted would you get if the life of the person you loved most in the world was on the line when you took the test the next day. My guess is that, no matter how much you loved pizza and how much you enjoyed your friends, the dinner with your friends could not possibly distract you from studying for the exam. As we make stronger personal commitments to a goal, the less likely we are to get distracted from that goal.

Accountability: When my kids started college, I had a clever plan to keep them from getting too distracted from their studies. It cost me $20 per week per child. I told them that I would give them $20 every week if they would just sit down and tell me how things were going in each of their classes. They thought it was a good deal. For a mere ten minutes of their time, they could make $20. To me though, I knew I wasn't just buying that ten minutes of their time. I knew I would be spending time in their heads all week long. When they were studying, they always knew in the back of their minds that they were going to have to explain to me how they did in the class they were studying for. That mere fact that they were going to share with me what happened would give them a little extra motivation to stay focused. In the end, they all did very well in college. Sometimes just having a person that we share our goals with will keep us on track. If distractions are a huge problem, we should have someone ask us on a regular basis how well we are doing at staying on track.

Written Goals: Psychological researchers have found an interesting quirk in human nature. If we write something down, we develop much stronger commitments to it. If we don't want another person to hold us accountable, we can just let a slip of paper do it. There is something about written goals that keep us on track. In the time management class I teach, many of my college students hate it when I make them write down their goals for the day. Even if I tell them that they can throw the paper away or not look at it ever again, some students still hate it. It isn't the time it takes to do because it doesn't take that long. The reason they hate it is because of the way it makes them feel. They tell me that once they have written something down, they feel compelled to do it. I tell them that they don't have to do it but they tell me it doesn't matter. If the piece of paper is telling them to do it, they feel as though they are tied to it in some way. As long as they keep the things they want to do in their head, they can get distracted all day without feeling guilty at all. But the second they write them down, everything changes. Now they have to get them done. They hate it when I make them write their goals for the day down because I make them feel guilty when they find themselves getting distracted.

Time Constraints: Every time I plan my day, I don't just make a list of things I need to get done. I also go down that list and place estimated times by each task that I have given to myself. Then, when I start the task, I start a timer. It is amazing how something as silly as a timer will keep me focused and on track. Later when we discuss The Efficiency Principle, we will look at how placing constraints on our time is so much better than just letting us take as long as we want to do something. Even as I write this chapter, I have placed a very tight time constraint on myself and it just kept me from getting distracted. Time constraints are powerful weapons to fight distractions.

Barriers: According to what people say on the internet, the biggest distraction we face is the internet. That could be selection bias. Who gets distracted by the internet? I would guess that it is probably people who are on the internet. So whether or not it is the biggest distraction challenge, I don't know. But I do know that it is a huge one for me. There are three sites in particular that give me problems: Facebook, NBA. com, and Google News. Knowing this, I have gone into the antivirus program on my office computer and blocked these three sites. I have put an e-barrier between me and those three distracting sites. I like barriers much better than will power. If I know I have access to my favorite sites, all day long I am fighting the temptation to stop working and start surfing. But if they aren't available to me, the temptation to be distracted is not even there. We will discuss the concept later when we cover The Discipline Principle.

Staying Focused

People who know how to manage their time understand that they cannot give into temptation every time they happen upon a trail that looks more interesting, easy, or fun than the one they are on. Most of our days are full of very tempting opportunities to get distracted. If we can't conquer these temptations, our lives will be caught up in a flurry of useless activity—moving fast but never getting where we want to go.

The Distraction Challenge:
Resolve to choose the trail that actually is right
over the one that simply looks right.

Focus

The Chaos Principle:
The Pull In Life Is Always Towards
Chaos and Never Towards Order

The NYCNO Principle:
The Value In Planning Comes From the
Process Not the Plan

The Process Principle:
Master the Process and the Results
Will Take Care of Themselves

The System Principle:
Any System Is Better than No System

The Hard Time Principle:
Hard Time Crowds Out Soft Time

The Efficiency Principle:
If You Are Always Working You
Don't Have to Be Efficient

Part 2

Focus

Imagine you are standing at the tee box on a golf course. The first thing you do is look for the green and see where you want to go with the ball. Then you look around to see what problems you may face in getting there—problems such as water and sand traps. Finally, you develop a strategy in your mind about how to get there. What you are doing is developing your vision for the hole. If you don't develop the vision, you will just be out there randomly hitting the golf ball around the course with no chance of making it into the cup.

Back when I played golf that was my favorite part of the game. I would step up to a 400 yard par four. I knew exactly what to do. I will just use my driver to hit a 220 yards shot a little to the left. That will send me over the water and keep me clear of the bunkers on the right. From there, I will use my three or four iron to get it up onto the center right side of the green slightly down-hill from the pin. Then with one putt, I will be out of there with a birdy.

My vision was perfect every time. I could see the big picture. If the game ended there, I could have been on the PGA Tour. But then came the hard part. It was time to focus on the little things. Specifically, I had to focus on that little white ball sitting on the ground in front of me. I had my vision of what I wanted to do. Now I actually had to do it.

When I moved from the big vision to the narrow focus, here is how things would go. I would start by duffing my ball on the tee shot. From about twenty yards down the fairway, I would send it chasing some squirrels out in the woods. After thoroughly exploring nature for a while, I would start my aquatic adventure. Remember the water trap? I would donate three or four golf balls to it. Then it was off to play in the sand for a while. Upon finally making it to the green, hope was in sight. If I could three-putt the green, I could keep my score for the hole in double digits.

Why was my golf game so awful? Here is where I went wrong. I never took golf lessons. I never learned the basics of golf. I figured that, if I would get myself some golf equipment, I would be a golfer. I bought some clubs and started hacking my way around the course. I wasn't a golfer. I was just a guy with some sticks randomly whacking away at some little white ball. I wasn't even good enough to be called a duffer. I was a person with some clubs who didn't know the first thing about actually playing golf.

I learned two important lessons from my days playing golf. One lesson was that I should stick to basketball where, if you are tall enough, you don't need much skill. The more important lesson I learned was that you can't move from vision directly to action. You need to learn some basics. I decided that I would never play golf again until I took golf lessons. If I ever wanted to play golf, I would learn the basics of golf.

Many people make the same mistake in time management that I made in golf. They can understand that they need to manage their time. They may even have a good idea of what they want to do with their time. They develop their vision and so they head into action. They get some equipment—calendars, day planners, time management software, to-do lists, etc.—and they start hacking away at their schedule. Time management moves from a vision of what they want to do with their life to focusing in on the moment. When we don't learn the basics of focus, time management can break down.

In the current section, we will learn the six basics of focus. We need to know what we will see when we focus in on the day's activities. We will be looking chaos square in the eye. So we will start our discussion of focus by looking at what to do when chaos is staring back at us.

We will then cover the three basics which can guide us in beating back chaos. We will look at planning, processes, and systems. Our #1 weapon against chaos is planning. To fight chaos, we must plan. Effective planning occurs when we understand processes. There is a process to achieve almost any result we want. We don't need to worry about the results if we follow the process. The results will take care of themselves. So how do we make sure we follow the process? We need a system. We will discuss how we can build a system that fits our unique needs.

To end our discussion of focus, we will talk about two very important basics to understand about our schedules. First, we all have to face the fact that others may have more control over our schedules than we do. This happens because of the commitments we make. We will explore how to balance such commitments against the need for flexibility in managing our time. Second, we will see why scheduling in more work time doesn't always translate into getting more work done.

Through understanding the material in Part 2, you will be better prepared to move from having a vision to providing focus for your daily activities. You will know how to use planning, processes, and systems to beat back chaos. You will also know what you should and should not do with a tight schedule. The six basics of focus will enable you to turn your time management vision into a daily reality.

7
Chaos

The Chaos Principle:
The Pull In Life Is Always Towards Chaos and
Never Towards Order

Before we look at how to manage our schedule, we have to understand what we are up against. If the world we lived in was a naturally ordered place, time management would be easy. But it is not. I look at pictures out into the universe from the most advanced telescopes and I am amazed at the order. I talk to a biochemist and he explains in incredible detail the order that occurs at the smallest levels of life. Whether it is the massive universe or the smallest cluster of atoms, everything seems to have this intricate order and structure to it. That is, everything except my daily life.

In my life, chaos abounds. I look at any typical day and I see a lot more chaos than order. NASA may be able to show us phenomenal order in something as large as the universe. The scientist in a biochemistry lab may discover that everything is structured perfectly in something as small as the molecular building blocks of life. But here in the real world, somewhere between galaxies and atoms, chaos seems to be the natural state of things.

When I cover this concept in class, I tell my students to look out the window. There they can see this beautifully manicured lawn surrounded by well-kept landscaping. I ask them how the field can stay so beautiful. It is because we have a team of diligent workers on campus whose sole purpose is to beat back chaos. Left to itself, that beautiful lawn would quickly become a totally overgrown mess.

Chaos seems to show up any time we go to work. Think about something as simple as cooking a meal. The kitchen can be so neat and clean. Then we walk in. The more we work, the more the kitchen moves from order to chaos. We are simply trying to fix ourselves something to eat. Chaos is trying to destroy the kitchen in the process. Unless we fight back, that nice, orderly kitchen we started with will be a total mess by the time chaos is done with it. So we cook a little and fight back chaos a little, cook a little, fight back chaos a little… When we cook, we are probably spending more time beating back chaos than we are focusing on the meal.

In the world where we live, the pull in life is always towards chaos and never towards order. We cannot eliminate chaos. Chaos will always exist and it will always find a way to come storming into our lives at the most inopportune times. The challenge is to manage chaos at the appropriate level. Our challenge is to position ourselves so that we can deal with chaos when it inevitably comes our way.

How People Deal With Chaos

So how do people deal with chaos? It depends on the person. Some people are OK with chaos. In fact, they may even enjoy living a chaotic life. Others get discouraged and disgruntled by chaos. Chaos beats them down. Then there are those who know how to deal with chaos. They neither embrace it nor let it beat them down. They keep it at just the right level in their life. Let's spend a little time exploring these three responses to chaos.

Some People Enjoy Chaos

I am sure we can all think of people who thrive on chaos. I think of a friend of mine named Raj. As a professor, he is a very productive researcher and an outstanding classroom teacher. He has a brilliant, creative mind and he is always on the go. Any time we wanted to get together for a meeting though, I always insisted that we meet in my office. My motto is, "A place for everything and everything in its place." Raj's motto is, "A place for everything but that's irrelevant." I didn't like going into his office for fear that some unexpected noise might cause an avalanche and I would be forever buried under research papers, surveys, and term projects.

It would be hard to say that all the chaos in Raj's life hurt him. He is very productive. It certainly didn't seem to bother him. That's the way certain people are. Chaos doesn't bother them. They operate quite well in a chaotic environment. In fact, I bet he didn't like coming to my office much more than I liked going to his. The most common statement I get from students who visit my office is, "Wow, this is neat. None of my other professor's office is this orderly." I bet Raj wouldn't use the word "orderly" to describe my office. He would probably use the word "sterile."

If I were to take all the chaos out of Raj's life, it wouldn't make him productive. He's already productive. It would make him bored. It would make him miserable. He enjoys a certain level of chaos. To expect someone like Raj to live a perfectly orderly life would be unfair, unrealistic, and counterproductive. He is made for chaos.

On the other hand, even someone like Raj cannot let chaos totally take over his life. At a certain point, no matter how much you thrive on chaos, it can become dysfunctional. For the Raj's of the world, the goal isn't to get rid of chaos but to keep it down to a manageable level. What is that manageable level? That manageable level for him is a much higher level than it is for me. Still, even someone like Raj can only manage so much chaos. No matter how much fun chaos may be to him, too much is still too much.

Some People Are Discouraged By Chaos

Not all people are as welcoming of chaos as is Raj. Some people are discouraged by it. Personally, I find it hard to operate in a chaotic environment. If I were to have an office like Raj's, I wouldn't get a thing done. I would walk in, see the mess, and become immobilized by it. I would probably sit there drooling all over myself, totally unable to move or function. I operate best when everything is in order. I get this nice, warm, fuzzy feeling inside when I get everything in my life set up just right. The office is set up right. My day is planned. My business cards are all alphabetized. Everything is fine and wonderful. Once I get it all set up that way, I am ready to go. I am excited. I am energized. I am going full speed because everything is in order. That is the way I like living my life.

There are two problems for people like me. First, no matter how hard we try to fight off chaos, it will still come creeping into our lives. Sometimes, it doesn't creep at all. Sometimes it comes crashing in. When it does, it can really rock our world. People like me need to learn not to be discouraged by the inevitable flow of chaos into our lives.

There is an even bigger problem with people like me. When we aren't willing to venture anywhere near chaos for fear of the psychological distress it may cause, we may be limiting our potential to achieve. Many of the best things in life reside right on the edge of chaos. Productivity can be enhanced by order but sometimes breakthroughs only come through chaos.

Some People Adjust to Chaos

There are those who seem to have mastered a perfect balance between chaos and order. Chaos is not something they embraced nor is it something they avoid. It is something they learn to adjust to. They don't let it run free and totally destroy their schedule. On the other hand, they don't try to eliminate it completely from their lives. In fact, at times, they may even welcome it. However, when order is needed, they fight back against chaos. They seem to have a better handle on chaos than other people. They can adjust to the absence of chaos better than people like Raj who need chaos to flourish. They can deal with the presence of chaos better than people like me who seem to be shut-down by chaos. If their world is chaotic, they are fine. But they keep chaos at a manageable level. They keep a great balance between chaos and order.

Expect Chaos

A big part of dealing with something is to expect it. A boxer will tell you that it isn't the hardest punch that takes you out. It is the one you don't expect. It isn't the most chaotic situations that take us out. It is the ones we don't expect.

Chaos is like the weather. Some days it rains. Some days the sun shines. Some days it snows and some days it is hot. We don't let the weather ruin our lives. We learn to adjust. We have an umbrella for the rainy days, sunscreen for the sunny ones. We have air conditioning for the hot days and heaters for the cold snowy days. We haven't learned to change the weather but we have learned how to go about our lives regardless of the weather.

That is how it should be with chaos. Some days are nice and orderly. We start the day with a clear picture of what we want to accomplish. Things go as planned and by the end of the day, we have checked everything off of our to-do list. There are no major interruptions and the only people who take any of our time are the ones we planned to see.

Other days are chaotic from the time our feet hit the floor. The car doesn't start or there is a wreck on the freeway that has us running late. When we get into work, we are met by one crisis after another, all of which demand our immediate attention. On the way home, we get a call reminding us of an engagement that we had forgotten. We can use today's to-do list tomorrow since we didn't get to a single item on it.

Too bad we can't have a chaos forecast like we have weather forecasts. What if we could go to our cell phone and pull up our chaos forecast. "Things should be orderly this morning but we will have some chaos moving in by early afternoon. After 3:00 PM there will be an 80% chance of chaos." Then we could plan our days around chaos. Unfortunately we don't know when chaos is going to happen. Fortunately, we can know what kind of chaos is most likely to hit our lives. That's because different people can usually expect different forms of chaos.

Again, it is like the weather. I live on the Georgia / Florida border. We don't get snow and so that isn't something that we have to prepare for. A hard freeze for us is if it dips into the 20's on a "cold" winter night (I am sure those of you from up north would consider it humorous that we would call that "cold"). In the summer, however, we just plan for the heat. We generally plan to stay inside in the air conditioning between about 11:00 AM and 6:00 PM. And though we don't have to deal with snow storms, we do have hurricanes blow through here on a regular basis.

It would be crazy to live in North Dakota and have the indifferent attitude towards snow that we have here in the Deep South. It would also be pointless to live in North Dakota and come up with hurricane evacuation plans like we need here in South Georgia. Every place has its own unique weather challenges and we just learn to adjust to what nature will most likely throw our way. When you move, you don't get rid of weather challenges. You simply trade in one challenge for another.

Chaos is the same way. We can't say when it will hit but we know it will hit. The type of chaos that will happen is somewhat predictable. A college student will face different kinds of chaos than will the parent of a small child. A corporate executive will deal with a different kind of chaos than will the manager of a restaurant. We can't escape chaos by quitting school, changing jobs, or shipping the kids off to some remote island to be raised by natives. We just trade in one form of chaos for another.

Keys for Dealing with Chaos

We cannot eliminate chaos. In fact, it isn't a good idea to even try. Rather than trying to keep a totally orderly life, we need to set ourselves up to deal with chaos when it happens. In South Georgia, we have a hurricane plan. In North Dakota, they have a blizzard plan. We need to set ourselves up to deal with the inevitable chaos that will come our way. What do we do to prepare for chaos? Let's look at a few suggestions.

Stay Organized

A major theory that cuts across several different scientific disciplines is chaos theory. The foundation of chaos theory says that how things start can have a massive impact on how things end. I am sure you have heard of the butterfly effect. That is chaos theory. It says that something as small as the movement of a butterfly's wing can cause a hurricane half-way around the world. A small change in how something starts can have a huge impact on things later in time.

What happens if our life is already in chaos when we are hit with a chaotic event? We are adding chaos on top of chaos. Unfortunately, the mathematics of chaos isn't addition. Chaos doesn't add; it multiplies. The chaos compounds and we have a huge mess. But what if we already have order when chaos starts? It is a lot easier to return to order if we start from a state of order. If we are disciplined in living an organized, orderly life before chaos hits, then when it does, we will better be able to ride it out.

Be Prepared to Ride It Out

I have heard that a Grand Canyon rafting trip is a unique experience. As you go through the Grand Canyon, most of the trip is smooth and uneventful. You get to spend most of your time admiring one of the most beautiful creations on this earth. Then there are moments when the smooth flowing water turns into a white-water frenzy. Water is rushing through the rapids, crashing into rocks on all sides. Eventually, you make it through the rapids and you return to a period of smooth waters. When you are in the middle of the rapids, you don't try to turn the raft around and paddle back up-river. You ride them out and try to avoid any serious damage.

That's how life is. Sometimes things are going along very smoothly and then chaos happens. What do we do? It is usually best just to try to ride it out and avoid any serious damage. It's hard to imagine a smooth life when you are in the middle of chaos. At times like these it is good to know that life won't always be such a challenge. We will only be in chaos for a season and then things will smooth out. Chaos doesn't last forever. Whatever is causing our chaos will pass. Eventually, the project will be turned in. The equipment will be fixed. The selling season will be over. The kids will get over the flu. The boss will go on vacation. The exams will be taken. Even the robo-politicians will stop calling you once the election is over. Have you ever heard that all good things must end? Fortunately that also applies to chaos. Eventually, it will be over and life will return to normal again.

In the midst of chaos, the worst thing we can do is to try and turn the raft around and head back upstream. If we ride it out, we will eventually come out on the other side. We need to learn to expect chaos, be prepared for chaos, and then ride it out until we can find a smooth place to begin preparing for the next period of chaos in our life.

Don't Live on the Margin

I have three kids right now who are in college. For the most part, they are not satisfied with anything but A's in all their classes. That makes for some interesting times around final exams. They have all learned that it is much better not to go into finals "on the margin." It is no fun going into finals wanting all A's when you have a couple classes right on the line between an A and a B. It is much more fun having a 98 average and only needing to make a 32 on the final to make an A in the class. Living on the margin is tough because if anything goes wrong, things can turn ugly very quickly. Having a large margin for error makes things a lot easier, especially when life starts pulling us into chaos.

Another example of the risks of living on the margin can be seen if we have too much debt. I loved an analogy that Warren Buffet gave for the problems this creates. He said that living with high levels of debt is like driving a car with a sharp stake coming out from the steering wheel pointed directly at your heart. As long as the road is smooth and nothing unexpected happens, you can drive that way. But a bump in the road can be dangerous and a crash means certain disaster.

If our schedule is all maxed out with no room for error, we can survive in a world without chaos. In a perfect world where chaos doesn't exist, we might be able to handle two bowling leagues, a second part-time job, the kid's soccer games, and still have time to be president of the PTA. But what happens if our schedule is already maxed out and chaos happens? Living a busy life is good. What is not good is living such a busy a life that we don't have the time to deal with the unexpected chaos that will inevitably come our way.

The Chaos Cycle

I have a trick question I like to ask my students when we are talking about the economic cycle. I ask them to discuss who was to blame for a specific recession. They usually start blaming the politicians or political party that they don't like. Then I tell them that no one is to blame. Recessions are part of the economic cycle. That's why we call it a "cycle." Certainly politicians can take an economic downturn and make it last longer than it should. Misguided economic policies can definitely make a recession deeper than it should be. But no politician can eliminate the ups and downs of the economic cycle. That's just economics.

Even if we are managing our time perfectly, there will be a cycle of chaos in our lives. If we are doing anything significant with our lives, we will be in one of three stages of the chaos cycle. We are either in the midst of chaos, we have just come out of chaos, or chaos is awaiting us in the not-too-distant future. The pull in life is always towards chaos and never towards order. We cannot blame the chaos on anyone or anything. It just happens. We cannot eliminate the chaos cycle.

But, just like politicians can make a bad economic situation worse, we can do the same thing with the chaos in our lives. We can make our periods of chaos longer than they should be. We can make the chaos more damaging than it should be. We must fight to keep excess chaos out of our lives but we must not be so naive as to believe we can eliminate it completely. Chaos happens.

The Chaos Challenge:
Resolve to prepare daily for chaos and then be ready to ride it out.

8
NYCNO

The NYCNO Principle:
The Value In Planning Comes From the
Process Not the Plan

Chaos can show up at any moment and thus the idiom, "the best-laid plans of mice and men." If our plans can so quickly go astray, what good is planning? That is the question we will explore in this chapter.

A Tale of Two Cities

In the year 2000, the Federal Emergency Management Agency came up with a list of the three biggest potential disasters that could strike the United States. They were a hurricane strike on New Orleans, a large earthquake in California, and a terrorist attack on New York City. Within just a few years, two of these three disasters occurred. In 2001, a terrorist attack destroyed the very center of the New York City (NYC) financial district and then in 2005, a hurricane devastated miles upon miles of the gulf coast including the city of New Orleans (NO).

When Hurricane Katrina hit, the whole world watched in total dismay over how unprepared New Orleans was for this disaster. How could there be such a lack of readiness for something everyone knew would eventually happen? There is one certainty of living on the gulf coast. If you stay there long enough, you will get smacked by a big, bad hurricane. The vulnerability of New Orleans to such a hurricane was well known. In fact, in the years leading up to Katrina, both *National Geographic* and *Scientific American* had feature articles on the potential catastrophic effects of New Orleans taking a direct hit. And yet, despite knowing of this impending threat, about the only strategy in place seemed to be, "Meet me at the Superdome and we'll ride this thing out."

This was in stark contrast to what we had witnessed just a few years earlier when New York was hit with the 9/11 terrorist attacks. Everyone watched in amazement at how well New York City responded. The very core of NYC's financial district was totally destroyed, almost 350 firefighters lost their lives, and soot and debris from the collapse of the towers blanketed the whole area. Despite this, Manhattan was evacuated in an orderly manner, Wall Street was back in operation in about a week, and New York City, though bruised and battered, returned to a sense of normalcy in very quick order.

I had the opportunity to hear Rudy Giuliani speak about what it was like to be mayor of NYC on 9/11/2001. He said that the thought never crossed anyone's mind that someone might take commercial jetliners and crash them into buildings. They didn't have an "airplanes destroy buildings" plan. The events of 9/11 caught them by total surprise. How, then, did they handle the crisis so well? Though they didn't anticipate the attacks on the World Trade Center, here is what they did do in the years leading up to 9/11. They tried to think of anything that might happen and they planned their responses. They planned for terrorists attacking the subways, a dirty bomb going off in Time Square, a major storm directly hitting them, etc. Giuliani said that everything that they did in response to 9/11 was a direct result of this planning. They planned for everything they could possibly anticipate and that prepared them for the unexpected.

In contrast, New Orleans didn't seem to have a plan at all for something that they knew would eventually happen. If New Orleans needed anything, it needed a hurricane plan. And yet it was as if they were totally caught off guard by Katrina. Just a little bit of planning before Katrina hit would have prevented so much of the grief that Katrina left behind.

NYC had a plan. NO did not. NYC responded well to something they didn't see coming. NO reacted terribly to something they knew would eventually happen. That is the nature of the NYCNO principle (pronounced "nice" and "know"). The value in planning comes from the process and not the plan.

Planning Is Everything

A number of years ago, researchers did a study of new, startup businesses. They found that some of them had business plans and some of them did not. A few years later the researchers went back to see which companies had become successful and which companies were no longer around. To no one's surprise, the companies that had business plans were much more likely to have survived than those that did not. Obviously there was great value in planning.

These researchers then studied the businesses that started with a business plan. They asked them whether or not they actually followed their plans. What they discovered was that there was no relationship whatsoever between the profitability of the companies and whether or not they actually followed their plans. How could this be? How could it be so important to plan but so unimportant to follow the plan?

Let's take this out of the business world and see if it makes sense in sports. On a warm September evening, deep in the heart of Georgia, two high school football teams take the field. The teams are equally talented. The only difference between the two teams is this. The coaching staff for one team spent all week planning for the game. They assessed their own strengths and weaknesses. They looked at the other team's strengths and weaknesses. They developed a game plan for Friday night that they felt would give them the best chance to win. The other team's coaching staff engaged in no planning. Which of these Georgia teams do you think is probably going to win? My guess is that the team that engaged in planning had a significant advantage over the team that did not. Planning definitely gives us an advantage.

Now, let's move a little further south. On that same warm September evening deep in the heart of Florida, two different football teams meet. The coaching staffs for both of the teams spend all week preparing and planning for their matchup. The coaches for both sides assess the other team's strengths and the other team's weaknesses and they both come up with plans that they think will give them the biggest chance to come out victorious on Friday. When Friday arrives, one team sticks to the plan regardless of what happens on the field. The other team is willing to deviate from the plan, or maybe even abandon the plan altogether, based on what is happening on the field. Which of these teams is most likely to win? It is the team that is willing to deviate from its plan.

The Georgia game teaches us that there is great value in planning. The Florida game teaches us that there is great danger in mindlessly sticking to the plan. The value of planning isn't so that we can have a plan that is carved in stone. The value of planning comes from the planning process itself.

The Value of Planning

We undervalue the process of planning and we overvalue the plans we come up with. We could go through the planning process, throw the plan in the trash can, and still be very well prepared. On the other hand, someone could hand us an absolutely wonderful plan and we would benefit very little from it because we did not go through the process of coming up with the plan. We gain much more from going through the planning process than we do from actually having a plan to implement. Why is that so?

Planning Clarifies Our Thinking

First and foremost, it is through the process of planning that we start to gain a clearer picture of what we are facing in the future. Think back to NYC on 9/11. There were a lot of things that have to be done when a disaster of that magnitude strikes. How can you evacuate Lower Manhattan in an orderly way? How can you mobilize for a recovery of the financial district? How can you deal with the loss of hundreds of firefighters or police officers? All of these things are difficult to figure out on the fly in the middle of a disaster. But, if you've thought them through in advance, then you are much better prepared for something that you never even anticipated.

Now, on the other hand, think of NO and Katrina. You may have seen the pictures of the school busses that never made it out. They were destroyed by the flood waters. Perhaps a little planning could have helped them figure out how to use the school busses to evacuate the people who didn't have access to transportation. Doing so would not be an easy task. In the two days leading up to Katrina's landfall, you probably couldn't have worked out all of the details involved in getting drivers, picking everyone up, and getting them to safe shelters away from the storm. But, if you had been working on a plan in the years leading up to Katrina, you probably would have been able to pull it off.

Planning Gets Us Thinking About the Future

In a similar way, planning gets us thinking about the future rather than simply being caught in the past. Planning takes all we know about the past and all we know about the present and uses this information to look towards the future. We cannot do anything about the past other than learn from it. The present is important because it is the only moment we have. However, what we do in the present should be affected by where we are going. Planning takes our focus off of the past that we cannot do anything about and puts it on the future that we can change. It is useless to dream of a brighter yesterday but anybody can create a better tomorrow.

There is a huge danger of planning for the future. As we are looking towards the future, we must to resist the temptation to fall in love with our plans. There are certainly reasons why we would do so. Planning done right requires great effort and so the plan we come up with is born out of a lot of hard work. We put all our best thinking into the plan. We start to see the plan as part of us and a reflection of our ability to think. We then tie our heart and ego to the plan.

But before we commit too deeply to a specific plan, here is what we must remember. We are planners, not soothsayers. We are not predicting the future. We are giving it our best, informed guess. When planning, we must make some assumptions about what may happen in the future. Nobody knows exactly what will happen. It is useful to think through what could happen in the future but we must also remain flexible in case our best guesses are wrong. We want to hold off on making our final decision until we have the most information. And when do we have the most relevant information? Is it when we are planning or is it when it is time to act? Obviously, we will seldom have the best information while we are still in the planning phase.

Planning Helps Us Acquire Resources

Even if we don't know exactly what we are going to do, it is certainly useful to have the resources we might need at our disposal. Surgeons don't always know what they will find once they open the patient up but they want to have everything they may need easily available to them. They stick out their hand, say "scalpel" and it is quickly placed in their hand, they say, "suture" and there it is... Imagine what surgery would be like if the surgeon had to say, "Go fetch me a scalpel" and then wait ten minutes while the nurse rounded up the right scalpel. Then the surgeon says, "Go see if you can find any sutures" only to have the nurse return and say that they were out but some are being delivered on next Thursday's truck. Planning helps us get the resources we need for whatever may happen. If we wait until we need the resources to acquire them, it is probably too late.

Dwight Eisenhower was in command of the Allied invasion of Normandy. He said that, "Plans are worthless but planning is everything." I am sure everything didn't work out exactly as planned once the invasion started. In fact, I am certain that many changes had to be made to the battle plan leading up to D-Day. But even though his plans were constantly evolving, Eisenhower just kept on planning. What was the alternative? They needed thousands of boats and planes, tens of thousands of vehicles, and hundreds of thousands of troops. It took a lot of planning to get all the resources ready, even if they didn't know exactly what they were going to do with them. Then obviously there was a lot of planning that went into the invasion itself. I doubt if D-Day would have been much of a success if Eisenhower had said, "Y'all just meet me in Normandy and we will figure out what to do when we get there."

One thing that is really important is that we have the resources we need when we need them. Planning forces us to think through what those resources will likely be. Even if things don't unfold exactly like we planned, we will probably need many of the same resources. Most of the resources NYC used to handle 9/11 were available from the preparation and planning that was done for other potential disasters.

Planning Helps Us Eliminate Bad Choices

Planning helps us gather information and eliminate bad choices. It also forces us to evaluate our strengths and weaknesses. In the end, we may not necessarily do exactly what we planned to do. But we probably have a very good idea of what we shouldn't do. We don't have to go through the process of trial and error if we have already figured out that certain things won't work under any circumstances.

We tend to think that our planning was only useful if we followed our plan. That is a mistake. Our goal in planning isn't to have something that will tell us exactly what to do regardless of what may come our way. We plan so we can make better decisions. We may not always zero in on the best alternative until we are actually in the process of implementing our plans. However, if we are able to eliminate some of the bad choices before we even get to the implementation stage, then we will definitely make better choices. When we plan, we eliminate bad alternatives making it easier to find the best alternative.

Planning Gives Us Confidence

Finally, planning does this very important thing. It gives us confidence. I have had the opportunity to work extensively with new salespeople. The biggest challenge I face is helping them get over their call reluctance. People who have no problem whatsoever talking to a perfect stranger will freeze up when they are talking to someone on a "sales call." A person can talk to his brother every day of his life and not think twice about what he should say. But suggest that he try to sell him something and he will freeze up thinking, "I don't know what to say." How can I overcome that?

I give the new salesperson a plan. Now I know that thirty seconds into the conversation, the plan will be out the window and they will be talking like they have for their whole life. But I don't worry about that. I know that giving them a plan gives them the confidence they need to get the conversation started. There is something comforting about a plan, especially if we are in an area where we are lacking in confidence.

Implications of NYCNO

Understanding that the value of planning comes from the process and not the plan has two very significant implications for managing our time.

Have Flexible Plans

One thing that NYCNO teaches us is that we need to be flexible with our plans. Since I am a government employee, quite often I get to see just how silly it is to stick to a plan regardless of whether or not that plan still makes sense. For example, a budget is nothing more than a financial plan for a specific period of time. However around large organizations, a budget can take on a life of its own. I remember one year, the university where I was teaching was facing major financial challenges. Employees were being furloughed. Programs were on the chopping block. But, as the end of the year approached, the grounds people bought three very expensive new lawn mowers even though they didn't have the people to use them.

So why did they buy the lawn mowers? Because the money was in the budget and their department had to spend it. About eighteen months earlier, somebody took all the information they had at the time and decided that the university had a certain amount of money to spend in the next fiscal year. They then determined that the grounds crew should be given a certain amount of that money. But in the next eighteen months, things happened that they didn't anticipate. The economy tanked, state revenues took a nose dive, and there weren't even as many people working on the grounds crew as there were when the financial plan was set in place. Still because of the inflexibility built into the state's budget planning process, the money had to be spent. So, they followed the plan even though the plan no longer made any sense.

Does that mean that there wasn't value in their planning? No, of course not. You cannot run a large organization without a financial plan. How would that work? Can a university that serves tens of thousands of students just spend money until it runs out? That would be crazy. Thinking about the future is a must. Planning is a must. What is also crazy though is how these financial plans get written in stone. Throw in a little government red tape passed down from the state and you can't even move money from one account to another. Planning is essential. The madness is all the structure and bureaucracy that makes it necessary to follow plans that no longer make any sense.

Don't Get Discouraged

The other thing that NYCNO teaches us is to not get discouraged when things don't work out as planned. As we will discover in the next two chapters, it is crucial to have a time management system. Any viable system will require some planning. Here is what I have discovered. Probably the biggest barrier to planning comes when people get discouraged that things didn't work out as planned. We take time out of our busy schedules to plan our day and then we never seem to follow the plan. So we get discouraged and start thinking that our planning was a waste of time.

Such discouragement is misdirected. We think that the only value in planning is that it allows us to anticipate what is to come. Actually, the real value in planning is that it allows us to deal with what we did not anticipate. In the unlikely event that we actually do anticipate everything that will happen in the future, then we will know how to respond. But in the more likely event that unanticipated things will blow our plans totally out of the water, then we will still have benefited from planning. The value of planning our day comes from thinking through what things we need to do, scheduling when we should do those things, and wrestling with the question of how to fit them all in a twenty-four hour time period. Then, even if things don't work out as planned, we still have an idea of what our priorities are. We still know the things we don't have time to do. And then, when we are implementing our plan and things start to get crowded, we know what to let get crowded out.

We Succeed Even When Plans Fail

We must learn to not get discouraged when things don't work out as planned. I use the term NYCNO to remind myself of this. I have NYCNO days which are days when my plans need to be adjusted early and often. It reminds me that at least I had a plan. I say NYCNO hit which means my plans totally fell apart. It reminds me that at least I went through the planning process. I use NYCNO to help me remember that, even when things don't work out as planned, it's OK. I did what I was supposed to do. I planned. NYCNO lets me know that planning is the important thing. That is nice to know.

The NYCNO Challenge:
Resolve to fall in love with planning and
not with your plans.

9
Process

The Process Principle:
Master the Process and the Results Will Take
Care of Themselves

Successful people have a plan. The plan may evolve and change from moment to moment but they have a plan. It may be as simple as writing down what they want to do for the day and then working from that list. A number of years ago, I heard a Washington reporter ridicule the President of the United States. What this reporter thought was so strange was that the President kept a to-do list in his shirt pocket. All day long, the President would refer back to his to-do list, adding things to it and checking things off as he went. The reporter said he couldn't believe someone with all the power and prestige of the presidency would plan his day by a to-do list.

When I heard that, I couldn't help but laugh. The President was flying around in Air Force One. The reporter was probably stuck in long-term parking at the airport. The President was living in the White House. The reporter was probably living in some one bedroom flat on the outskirts of town. The President was daily making decisions which were affecting the lives of millions. This reporter was watching these decisions from the sidelines and writing about them. I thought to myself, maybe that reporter needs to start making a to-do list.

That President had gone through a process to get to the White House. The to-do list was part of the process. The reporter thought that the President of the United States should be above following such a simple process for deciding what needs to be done next. What that reporter failed to understand is that we all need a process for planning our time. The need for a process to plan our time doesn't end just because you become President. In fact, without some process for planning our time, it is difficult to become President of the Dog Catchers Society much less President of the United States.

Results Come from Processes

A process is nothing more than a series of events, actions, and reactions that occur in a regular and predictable way. A perfect example of a process can be seen in the baking of a cake. You mix certain ingredients together in a certain way and you will get the batter. It will have a certain consistency and color to it. Every time you mix the same ingredients together in the same way, you will always get a batter that looks and feels the same. You then add heat. It changes the thick liquid into a fluffy solid. That is the natural outcome of mixing and heating. If you like the outcome, you can do the same thing again and again, and you will always get the same results. In fact, even if you don't like the outcome, if you do the same thing again, you will still get the same result. A process produces predictable results. Master the process and the results will take care of themselves.

Breakthroughs happen when people master processes. Automobiles went from being a luxury that only the rich could afford to a necessity for the common person when Henry Ford figured out a process for mass producing them. On a quite different note, the biggest breakthrough in the history of treating addictions came when Bill W. and Dr. Bob wrote a book laying out a twelve-step process for overcoming alcoholism. Everything from making automobiles to overcoming addictions needs a process.

We need to be students of process. Here is why. When somebody has accomplished something we admire or desire, we can be certain that they did so through following a process. If we can figure out the process they followed, then we can get the same results they do. We just need to follow the process. Success is a process. Master the process and you achieve success. Beware though because there is also a dark side to the Process Principle. Failure is a process too. If we follow the process of people who fail, we too will fail.

Endocrinologist Michael Jensen wanted to conduct a research study to see what is happening in our bodies when we gain weight. To do so he recruited 28 volunteers. He developed a process to fatten them up. For eight weeks, these volunteers were encouraged to eat and drink almost anything they wanted including high calorie drinks, giant candy bars, and lots of ice cream. It worked. On average, these volunteers gained almost a pound per week. I know there are a few blessed souls who can eat like that and stay thin but, for us mere mortals, Dr. Jensen developed an outstanding process for putting on the pounds. Follow his process and the pounds will be sure to show up.

Here is what would be crazy—trying to lose weight following Dr. Jensen's process. You aren't going to lose weight following a process designed to build fat. There is a process for packing on the pounds and a process for taking off the weight. Whether you put weight on or take weight off depends on which process you follow. Following the wrong process is very discouraging. Imagine how discouraging it would be if we were trying to lose weight by following Dr. Jensen's weight gain process.

For any activity or goal, there is usually a process for success and several processes for failure. There is a process for doing well in college but there are several processes for flunking out. I have seen students show up their freshman year, spend their evenings at parties and their days in bed recovering from the parties. Between going to the parties and recovering from the parties, they don't have much time for studying and going to class. That is an outstanding process for flunking out of college. If we follow that process, the results will take care of themselves. The Dean will send us a letter explaining that our time at the university is over long before we graduate. On the other hand, there is also a process for doing well in college. It involves spending days going to class and evenings studying. If we follow that process, we will likely get a letter from the Dean but it will be a much different letter. It will congratulate us for making the Dean's List.

I enjoy studying economics. When I see economic differences, I always look for process differences. They are easy to find. Warren Buffett went through a process to acquire his billions. The process started when he was a child. While others were playing games, he was making money. It continued through school when he got an education from a couple of the best business schools in the country. The process went on when he would spend very little of his income on luxuries preferring to invest his money instead. That's a pretty good process for succeeding at something. Spend your life studying it and working as hard as you can at it without getting distracted. He applied that process to money and he made lots of it.

If your goal was to end up in poverty, there are processes for that too. Here's one. Drop out of school at an early age. Make sure you think you are too smart to learn from anyone else. Staying ignorant is a wonderful addition to the process. Spend all the money you have and all you can borrow on useless trinkets to impress your friends. Get fired from several jobs until no one wants to hire you. Follow that process and the results will take care of themselves. You will have all the poverty you want and even more.

Now, lest I be misunderstood, let me make something completely clear here. I am not saying that everyone in poverty is following this poverty process. There are many factors that come into play. It is easy to imagine special circumstances such as health problems where people didn't follow this poverty process yet still ended up in poverty. On the other hand, here is something I cannot imagine. I cannot imagine someone following the poverty process and ending up with more money than the person who followed the process Warren Buffett did for acquiring his wealth.

Most people see wealth and poverty as these mysterious things that just happen. That is because they don't understand processes. When it comes to money, wealth is the end result of a wealth process and poverty is the end result of a poverty process. If we master the wealth process, we will most likely end up wealthy. If we master the poverty process, we will always end up in poverty.

This doesn't just apply to people. It applies to whole economies as well. I am convinced that any country on this planet can develop and flourish economically. It just needs to develop a process of encouraging innovation and ownership. The process needs to make sure that people who get results are rewarded for their results. Some countries have built such economic processes into their system and it is amazing how fast their economies develop. Then there are the countries that pick a different process. They develop a process that discourages innovation, prevents ownership, and withholds rewards from those who contribute the most. Without exception, those countries who adopt these processes experience an economic nose dive.

Study economic history for yourself. See if you can find any country flourishing while discouraging innovation, preventing ownership, and withholding rewards. It is absurd to expect economic prosperity if we build a lot of processes into our economy that discourage innovation, take away from private ownership, and minimize the rewards of those who are most productive. That is expecting success from a process that has been shown to fail every time it has been tried.

Finding the Right Process

One of the biggest mistakes in life is to desire success while ignoring the process that makes it happen. The question isn't whether we can have what we want in life. We can. The real question is whether or not we are willing to follow the process it takes to produce success. Of course this assumes we know what that process is. But what if we don't know the process? What can we do then? Well, there are a couple ways to find the process that will give us what we want.

See What Is Working for Others

Since I teach marketing and sales, I often have students come up to me and ask me about an opportunity they have seen in the direct selling industry. They ask me if people actually make money in direct selling. I say, "You tell me. The direct selling industry did over $100 billion in sales last year with over $30 billion of that being done in the United States."

Often, they will respond with, "Well, I had a brother-in-law who said he tried direct selling and he didn't make any money at it." They act as if that is some sort of evidence that you cannot make money in direct selling. That is like pointing to the desert as proof that there is no such thing as an ocean. There may not be water in the desert but there is plenty of it elsewhere. Just because somebody's brother-in-law followed a failure process doesn't mean that a success process doesn't exist. There must be a success process somewhere in direct selling. How else could you explain the billions of dollars in sales every year?

So, when somebody says that they know somebody who failed in direct selling, I always reply with, "Well, I guess I wouldn't follow his process. I would find somebody who made money and try to figure out what process he or she followed." I find that most people who get into direct selling have strongly held but totally wrong opinions about how to make money in the industry. They insist on following the process that makes sense to them rather than a process that has been proven to work for others. Then, when they fail, they blame the industry and not the process they chose. Are there processes that won't work in direct selling? Of course there are. But to assume that something doesn't work just because somebody figured out a way to fail at it is totally absurd. Just like everything else, there is a process for success in direct selling and there is a process for failure.

Besides the fact that I teach selling, here is why I use the direct selling industry as an example. In direct selling we are almost always able to learn from people who have had consistent long term success in the industry. That is because the industry is set up so that people succeed when they teach others to succeed. Learning the process of success from people who have had success is the easiest and best way to achieve success ourselves. So, if someone is willing to teach us a process that worked for them, then we shouldn't be too smart to learn.

Unfortunately, the whole world is not like direct selling. In a competitive world, it is more often the case where people are hiding their success processes. When Sam Walton started opening retail stores, his competitors weren't lining up to show him how he could attract their customers away from them. The people who were already successful weren't very interested in showing Walton their success processes. Still, he put together a process for moving merchandise unmatched in the history of the world. In fact, it is estimated that 25% of the total economic productivity gains that occurred in the 1990's came from the Wal-Mart model. And where did he get his model? He didn't figure it all out on his own. He shopped around at everyone else's stores and saw what was working for them. Sam Walton didn't invent much. He simply observed the processes that worked for others and followed them himself.

So the easiest way to learn a process from someone else is to let them teach it to us. But, if they aren't willing to teach us, we can still observe what they are doing. By being good students and great observers we can discover the processes that work for others.

See What is Working for Us

It is often said that success comes from making good decisions, good decisions come from experience, and experience comes from making bad decisions. We cannot avoid making bad decisions. What we can avoid is making the same bad decision twice. We should learn from everything we do whether it is good or bad. When we do something and we get what we want, we need to learn from that success process. We learn success processes so that we can do them over and over. When we do something and we don't get what we want, we need to learn from that process too. We need to realize that we have discovered a failure process. We don't need to follow that exact process again. We should assume that the good things we have achieved in life came from success processes. We should also assume that the bad things we have brought into our lives came from failure processes. It is useful to learn which processes are success processes and which ones are failure processes.

As I've gotten older, I have discovered that feeling good is a process. So is feeling terrible. There is a process I go through that includes getting the right nutrients into my body, exercising, and getting adequate rest. When I follow that process, the results take care of themselves. I feel great. Then there is another process I often follow. I don't eat right. I don't exercise. I don't get enough rest. When I follow that process, the results take care of themselves too. I feel terrible. I know both of these processes well because I switch between them on a regular basis. At some point, I am going to learn to always choose my process based on observing the results. I need to quit choosing my health process based on how delicious the ice cream looks in the evening and how great the bed feels in the morning.

Be Patient

The essence of the Process Principle is that we have to give the process time to work. Returning to Warren Buffett, his success came from a process called "value investing." In short, this process involves finding good investment deals and holding on to them for a long time. So why don't all investment firms follow Buffett's process? After all, it made Warren Buffett the wealthiest investor in the world. Here is the problem. Very few investment managers are patient enough to try Buffett's approach. So, because few people have the patience of Warren Buffett, few people get the returns he does. They just aren't patient enough.

The Process Principle only works if we are willing to be patient enough to let it work. Follow the process and, given enough time, the results will take care of themselves. Farmers know that a bountiful harvest time isn't the result of magic, luck, or chance. It is the result of process and patience. They go through the process of preparing the soil, planting the seed, fighting off the weeds and pests, providing nutrients and water, etc. Eventually that process will result in crops. But what would happen if the farmer planted the seeds and then ran out to the field the next day and started digging them up to see if they were growing yet? How well would that process work? You can kill the product by constantly checking the process for results.

Let me give another example that a lot of us can relate to. Taking weight off is a slow process. I remember talking with someone who was discouraged by how long it took to lose weight. I said, "Isn't it a good thing that the weight doesn't come on as fast as we want it to come off?" Putting on weight is a slow process. Even the people who were pigging out in the weight gain study put on less than one pound a week. So taking it off is a slow process too. The surest way to short-circuit any process is to get discouraged because it takes too long.

All processes work and they always work in the same direction. However, they don't necessarily work for all of us in the same magnitude or at the same speed. I could follow Buffett's process for wealth creation and I probably wouldn't make as much money as he did. Why? Because I am not as smart as he is. But had I followed his process across the past several years, I would have a lot more money than I do today. Buffett's process doesn't make everyone a billionaire but it does make everyone money.

I played basketball in the days of Magic Johnson and Larry Bird. I could have followed their workout processes to the letter and I would have never been nearly as good as either of them. Why? Because I didn't have the natural talent they had. Still, if I had followed their processes, I would have been a much better basketball player than I was. Following a great practice process doesn't make everyone a super-star but it does make everyone better.

Watching Our Process Unfold

I am not really that patient. Here is the problem. Being the impatient person that I am, how do I stay focused on a process long enough to let it work? Here is what I do. When I start a major project, I decide how long I think it is going to take to complete it. For example, a few months ago, I started a project and I estimated that it would take 1,000 hours to complete from start to finish. I have a process that I know will result in success and the only ingredient I have to add is time working the process. In this case, I need to add a lot of time (1,000 hours) to complete the process and get the results.

On my desk, I have two clear bowls that stack on top of each other. I also have a bunch of decorative pebbles I purchased from the craft store. Before I started this project, I put 1,000 of these pebbles in one of the bowls. Every time I work an hour on the project, I move one pebble from that bowl to the other one. Once I have spent 1,000 hours on the project, I will have moved all of the pebbles from one bowl to the other.

Now, I am free from worrying about the results which are quite a ways down the road. I just think about moving pebbles. I focus on the process and I know that the results will take care of themselves. One thousand pebbles from now, the process will have worked and I will have the reward. Actually, these pebbles are a simple "system" I have for making sure I follow the right process. In the next chapter, we will finally get to discussing time management systems. All systems are built to take advantage of processes. We almost always do a better job of making a process work in our favor when we have a system. There is no perfect system but there is no success without an imperfect system. So let's see how processes and systems work together to help us manage our time

The Process Challenge:
Resolve to find the right processes and be
patient enough to let them work.

10
System

The System Principle:
Any System Is Better than No System

Once we identify a success process, we need a system to make sure we follow it. A system is just a regular, organized way of doing something. You already have systems in your life for doing many repetitive things. If you do something as simple as fixing yourself a pot of coffee every morning, you have a system for gathering together everything you need to do so.

Every morning, you go to the same places, probably in the same order, to get what you need to make coffee. When you are done making your coffee, you go back to those places and return everything. Without a system, you would just place everything in random spots. Every morning you would rummage through your house looking for the coffee, filters, your coffee mug, and the coffee pot. Let me see, where are they today? Is the coffee pot under the cabinet or is it in the guest bedroom? How about the filters, where are they? Maybe I put them over the washer or maybe I put them in the glove box of my car. Whatever your system is, it is better than approaching the task in a random, haphazard way.

You wouldn't want to wander the house every morning for thirty minutes finding what you need to make coffee. If you had to do that, you might give up coffee. You enjoy your morning cup of coffee because you have a system that makes brewing it a simple process. We do things that are simple. We avoid things that are complex. We will not trudge through complex processes but we will follow simple systems. Systems can make complex processes simple to follow.

Why We Need Systems

Even if you found a great process for managing your time, if it were too complex and difficult to follow, you wouldn't follow it. That is why we need simple systems. They make it easy for us to follow complex processes. If you don't plan your week and plan your day on a regular basis, it may be because you don't have a simple system for doing so. If you don't keep up with your contacts, it might be because you don't have the right contact management system. If you have something you always wanted to do but you never got around to doing, it might be because you never found a system to follow in doing it. Perhaps you wanted to write a book, get in shape to run a marathon, learn a second language, get another degree, or start playing a musical instrument. Trying to accomplish any of these without some system is about like trying to make a pot of coffee when you don't know where you put everything.

We need them because, as we saw in the last chapter, everything we get comes at the end of a process. Brewing a pot of coffee comes at the end of a process. It is a process of gathering the coffee, pot, filter, and water together. If we master the process, we get the results. How do we make sure we follow the process in the most effective and efficient way possible? We find a system for doing so. A system is simply the tool we use to keep us on track in following a process. That's all there is to a system. Without a system, how do we know if we are following the process that will lead to success? We don't. The only way to make sure we follow a process is by having a system for doing so.

Things Work Better With a System

Whether you are making your morning pot of coffee or running a huge factory, things work better with a system. The system doesn't even need to be that complicated. In fact, as we will discuss later, it is probably better if it is very simple. I heard a story once of a consultant who visited his friend who was the general manager of a large factory. Everything was in total chaos. The general manager couldn't seem to pull things out of chaos and so he wanted to hire the consultant to try to straighten things out. This consultant said that he would be glad to work with him but he wanted him to try something first.

The consultant told his friend to pull out a sheet of paper. He told him to write on that sheet of paper the six most important things he would like to accomplish that day. He then told the manager to rank these six things from the most important to the least important.

Next the consultant told the manager what to do with the list:

> Go to work on #1. Don't even think about #2 through #6 until you finish #1. Important things will pull you away from #1. That's OK. That's expected. Go take care of them. But when you are done, as quickly as you can, get back to #1. Stay with #1 until you are done. Then, go to work on #2. Do the same thing with it. Don't worry whether

or not you even get to #6. Just make sure that you don't work on #2 until you have finished #1, that you don't work on #3 until you have finished #2, etc. Tomorrow, I want you to pull out another sheet of paper. Follow this process again. Keep following it every day and see how it works.

As the story goes, the consultant didn't charge for this little advice. He just told the plant manager to try the system for a while and pay him whatever it was worth.

A few months later, the consultant received a check from the plant manager for $10,000. He quickly called his friend down at the plant and asked him about it. The plant manager said that the little system he gave him was easily worth $10,000. He put it into place in his office and quickly got control of everything. He then brought it in and taught it to all the managers he had working for him. They put it in place too. Eventually the whole plant was running on this simple system and the chaos was gone. Now the factory was running in perfect order. It wasn't that complicated of a system but it certainly was better than no system.

What Is A Good System?

There are many types of systems. What we have said so far in this chapter relates to any system. Let's narrow our discussion now and look specifically at time management systems. A time management system should provide us with a regular way for planning our weeks and days so that we will get the most from them. It should also help us stay on track or get back on track when we are pulled away from what we should be doing. Think of what the consultant gave the plant manager. It was a time management system. It showed him a way to figure out what he needed to be doing every day. It helped him focus on the most important things that needed to get done. Finally, when he had to put out the daily fires that arose, it helped him get back to work after the fires were out.

The purpose of a time management system isn't to have an impressive looking folio with several rings holding together a really intimidating calendar and a bunch of planning pages. There isn't anything wrong with such a system. It works great for some people. But there are a lot of people who simply aren't the folio types. They need a system too. What should their system look like? There are five things that we can use to evaluate any time management system.

Simplicity

A good system is one that we will use. For most of us, the more complex the system, the less likely it is that we will use it. People want to manage their time so that they will get more done. There is something disheartening about a system that takes away from us the very thing we want—more time. In sales, we have a principle. We say that a salesperson should say the least amount possible to get the desired results. The same idea applies to developing a time management system. We should have the simplest system possible to get the desired results.

This is especially true when we are just getting started using a system to manage our time. If I tried to hand you my time management system and make you follow it, you would probably swear off all time management systems forever. Why? It is too complicated. It is a system I have refined over decades. Thirty years ago, if I would have tried to manage my time the way I do today, I couldn't have done it. It would have been way too complicated. As I mastered a few things, I could do them with little or no thinking. I would then add other components to my system. Over time, I have developed a fairly complex system but it certainly didn't start that way. And, because I have been doing it for so long, it isn't complicated to me. It is actually very simple for me to use.

This gets to a question that always seems to arise when I teach time management. People want to know which system they should buy. They are assuming that they need to buy a system. The advantage of buying someone else's system is that it is simple to acquire but the disadvantage is that it is hard to learn. On the other hand, we can develop our own system. Personal systems that we make ourselves are more difficult to develop but they are easier to learn.

Clarity

The purpose of a time management system is to help us clearly see what we must be doing right now to be where we want to be at some point in the future. We can be so busy taking care of "important" things that we never step back to see if they are the most important things we should be doing. Something as simple as a prioritized to-do list can force us to clarify what really is important and what is not. A good system takes us to some point in the future. We look at where we need to be then and we work backwards. If we have a good system, it should give us specific instructions about what we need to do today to achieve tomorrow's goals.

Flexibility

One of the most important things to remember about our system is that it should be our servant and not our master. A system needs to be flexible enough for us to take it in a different direction if need be. For example, if our system involves blocking off parts of our days, we need to be able to adjust if something messes up one of the time blocks. Let's say I have everything in my day blocked off to happen at certain times. The most important thing I need to get done is scheduled for the first thing in the morning right when I get into the office. What if the freeway shuts down and I am an hour late making it to work? Can my system adjust? I probably will not want to just throw out my most important task for the day just because I didn't get to it when it was scheduled. How difficult will it be for me to move the other things in my day around to make room for that important task? If it is too complicated to do so, I might throw my system out the window. Remember, we will follow simple systems but we will not use complex ones.

Do I actually think we would throw out a system just because there was one traffic jam on the freeway? No. If it worked great every other day, one bad day isn't a big deal. But if one traffic jam is too much for our system to handle, imagine all of the other things it won't be able to adjust to. As we just covered in the previous few chapters, things never work out as planned. The pull in life is always towards chaos. A traffic jam is just one way chaos can mess up our day. There are so many others. If our system cannot handle the chaos, NYCNO days, etc., then it is not very useful.

Expandability

There is another way that our system needs to be flexible. Our system needs to change over time as our responsibilities grow. As we move through life, two things will happen. Our family responsibilities will increase and we will be given more and more responsibilities in our jobs. We need a system that can expand to handle these greater responsibilities. Can our system handle the promotion at work and the new baby at home? Even if we don't get a promotion, there can be seasons when our responsibilities grow. Our systems need to be able to handle all times including prime time. An accountant needs a system that can handle April, a retailer needs a system that can handle December, and a professor needs a system that can handle the end of the semester.

We don't want to have to reinvent our system every time our responsibilities change and here is why. When our responsibilities increase, we are already short on time. It's not the best time to find a new system. We want a system that helps us make a seamless transition into greater responsibilities. We don't want one that will be an added burden to our new, busier schedule.

Portability

The other thing we should consider is how much we need to be able to move our system around. It probably isn't a good idea to manage our time in our heads. However, keeping it in our heads does have one big advantage. It is the ultimate in portability. Wherever we are, there it is. At the other extreme, we have systems that are on our desktop computers. They work if we are always at the computer. If we need to move, they cannot move with us.

The real question is, "How much portability do we need?" We have so many options today. We can buy binders. We can buy pocket systems. We can put things on our cell phones. We can put them on our desktop computer. We can put them on our laptops or tablets. Each of these has its advantages and disadvantages. Fortunately, with the way various devices easily sync up, we can keep them in multiple places at the same time.

Personally, I like doing all of my planning on my desktop computer and then having it automatically sync with my tablet and cell phone. It also syncs between the desktop computers at both of my offices and my laptop. That gives me the best of all worlds. I have the power and size of my desktop computer and I have the portability of the phone and tablet. My system is anywhere I am. It actually took some creativity to get three different operating systems talking to each other but it was well worth the challenge.

More Than a System

When I played basketball back in school, my coaches had systems we were taught to follow. We had specific plays we ran. There were specific places we were expected to be. I was a big man and so I was expected to be around the rim rebounding and blocking shots. The guards were expected to be outside shooting and guarding against the fast break. We had to learn to run the plays. If we didn't learn the system, the coaches wouldn't let us play.

But there was a lot more to playing basketball than just learning the system. We had to do conditioning and strength training to get our bodies in shape. We had to learn to dribble, shoot, rebound, and screen. If I can jump, shoot, dribble, rebound, etc., then the system is useful. It will tell me when and where to do those things. But if all I did was learn the plays, no coach would want me on his team. A system is essential for any team to win. But no coach would think of using a system in place of fundamentals. If you know the fundamentals, a system is key to managing your time. Without the fundamentals, a system is useless.

Here is a problem I see that people have when they discover the need to manage their time. They jump straight to the system and they skip the fundamentals. They know they need to get control of their time. They hear somebody talk about some great time management system and so they buy it. The system can tell them when to be where but without a mastery of the fundamentals, they don't know what to do when they get there.

The fundamentals in basketball are dribbling, shooting, rebounding, screening, and defense. What are the fundamentals in managing our time? They are the time basics presented in this book. We must learn to value our time. We must learn to deal with chaos. We must learn how to respond when things don't work out as planned. We need to learn self-discipline. We need to learn how to gain clarity. We need to learn how to involve others. We need to learn how to avoid the crowd-out effect of hard time. We need to learn balance. If we don't learn these fundamentals, we are like the basketball player who knows the plays but doesn't know how to dribble or rebound. No system can make up for a lack of understanding of the fundamentals.

That said, this doesn't mean that we wait until we master all the fundamentals before we start developing and using a system. I didn't' wait to play basketball until my shot was fully developed. Actually the experience of playing games helped me develop the fundamentals. In a similar way, one way we learn the time basics is by developing our system. The time challenges we face as we develop our system will help us learn the basics. Also, learning the basics will help us develop our system. So we need to do both. Just as we don't want a system without learning the principles, we also don't want to learn the principles in a vacuum, devoid of a system. They go hand in hand. Which is more important to managing our time--the system or the principles? Returning to the breathing analogy, which is more important—inhaling or exhaling. Try breathing without either. You need them both.

Finding Your System

Where can you go to find a time management system? There are a lot of books that have been written on time management. Many of them take the approach of giving you a system and telling you how to use it. These books can certainly be a starting point for developing your own system. However, in the end, you don't need some author's system. You need your own system that fits your needs. I find these types of books much more useful for gaining ideas than for providing me with a preassembled turn-key system.

Also, we have developed some resources that can give you some great ideas for developing your system. You can find these resources at *timebasics.com*. Of particular note, you may want to get *Living the Basics* which is the workbook that accompanies *Time Basics*. Many of the exercises in it will help you develop your own system. The advantage of the workbook is that it doesn't give you somebody else's system. It helps you develop your own.

Wherever you get your system, remember this. Great systems develop over time. The goal isn't to come up with the perfect system before you start using it. That would take too long. The goal is to come up with a workable system and then get to work. Some people are looking for the perfect time management system. They should settle on an imperfect system and start using it. Any system is better than no system. Over time, a good system will evolve into a great system. We shouldn't worry that we don't have the perfect time management system. We should worry if we don't have one at all.

The System Challenge:
Resolve to have a good system today and a better system tomorrow.

11
Hard Time

The Hard Time Principle:
Hard Time Crowds Out Soft Time

Up to this point, we have been treating our time as if we have control over all of it. We know that isn't so. Others seem to own more chunks of our schedules than we do. We have jobs and they take huge chunks. We have family obligations like the kids soccer games. Then there is the church or civic clubs we belong to. They get chunks of our time. Join the bowling league or a softball team and more chunks of our time are gone. If we aren't careful, we can give away so many chunks of our time that we don't have any time to manage.

There is a concept in economics called discretionary income. Economists recognize that there is a huge difference between the money you make and the money you can spend. Discretionary income is the money *you* get to spend. You only get to start spending your money after the government gets some, your landlord or mortgage company gets some, the utility companies get some, the insurance companies get some, whoever you owe money to gets some, etc. Have you ever thought how wonderful it would be to get one paycheck that was actually all yours to spend? You might feel like you won the lottery.

What if the politicians decided they didn't need so much of our money, our mortgage was paid off, our house was well insulated, our insurance needs were small, and we didn't have any other loans or financial obligations? We could enjoy our paychecks a lot more than we do now. The less of our paychecks we have obligated to others, the more of it we control. The same concept applies to our time. The less of our schedules we have obligated to others, the more we get to choose what to do with our time. That is why we need to understand the concept of "hard time."

Hard Time Versus Soft Time

When we look at our schedules, we see some blocks of time where we have to be at a specific place doing a specific thing. These committed times are what we call "hard time." As we plan our days, we build everything around this hard time. After we have made room for our hard time, we can then go about planning our soft time. Our soft time is made up of those blocks of time when we have more flexibility over what we do and where we are. Soft time doesn't mean that we aren't doing anything productive. It just means that we have more discretion over what we are doing at that moment.

As I write this chapter, I am doing so early in the morning during some soft time. It's 6:30 AM and most of the rest of the world is just now beginning to stir. By getting up early, I found that I can get to my schedule before anyone or anything else does. I can work on whatever I choose to work on. I cherish this early morning soft time. In a couple of hours, my first class of the day starts. When it does, my schedule moves from soft time to hard time. At 8:30 AM on Mondays, Wednesdays, and Fridays, I don't have any say over where I will be and what I will be doing. I will be in whatever classroom the university tells me to be in and I will be teaching whichever students signed up for the class. In my world, class time is hard time.

For most of us, the biggest blocks of hard time are gobbled up by our professions. We build everything in our days around our jobs. If we want to do anything significant outside our career, we usually have to make other hard time commitments. If we make commitments to a group, it almost always requires hard time. There is nothing inherently wrong with such hard time commitments. We all make them. We just need to understand something about hard time. Hard time crowds out soft time.

What Is Hard and What Is Soft?

We all have things we need to accomplish. Very few of us sit around all day with nothing to do. In fact, most of us have more than twenty-four hours of stuff we would like to do on any given day. That is why it is important to look at our schedule and ask what should be hard time and what should be soft time. We always find ways to meet all our hard time commitments. If something in our schedule has to give, it's not hard time. Soft time is always the giver. The problem comes from the fact that not all hard time commitments are as important as some soft time activities. When we start making time for relatively trivial hard time activities at the expense of very important soft time activities, then we are not going to get the most out of our twenty-four hours.

For example, most of us make the time for our jobs hard time and the time for our families soft time. Are our jobs more important than our families? Are we going to make a bigger impact on the world through our jobs or through our families? For the vast majority of us, the most important long-term impact we will have on this world will be through what we do at home. But, because the job time is hard time, when it comes time to choose, work takes precedence over family. This doesn't happen because work is more important than family. It happens because work is hard time and family is soft time. I am not saying that we should change this and start making our job time soft time. What would that do to our family? After all, our kids do need to eat and to have a roof over their heads. I am just saying this to help us understand the challenge we face in carving out adequate time for the most important things in our lives.

In theory, our schedule should be ordered with the more important things taking precedence over less important things. In reality, it doesn't work that way. In the real world, our schedules are ordered where hard time takes precedence over soft time. That is the case regardless of how trivial the hard time commitments are or how important the soft time commitments are. If something is important, we must make sure that it doesn't get crowded out by some unimportant hard time commitment.

Understanding Hard Time

Here is how hard time works. Hard time commitments usually arise out of *external constraints* that come with *consequences* so we make *commitments* which *crowd out* everything else. Those are the four C's of hard time. Let's look at each of them individually.

Constraints

Hard time usually arises out of external constraints that are placed upon us. The most common one comes from employers. Usually, when we go to work for someone, they expect us to be at a certain place at a certain time. That creates a huge hard time commitment. Some people think they can avoid that hard time commitment by going to work for themselves. However, most people who are self-employed have to make hard time commitments to their customers or their employees. Work isn't the only thing that creates hard time commitments. Any time we join a group or a team, it usually comes with hard time commitments. What that means is that our soft time is usually what's left over after our boss takes his chunk out of our schedule, the softball league takes its chunk out of our schedule, and the civic or religious groups that we're a part of take their chunks out of our schedule. We are free to do whatever we want with whatever soft time is left over.

Consequences

The thing that makes a hard time commitments "hard" is the consequences that come with it. These consequences are usually immediate and they can be quite severe. I heard a story about a guy who was laying there with his bed sheets pulled up over his head when his mother came in and told him that it was time for him to get up and go to church. He told her that he wasn't going unless she could give him three good reasons why he should go. She said 1) God wants you to go, 2) I want you to go, and 3) since you are the pastor, the people expect you to be there. Obviously there would be consequences for him not going to church that Sunday morning and they would probably be greater consequences than for anyone else in the congregation. For that reason, Sunday morning is more of a hard time commitment to the pastor than to the person just sitting in the pew.

Failure to keep certain soft time commitments will also come with consequences. In fact, these consequences may be much more severe than the consequences that come with our hard time commitments. But they are seldom as immediate. In our minds, they probably aren't as certain. For example, if I don't keep my hard time commitments to work, I get fired. That means I will have to find a new job and I will suffer financially. On the other hand, if I don't keep my soft time commitment to exercise, I may have a heart attack. Now I would much rather face the unemployment line than a heart attack. But the unemployment line is just a few days away if I don't keep my hard time commitments to work and the heart attack is years away if I don't keep my soft time commitment to exercise. So work crowds out exercise.

Commitments

About the only students you will find at our campus recreation center at 6:00 AM are the student workers and the ones that have other hard time commitments to be there. For example, you might find the ROTC cadets working out at 6:00 AM. Is that because these ROTC cadets see greater value in physical fitness than the rest of the campus? I don't think so. They are there because they are committed to ROTC and not to their own physical health.

Crowds Out

This is the very nature of the Hard Time Principle. Hard time gets its way because it crowds out soft time. Now is that good or bad? Well, that depends on what we want to get crowded out. If we can find a way to make the most important things in our life hard time commitments, then we will spend our life doing more important things. But if the most important things in our life end up in the soft time category, then we may have a problem.

Hard Time Commitments to Make

If we want to really commit to something, we can do so by finding a way to make it a hard time commitment. Because it has a hard time commitment, it will take precedent over anything else that we may be tempted to do with that time. There are four hard time commitments that we should be willing to make.

Things That Require Self-Discipline

We should look for ways of making hard time commitments to important things which require self-discipline. One of the top distance runners of the 1980's was Toshihiko Seko. He burst onto the world running scene by winning the Fukuoka Marathon for three straight years. The next year, when he won the Boston Marathon for the first time (he won it twice), people began to try to figure out what his secret was. What shoes did he wear? What strength training did he do? Who coached him? Whenever asked about his training, Seko would always say the same thing. "Every day, I run ten kilometers in the morning and twenty kilometers in the evening." That was it. That was the sum total of his strategy, training, coaching, and conditioning all wrapped up in one.

What was the most important part of this simple strategy? It was the fact that he ran every single day, 365 days every year. If he felt good, Seko would run his 10k/20k. If he felt terrible, Seko would run his 10k/20k. If the weather was beautiful outside, Seko would run his 10k/20k. If the weather was terrible outside, Seko would run his 10k/20k. Here was the real challenge. When other things tried to take the time he had set aside for his 10k/20k run, he didn't let them. He didn't work in his runs around the other things in his schedule. He worked everything in his schedule around his morning and evening runs. To Seko, the time set aside for these two runs was hard time and nothing ever got in its way.

Seko made his hard time commitments to himself. For those of us who aren't so disciplined, we may need to make hard time commitments to others. That can be done in the form of a workout partner, accountability partner, etc. I may not have the discipline to go by myself to the gym at 6:00 AM but I won't want to let my workout partner down if he is waiting for me.

Team Time

A second hard time commitment we should be willing to make is team time. As we will discuss when we cover the Team Principle, we can accomplish so much more by being part of the team than we can by going it on our own. One of the things about being a team member is that there needs to be times when the team gets together. That means the team members must be willing to set aside their own personal activities and commit to specific times that they will meet with the team. If we are going to be part of a team, we must be willing to make hard time commitments to the team. To avoid making these commitments, some people choose to go it alone. That isn't very wise though because there are so many advantages of being part of a team. The hard time we spend with a team may be some of the most valuable time we have in our schedule.

Individual Time With Significant People

A third hard time commitment we should be willing to make is time set aside specifically for the important people in our lives. As we mentioned in several other places, relationships take time. Whether it's setting aside time for people to mentor us, setting aside time for key clients or customers, etc. we need to make sure that this important time doesn't slip away into the realm of soft time. "Let's get together sometime" is usually a fantasy unless it is followed up with, "I will give you a call so we can set up a time."

Family Time

Perhaps the biggest danger of a schedule filled with hard time is that it doesn't leave enough time for the family. This can be overcome simply by making some hard time commitments to the family. I had a job interview several years ago in Logan, UT. I was told that they didn't schedule things on Monday nights in Logan. The religious tradition there is that Monday nights are always set aside for family. They value family and so the whole community makes Monday nights hard time for the families. That's how it worked in Logan, UT. How can those of us who don't live in Logan UT make hard time commitments to our families? Some couples realize that they need to set aside one night of the week for "date night." Some families make dinner hard time. The whole family eats together at dinner and interruptions are not allowed. Our family ended every day with a spiritual devotion. We couldn't go to bed until we had come together for this family devotion time.

Hard Time Commitments We Should Avoid

There are also some hard time commitments that we should try our best to avoid. These fall into three categories.

Projects That Have No Impact

We must be very careful about what projects we get caught up in or what committees we become part of. When it comes time to promote people, you aren't going to be rewarded for heading the committee that decided where to place the garbage cans in the parking lot. Find projects and sit on committees that actually make an impact.

People Who Waste Our Time

Have you ever started a new job and, before you had been there a week, someone stopped by to "tell you how things work around here"? Let me give you a warning. That person is clueless. He doesn't know how things work around here. If he did, he would be working. That is one way that people waste our time. They seek to draw us into their unproductive world of inactivity. People who are doing nothing always seem to want to do it with someone else. People who aren't going anywhere have a lot of time to fill and they are looking for other people to fill it with. Don't be one of them. Don't let a slacker's soft time become your hard time.

Money That Flies Away

I've heard it said that the key to great wealth is to pick your grandparents very carefully. Most of us don't get to take that route to wealth. We have to earn whatever money we make. That means we will have to spend a big chunk of our lives taking our time and trading it for money. When we spend the money we've earned, we seldom make the connection that we were actually spending the time it took to make that money. For example, if I clear $25 per hour and I buy a car for $25,000 then that car has cost 1,000 hours of my life. If I work 40 hours per week, that means the car has taken about half a year of my career life.

Here is the reason I bring this up while talking about hard time. If we make money, it is probably because we have made a hard time commitment to work certain hours. If we take that money and blow it, our hard time commitment has also been wasted. Everyone needs a car and so to take 1,000 hours and invest it in a car is probably a good idea. But what if we are blowing our money on insignificant things that don't matter?

Every dollar we blow is hard time wasted—hard time that may have crowded out more significant soft time commitments. If we are wasting the money, we are wasting the time. And if the hard time commitments to work are pushing out a lot of more important soft time things we could be doing, then what? In a sense, the wasteful things we are buying are crowding out the more important things we could be doing with our time.

Given the Choice, Choose Soft Time

Here is the most important thing to understand about hard time. Hard time commitments are more of a burden on our schedule than soft time commitments. That is true *even when those soft time commitments require the same amount of our time.* Because it is flexible, a soft time commitment of three hours may be easier to manage than a hard time commitment of two hours. We can bend the soft time commitment to fit our schedule. But we must bend our schedule to fit our hard time commitments.

This is why we need to be certain that the hard time commitments deserve the inflexible time commitments we are giving to them. All other things being equal, we should prefer soft time commitments over hard time commitments. If I have the choice this week of playing two hours of league ball or two hours of pick-up ball at the rec center, I will choose the pick-up ball. With the league ball, I have to be at a specific place at a specific time. If it is rec center ball, I just show up when I feel like it. I have to make my schedule fit the league but I can make the rec center ball fit my schedule.

Things are not always equal and so there will always be hard time commitments in our lives to things of lesser importance. We just need to understand the burden hard time puts on our schedule and always remember that hard time crowds out soft time.

The Hard Time Challenge:
Resolve to avoid low value hard time
commitments.

12
Efficiency

The Efficiency Principle:
If You Are Always Working You Don't Have to
Be Efficient

Perhaps you read the previous chapter on hard time and thought, "But I have to make huge hard time commitments to my job. If I don't, I will never get all the work done." Maybe so. Maybe not. In this chapter, we will look at the possibility of getting more done at work with less time.

I heard a story of a wagon train that left Philadelphia for Denver during the great westward expansion. There were about fifty wagons in the train. When the first Sunday arrived, one group of people didn't want to move and the other group wanted to keep on going. So they split. By Saturday of the next week, the group that had rested had caught up with the group that kept on going. On Sunday morning, the same thing happened again. But the next week, the group that rested on Sunday caught up with the other group on Friday. These two groups eventually decided to go their separate ways. One traveled six days a week and the other traveled seven. The group that traveled six days a week arrived in Denver two weeks before the one that traveled seven days a week.

More With Less

We must be careful not to fall into the trap of thinking that the only way to accomplish more is to put in more hours. Early in my professional career, I worked all the time. I was always the first one in the office. I worked all day long. I would bring a big briefcase full of stuff home from the office and, unless my wife and I had something specific planned, I would work all evening too. I was working eighty to ninety hours in a typical week. Then our first child was born. I knew I needed to spend time with the family so I made a commitment to never work more than sixty hours a week. Though I was willing to let my productivity at work suffer, it didn't. To my surprise, I actually started getting more done. I discovered that spending less time working forced me to be efficient in what I did. When I was working all the time, I didn't have to be efficient. When I decided to start giving my time to something other than work, I was forced to be more efficient with the time I spent at work. This forced efficiency actually made me more productive with less time.

Something else happened about that time. Because I was starting to have some success in my career, I began to spend time with some unbelievably successful people. Since they had accomplished so much, I expected to find them working all the time. Such was not the case at all. One person that I had idolized for years because of his success was a weight lifter. He spent many hours in the gym. Another equally successful person was a huge jazz fan who spent hours expanding his jazz collection and attending concerts. Still another one of the most successful people I knew would spend hours restoring old cars. I found that such was the case with almost every highly successful person I met. They all had two things in common. First, they had all reached the absolute upper elite in terms of success in their respective fields. Second, they all had interests outside their vocations that took up substantial amounts of their time.

I was perplexed. Working extremely long hours didn't seem to do me much good. How could I cut back my work hours by twenty to thirty hours a week and still get as much done? Further, why could so many people who worked a lot less than me accomplish so much more than me? Then I read something in a book that completely rocked my world. It stated what I have labeled the Efficiency Principle. It said that, "If you are always working, you don't have to be efficient." That explained it. Because I thought I had all the time in the world to do my job, it took all the time in the world. I even found out that there was Parkinson's Law which stated that, "work expands so as to fill the time available for its completion." I had let myself become a victim of Parkinson's Law.

Two Ways of Viewing Time

Eventually, I began to realize that the way I viewed time was all wrong. Remember back to chemistry class? We learned the difference between solids, liquids, and gasses. There is this one property of gasses that has always intrigued me. A gas will take up all of the space of the container in which it is stored. Liquids and solids don't have that property. How much liquid can you get in a one-gallon container? About one gallon. That's because liquids take up a fixed amount of space. If we want to store more liquid, we need a bigger container.

That's not the way a gas works. Let's say you have a certain amount of oxygen in a one-gallon, air tight container. How much space will it take up? It will take up the whole container. Let's say we doubled the amount of oxygen in the container. How much space would it take up now? All of it. Let's say we cut the amount of oxygen in half, how much space would it take up then? All of it. As long as it doesn't explode the container, a gas will take up all of the space in whatever container it is placed.

My problem was that I viewed time like it was a liquid. I had a certain amount of productivity that I could fit into a certain amount of time. If I wanted to be twice as productive, I needed to spend twice as much time. I filled up my schedule to the top and then I had to get a bigger schedule. The only way to get more schedule was to work more hours. So I concluded that, if I needed to get more done, I had to work more hours. I thought it worked the other way too. If I worked fewer hours, I had a smaller schedule. Because my schedule was smaller, I wouldn't be able to put as much productivity into it. I wouldn't accomplish as much. I thought that the only way that others were more productive than me was that they used a bigger container. They spent more time working.

Here's what surprised me. Time actually acts a lot more like a gas. The work I wanted to accomplish would fill whatever container I put it in. My first child was born and so my work schedule became smaller. I didn't have as big of a container and yet my smaller container held just as much productivity. Then I started looking around and I found people whose schedules held a lot more productivity than mine did. I expected to find that they had these huge containers. Actually, what I found was that theirs were smaller than mine. I discovered that work will expand to fill whatever container we put it in.

How Things Fill Our Schedule

How does this happen? How can the same amount of work take up however much time we give it? It happens because we have two forces working against each other. They are the forces of *scheduled inefficiency* and *forced efficiency*.

Scheduled Inefficiency

To understand this, let's first look at what happens when we start spending all of our time at work. Let's say we have decided like I did early in my career, that we will spend most of our waking hours working. Under those circumstances, what will happen? First, we probably won't do a very good job of setting priorities. We don't have to. We can fill our work time with a bunch of unimportant things and still have time to get to the things we have to do. It will probably also be easier for us to get distracted. We have time to chase rabbits. We will also probably not work as hard and fast as we can. What all this means is that we never get any more done despite the fact that we are putting in the longer hours.

Forced Efficiency

Let's look at the other side of the coin. Let's say we make the decision that I did when my first child was born. We start working fewer hours. That forces us to look at our priorities and start scheduling around them. It forces us to look for ways to be more efficient. It also makes us take a hard look at what we are actually doing with our time. Don't get me wrong on this point. If we start working fewer hours, something in our schedule will have to give. We will have to let go of something. There won't be room for everything we had in our schedule. But that's really not a problem and here is why.

When things start to drop off of our schedule, it is the less important things that go. Say I have been spending one hour per week meeting with my most important client and one hour a week standing around the coffee machine talking about sports with my coworkers. Now one of them has to go. It won't be the time with my number one client. I may have to give up the joy of being the best Monday morning quarterback at the coffee machine but I will make that hard choice. That's the beauty of forced efficiency. We quit doing a bunch of stuff that wasn't really that important anyway.

There is another thing forced efficiency does. It helps us gain momentum. We will see how this works in a couple chapters when we cover the Momentum Principle.

Making Efficiency a Habit

Later in this book when we look at the Aristotle Principle, we will discuss the importance of breaking bad habits. The best way to deal with bad habits is to not form them in the first place. If we are not putting limits to how much time we spend on our work, we can develop some very bad time management habits. That is particularly true if we have the extra time to spend at work. When I was single, I didn't mind spending all of my time at work. Outside of church and a few hours at the gym, I didn't have anything else to do with my time. Unfortunately, when I needed to start keeping a tighter schedule, it was hard to break the bad habits I formed in those single years. How can we make sure we aren't wasting time at work just because we can?

Be Honest

We need to be honest about why we are working long hours. Success comes when we work to achieve and not when we work to avoid the alternative. Before I was married, I worked long hours on a busy university campus. That certainly beat spending those hours alone back at my apartment. If I took eighty hours to do forty hours of work, it wouldn't matter. The only reward I had for being efficient at the office was that I had to go home to an empty apartment. I could work forty hours, waste forty hours, and it didn't matter. I wasn't working those long hours because I was going somewhere with my career. I was working those long hours to keep from going somewhere I didn't want to be. So let's be honest. Are we working long hours because that's what we need to do to achieve success? Or are we working long hours to avoid something we really don't want to do?

Be Willing

We must be willing to put constraints on our time. When I started my career, I didn't have any constraints on my time. As long as I made some time to play basketball and go to church, I really didn't have anything else to do with my time but work. Then came the family and I had to start placing constraints on my time. As our life changes or as we step up and accept greater responsibility, we must be willing to tighten our schedule. Because a tighter schedule brings greater efficiency, constraining our time doesn't necessarily mean we will get less done. It may just mean that we will have to give up the luxury of being inefficient.

Be Creative

With a little creativity, it is amazing what we can do with our time. Let me give you an example. One of the things I love to do every semester is give a lecture on success to all of our sophomore business students. It is one of the highlights of my career. Much to my dismay, this semester the lecture was at the same time as a class I teach. My class schedule couldn't be changed and neither could the time of my success lecture. My immediate thought was that I couldn't give the success lecture because I couldn't be two places at once. Or could I? I decided to apply a little creativity to the problem.

I looked at what I needed to cover in my class on the day I wanted to speak on success to our sophomores. It just so happened to be that I needed to give an hour of straight lecture and follow that with a fifteen minute question and answer session. I decided to go into the studio, video the one hour lecture, and have my graduate assistant show the video to my class. I told the person coordinating the success lecture that I would need to shorten the lecture to less than an hour so that I could zip over to my classroom in time for the question and answer session. I actually was two places at once—sort of.

Adding efficiency to our schedule requires creativity. What kills that creativity is immediately assuming something cannot be done. Had I accepted my initial assessment of the situation, I would have never worked out this solution. I would have just resigned myself to giving up something I valued very much. But when I started with the assumption that I could do them both, my mind went to work on figuring out how. Here is the point. Perhaps the only reason we work long hours is because we assume we have to. We don't challenge our brains to creatively figure out how to do otherwise.

Be Careful

Though we can become more efficient, there are limits to what we can do. I had a student this semester who came up to me after class and asked for advice. She said that she was exhausted and hoped that my class on time management would help. She was only getting three hours of sleep per night. I asked her to lay out what she was doing with her time. Between school, work, and other hard time commitments, she had managed to schedule about twenty hours per day. Obviously that didn't leave much time for sleep. So I suggested that she start throwing things out. One by one, she explained how she absolutely could not drop anything she was doing. I said there isn't much advice I could give her. If you fill up twenty hours of your day with hard time commitments, you won't get eight hours of sleep per night. It is mathematically impossible. Asking me to show her how to fit twenty hours of commitments plus eight hours of sleep into a twenty-four hour day would be like asking me to show her how to make two plus two equal five.

We discussed the pros and cons of energy drinks and then I gave her this warning. She may need to trudge through the next two semesters at this pace trying just to survive. But she needed to make sure that what she was doing was for a reason and for a season. I told her that, once she graduated, she must be careful not to just continue life at this furious pace. It must not become her norm. She needed to make sure that, once this season of her life was over, she would be careful about what hard time commitments she made. She must not take the same approach to her career that she was taking to her education. It just wouldn't be sustainable over the long run and it could end up destroying her career and her health.

There are times when not even the greatest of creativity will change the fact that we just need to spend more time on our careers than is desirable. When this happens, we will do what we have to do. But, as I told my student, this increased work time must be for a reason and for a season. We must not let these new hours become the new norm.

Avoiding Baseline Creep

What we must avoid is the phenomenon called *baseline creep*. Here is how baseline creep works. Let's say you are currently working forty hours per week. You get promoted to a new position. Because you don't know the territory, you have to start working fifty-five hours per week. That is expected. However, what should also be expected is that, over time, you will become better at doing your new job. You should be improving your skills and so you should become more efficient. You should be training people around you so you should become better able to delegate. There is no reason why the fifty-five hour workweek should become the new norm unless you make it so. Over time, you should be able to drop back to forty hours.

Before the promotion, the baseline was forty hours. We must not let that baseline creep up to fifty-five hours. Fifty-five hours should be seen as a "transition" and not the new norm. If fifty-five hours becomes the new baseline for your workweek, that's what it will always be. As we are learning the new position, we must be willing to accept some fifty-five hour workweeks, but our goal should be to work things back down to forty hours. If we succeed in getting back to forty hours, then we will be accomplishing more with the same amount of time. If we don't get back to forty hours, baseline creep will rob us of fifteen hours of our life every week.

A big risk of baseline creep is that it can cause our career to dead-end. The only road to the next promotion is to become more efficient at our current job. If a promotion took fifteen hours out of our life, what will we do for the next promotion? Will we give it another fifteen hours? Will we work seventy hours a week for the next position? Then what about the next promotion? Will we work eighty-five hours a week? There are only so many chunks of our life that we can give up. If we keep raising the baseline every time we get promoted, we will eventually reach our limit. On the other hand, if we always keep working ourselves back to the forty hour baseline, we will always have the time we need to accept the greater responsibility of the next promotion.

It Is Not an Excuse

The Efficiency Principle should never be taken as an excuse for doing less than we should. We shouldn't drop our standards. We should create efficiency. When I was in the Ph.D. program, the culture was that we were to be totally sold out to it. We felt like we were expected to not have much of a life outside the program. I remember this one guy named Rob showing up who didn't fit that mold. He had a family. He had a life. He was an outstanding student but we had doubts that he would make it because he wasn't spending every waking hour on the program like the rest of us were.

Looking back, I now understand that Rob was as committed to his studies and other responsibilities as anyone else in the program. He was also committed to doing so while still being the father and husband he needed to be. Rob did graduate just like the rest of us did. He went on to become a highly respected researcher and Department Chair at a major state university.

In the end, the marketplace doesn't reward us for hard work or long hours. It rewards results. We need to worry less about being the hardest worker and more about being the most productive one. We will be applauded for working hard. We will be rewarded for getting results. So we need to be sure we are getting the most done, not just spending the most time.

Stop being the one who works the longest hours. Start being the one who gets the most done. Then, with the time you free up, take on a new project, pursue a new opportunity, spend more time with the family, or just take up an interesting hobby. You will get more done and you will become a more interesting and well-rounded person.

The Efficiency Challenge:
Resolve to choose efficiency and effectiveness
over hard work and long hours.

Speed

The Procrastination Principle:

An "I'll Do It Tomorrow" Attitude Can Yield "I Should Have Done It Yesterday" Results

---

The Momentum Principle:

To Keep Going, Get Moving and Don't Stop

The Clarity Principle:

Clarity Speeds Things Up. Confusion Slows Things Down.

The Andretti Principle:

If Everything Seems Under Control, You Just Aren't Going Fast Enough

---

The Discernment Principle:

Activity Does Not Mean Progress and Urgent Does Not Mean Important

---

The Principle of Useless Perfection:

Nothing Is as Useless as Doing Well That Which Should Not Be Done at All

Part 3

Speed

Not long ago I was giving a seminar on the time basics. Before the seminar began, I was chatting with some people in the audience. A woman told me how much she loves to manage her time. She said that the problem was that she spent so much time managing her time that she didn't have enough time to actually accomplish much.

She might have been great at organizing and systematizing but she wasn't very good at managing her time. She had great direction but no movement. That's like having a super-fast sports car but no fuel. You may feel pretty cool sitting there but you certainly aren't going anywhere. It doesn't even matter if the car is facing the direction you want to go. You aren't doing anything that will take you to where you want to be. Vision and focus will give us direction. Once we get direction, we need to get moving and pick up some speed.

Time management isn't just about having a vision and focus for our days. At some point it is about moving into action and picking up speed. The more we can get done in a day, the more things we can do with our time. Of course our actions need to be pointed in the right direction. But we don't want to just crawl along in the direction we are pointed. We want to get going and then make good time.

Part 3 is about moving into action and gaining speed. General George Patton once said that a good plan today is better than a perfect plan tomorrow. The perfect plan is useless if we never get around to putting it into practice. We will start out Part 3 by talking about the most common enemy of action. For most people, the enemy of action is procrastination. We can't gain speed if we never get going in the first place. We will look at how we can actually make procrastination our friend rather than our enemy.

The next three basics are about gaining speed. The first step in gaining speed is establishing momentum. With momentum, we can go even faster if we have clarity. Once we are going fast, things may get a little out of control. That doesn't mean we aren't managing our time. That just means we are going fast. We cannot slow down just so we can regain our feeling of control.

We finish Part 3 by looking at two things that will slow us down. We will lose significant speed if we are unable to discern progress from busyness or important from urgent. We also slow down when we spend more time on a job than is justified by the nature of the task.

Do you want to make time management much simpler? Here is all you have to do. Invent a time machine and go back to 1990. That would get rid of most of the things that slow us down. Back then, there were not nearly as many interruptions and distractions as there are today. If somebody wanted to interrupt our workflow in 1990, they had to either show up in person or call us on the landline telephone. Today technology has created so many more ways for us to be interrupted. Between the internet, cellular communication, email, voicemail, etc., our lives are flooded with things to slow us down and get us off track.

How can we move fast in a world that is constantly inventing new ways to slow us down? Again, it comes back to mastering a few basics. Let's explore what the basics of speed are. Make sure your seatbelts are securely fastened and your seatbacks and tray tables are in the upright and locked position. We are about to take off into the world of high speed time management. Hopefully when you finish this section, you will know how to keep up the pace in a world that is constantly inventing new ways to slow you down.

13
Procrastination

The Procrastination Principle:
An "I'll Do It Tomorrow" Attitude Can Yield
"I Should Have Done It Yesterday" Results

I have asked many groups of people what their biggest time management challenge is and I always get the same answer. It is procrastination. When I ask an audience to raise their hands if they struggle with procrastination, 90% of them do so. The other 10% might also raise their hands but they just don't get around to it. One person once replied that he doesn't have a problem with procrastination at all. He was a pro. He said that he was better at procrastinating than anyone else he knew.

Everyone Procrastinates

Even though I wrote a book and teach a class on time management, I procrastinate. In fact, I did so today. The scheduled topic for my time management class today was procrastination. I walked in and told the students that, in the spirit of the topic, we wouldn't get to it until next class period. I actually had a good reason to procrastinate on the procrastination lecture. But, then again, don't we always find ways to justify our procrastination?

In reality, unless you only have one thing to do in life, you must procrastinate. We have to procrastinate because we cannot do everything at once. I heard it said that God invented time so that everything wouldn't all happen at once. Time is a good thing. It keeps everything from happening at once. On the other hand, it also makes it impossible for us to do everything at the same time. And, since we usually have several things we need to do, we must procrastinate on something.

For example, I have two more things I need to do today. I need to exercise and I need to finish writing this chapter. Since I am writing this chapter, that means I am procrastinating on exercising. If I decided to go exercise, then I would be procrastinating on writing. I cannot exercise and write at the same time so I have to procrastinate on one of them. Anytime we have more than one thing to do, we must procrastinate on something.

Good and Bad Procrastination

Unless we learn how to be two places at one time, we have to choose what to procrastinate on. What we need to do is be thoughtful when we procrastinate. If we procrastinate on unimportant and insignificant stuff, it will free up our time to do the things we really should do. If we procrastinate on important things, our procrastination will come back to bite us. I had a colleague who can be used as an example of both. He was great at putting off small things so he could do big things. However, at times, he could put off things he really needed to do. I will call my friend Bart.

Bart was a very focused man. He would set huge goals and nothing would distract him from reaching them. He was an amazing researcher. One time, the top ten research articles published in the history of my discipline were identified. Bart had written four of them. He also had big things he was doing in the real world. Together with a couple other professors, he formed a consulting company. Many of the top executives at Fortune 500 companies would fly in to town just to have this group help them make major business decisions.

Procrastinating on the Right Things

The reason Bart could get so much done is because he was absolutely outstanding at procrastinating on the right things. If anything did not directly relate to either his research or consulting, he put it off until later. He wouldn't say no to things, just later. And because he put so many things off, he was able to focus on what mattered most to him which was his research and consulting.

For example, he really needed to buy a new car but he never got around to it. He could afford any car he wanted but he drove around in an old beat up station wagon. His procrastination kept him in an old clunker but that didn't bother Bart because he had better things to worry about than his car. It got so bad that the partners in his consulting company started to get on to Bart about his clunker. "How are you going to take out any of our clients in that old thing?" they would ask. Bart would tell them that he would get a new car but he never got around to doing so. He was too busy with his research and consulting.

Eventually, the partners decided that they would buy Bart a car. He was such an outstanding researcher that he had made way more money for them than any car would cost. They asked him what kind of car he wanted and he said he would like one of those cars with the "peace sign lookin' thing on it."

"OK," they said, "We will get you a Mercedes. Just go down to the dealership and pick one up. We will arrange all the details." Now all Bart needed to do was to drive his clunker onto the lot and drive away in his brand new Mercedes. However, between research and consulting commitments, he never made the time to even do that. Eventually, his procrastination got to the partners and they used the nuclear option. They changed the locks on their office and they wouldn't let Bart in until he picked out a car.

The next morning when Bart's graduate assistant (GA) came in to work, there was his usual to-do list from Bart waiting for him. There were three items on the list: 1) Run this data analysis on the computer; 2) Pick up this book from the library; 3) Get me a car from the Mercedes dealership. The GA quickly went into Bart's office. "What does this mean?" he asked pointing to item three on the list. Bart explained everything to him. Bart came out that evening, the GA showed him his new car and he drove it home.

Not Procrastinating on the Wrong Things

Bart was so good at research and consulting because he was so good at procrastinating on everything else. However, his procrastination also had a dark side to it and that dark side ended up costing Bart dearly. Regardless of how focused we need to be, there are some things we cannot procrastinate on. One such thing is our taxes. For several years, Bart never made time to file his taxes. He wasn't trying to evade paying taxes. He just didn't make the time to do them. Then one day he got a letter from the IRS asking him why they had not heard from him in a while. The letter turned into an appointment which turned into an audit which turned into an arrest which turned into a trial which turned into a change of residence. Bart ended up doing some significant jail time because he procrastinated on the wrong thing. Bart learned that the last thing you want to procrastinate on is your taxes. The IRS has a way of making such procrastination bite you.

Deciding When to Procrastinate

Bart was successful because he knew how to procrastinate on the right things. However, he blew it all because he never learned to not procrastinate on the wrong things. We need to know when to procrastinate and when not to procrastinate. How do we know when procrastination is right and when it is wrong? Let's look at three warning signs that we are procrastinating on the wrong things.

Some Things Don't Go Away

Sometimes we put off doing things that won't go away. Bart could procrastinate on his taxes but they weren't going away. If we are going to eventually have to do something anyway, we might as well do it now. It isn't like the things we are putting off will get any easier in the future. In fact, it is usually worse to look at them knowing we will have to do them eventually than it is to just go ahead and do them. Unpleasant things don't bother us the most when we are doing them. They bother us the most when we are putting them off.

A perfect example of this is the dishes in the sink. I remember a student sharing with our class a profound observation she read. She said that "the dishes in the sink only bother you when you aren't doing them." When she said that, I thought, "Wow, that is so true." When you know you need to do the dishes, it bothers you to see them sitting there in the sink. But the most amazing thing happens when you start to do them. You feel better. It isn't really that painful to clean the dishes or put them in the dishwasher. It actually feels good knowing that the kitchen is on its way to a nice clean look. It is all the dread leading up to the doing of the dishes that is painful.

Here is the sad part. The dishes aren't going away. Have you ever heard of someone having their house broken into by an intruder who just washed the dishes and left? Sooner or later, you are going to have to do them. The longer you wait, the harder the food is to get off. All procrastinating is doing is making the dread last longer and the job more difficult. That is how it is with many things we put off.

Procrastination doesn't make the job any easier. It usually makes it harder. Procrastination doesn't make the job go away. We just have to stare at it longer. If we want to make the job easier and the day more enjoyable, we need to go ahead and do what we don't want to do. When Brian Tracy wrote a book on procrastination, he called it *Eat That Frog*. Here's how he got the title. He said that, if you knew that sometime today you had to eat a frog, you should go ahead and eat it first thing in the morning. After all, if you know you have to eat a frog, you don't want to stare at it all day long. What is worse than eating a frog? Staring at a frog all day knowing you have to eat it.

Some Things Never Come Back

Sometimes we put off important things and we never get them back. One year in early November, I had a huge publication deadline.

I had to finish some things I was working on and the drop-dead date was quickly approaching. I was procrastinating on everything except my writing. There were days I wouldn't even shave. I would just throw on some blue jeans and any shirt I could find to teach my class. Then it was back to the computer to write. Despite the time crunch, I did not procrastinate on one particular thing. As I said, it was early November. It happened to be an election year. I take my responsibility to vote very seriously. I procrastinated right through early voting but, when Election Day arrived, I procrastinated no more. If I procrastinated that day, I wouldn't get another chance to vote in that election and I would probably remember that for the rest of my life. My chance to vote that year was going away and it wasn't coming back. Procrastination could cost me something very important.

Probably one of the most impactful songs in all of my generations' music was the 1974 folk rock song by Harry Chapin titled *Cat's in the Cradle*. It is about a father who kept telling his son, "We'll get together some time." They never did. The father didn't have time to watch his son grow up. He didn't have time to play catch with him. Well, finally by the time the kid is in college, the father has some time to spend with him. By then it is too late. The kid has better things to do. Finally, the father is retired and the kid has no time for him whatsoever. As a child, the son would say to his dad, "I'm going to be like you." Indeed, when he was grown, he was just like his father.

That was one of those songs that never went away. To this day, it is still being played on the radio and, when it is, it makes parents pause and evaluate their lives. It is amazing how quickly kids jump from being two to being twenty. Once those years are gone, we can never get them back. It is so easy to procrastinate those years away because ten year old Johnny seems like he will always be ten. Then, one day, we wake up and he's twenty.

Knowing what will never come back is what made Bart such a good procrastinator. People knew that, when Bart was working on a research or consulting project, they could count on him. In the fast paced world of business research and consulting, you only have a small window of opportunity to get things done. The only way Bart could thrive in such an environment is that he could save until later anything that he didn't absolutely have to do today. That made him the perfect business researcher and consultant. Because Bart could procrastinate so well on everything else, nobody ever had to worry about him procrastinating on his research projects or consulting.

Some Things Bite Us

Sometimes, by putting things off, we create problems for ourselves. It sent Bart to jail for tax evasion. He shouldn't have procrastinated on his taxes but he never meant to "evade" anything. Bart never cared about money one way or the other. As he found out, the IRS didn't share his cavalier attitude towards money. Not getting our money is a big deal to the IRS. Eventually, Bart's procrastination came around to bite him.

We don't need to go to jail for our procrastination to bite us. If the boss is on the phone screaming, "Where are those reports you promised me yesterday?" then we need to be more thoughtful in our procrastination. If our spouse can't remember the last date we had with him or her, we need to add thought to our procrastination. If our gym membership expired a few years back and we didn't even notice, we may need to start procrastinating on something other than our health. If we never seem to get around to planning our days but we always seem to get around to watching our favorite television programs, we may need to stop procrastinating on our time management system. When we are always playing catch-up, the effects of thoughtless procrastination may be catching up with us.

Do this. Think back to the last few times you procrastinated on some important thing and it ended up coming around to bite you. Think back to specific times you had that "I should have done it yesterday" feeling. Now, think back to the things that you did while you were procrastinating. Was the mess you found yourself in because you procrastinated on the wrong things? Were you in trouble because you put off important things to make time for television, video games, hanging out with friends, the internet, etc.? If so, then you have found your problem with procrastination. You found some things you need to get better at procrastinating on. You just need to get better at procrastinating on surfing the net, watching television, etc. Then you might stop procrastinating on the things that eventually come around and bite you. Seldom will you get in trouble because you procrastinated on playing a video game.

Sometimes we get in trouble for the things we do or don't do. Often we get in trouble for the things we do too late. Try remembering your anniversary just one day too late. You didn't forget. You just didn't remember on time. I am sure your spouse didn't give it a second thought. Enjoy the couch. That's the way procrastination is. Doing something too late can be just as bad as not doing it at all. When things are always coming around to bite you, you know that you are doing things too late.

What Does Procrastination Cost Us?

All procrastination has consequences but the consequences aren't always the same. If we procrastinate on certain things, the consequences will be huge. If we procrastinate on other things, the consequences will be small. In fact, there are some things that, if we procrastinate on them, the consequences will be positive, especially if we never get around to doing them. We need to start looking at what our procrastination is costing us and then procrastinate accordingly.

I had a student who said that she wanted to get her Ph.D. in an area where she would earn about $150,000 per year. She said that she wanted to take a couple of years off of school before getting her Ph.D. I asked her if she minded blowing a quarter of a million dollars. She looked at me with surprise on her face. She asked, "How would that be blowing almost a quarter of a million dollars?" I pointed out that, without the Ph.D., she would probably get a job for around $40,000 per year. The difference between two years at $40,000 per year and two years at $150,000 per year would come out to be around $220,000. Then I said, "Now I don't know if you consider $220,000 to be around a quarter of a million but it would be close enough to make me rethink putting off completing my education."

We need to always keep in mind what thoughtless procrastination costs us. Sometimes it is easy to calculate the monetary costs. If we put off doing something that will eventually make us an additional $24,000 per year, then our procrastination is costing us $2,000 per month or almost $500 per week. On a five day work week, we are costing ourselves nearly $100 per day. Try saying to yourself, "Go ahead and wait another day. After all, you have another $100 to blow." The problem is that we aren't paying the $100 out of our pocket today. We are taking it out of our pocket sometime in the future. So it doesn't really feel like it is costing us. That is how procrastination always is. Because we are putting things off to the future, we never have to pay the price today. We don't feel the pain so we think the pain doesn't exist. It doesn't but it will. We need to consider future pain, not just what hurts now.

It isn't just the financial costs that we need to see. What does procrastination at school cost us? Grades. What does procrastination at work cost us? Respect and influence. What does procrastination at home cost us? Relationships. What does procrastination in exercise cost us? Health. There is no important area of our life that can't be hurt by thoughtless procrastination. We need to be careful when we procrastinate. We may be putting off living a very good life.

What Procrastination Can Do

If you look carefully at the wording of the Procrastination Principle, it doesn't say that procrastination will bring regrets. It says that it can bring regrets. Every day Bart sat in that jail cell, I am sure he regretted procrastinating on his taxes. I am sure he wished he were back consulting and researching. Because he procrastinated on filing his taxes, that which meant the most to him was taken away. Procrastinating on the wrong things brought huge regrets to Bart.

On the other hand, procrastinating on the right things is not a problem. In fact, procrastinating on the right things can pay huge dividends. Bart procrastinated on so many trivial things, and even some not-so-trivial things, that he had plenty of time to become one of the best researchers in the history of my discipline. If Bart didn't have the ability to procrastinate, he wouldn't have possibly had such a huge impact on his profession.

Was Bart a great procrastinator? In a sense he was. That's what made him a great consultant and researcher. In a sense he wasn't and that's what cost him his job, his freedom, the respect of others, and the very thing he enjoyed most doing. Bart's story can serve as both an example and a warning. If you want to become great, procrastinate like Bart did. If you don't want to crash and burn, do not procrastinate like Bart did. Learn to procrastinate but learn not to procrastinate. Procrastination can be our best time management friend but it can be our worst time management enemy.

We need to be great at procrastination. We need to become so good at it that we will know exactly what we should put off doing. If procrastination is getting us in trouble, then it is because we just don't seem to know when to procrastinate. If we have an "I'll do it tomorrow" attitude on a bunch of unimportant things, then that's fine. But if that is our attitude towards the things that really matter, then we will live an "I should have done it yesterday" life.

The Procrastination Challenge:
Resolve to put off until tomorrow that which
would interfere with what should be done today.

14
Momentum

The Momentum Principle:
To Keep Going, Get Moving and Don't Stop

Baseball great Yogi Berra had some great quotes ascribed to him. Quotes like, "Nobody goes to that restaurant any more, it's too crowded," "Always go to other people's funerals, otherwise they won't come to yours," "The other teams could make trouble for us if they win," "You can observe a lot by just watching," "A nickel ain't worth a dime anymore," "You wouldn't have won if we'd beaten you," and, the best of all, "I never said most of the things I said."

When I look at the Momentum Principle, it looks like something Yogi Berra might have said. "To keep going, get moving and don't stop." Duh! However, when you think about it, the problem we have in completing any job is that we either never get started or something stops us. Conquer these two problems and you can do anything. How do we conquer them? We gain momentum and then we keep it. That's what momentum is and that is why it is so important to time management.

Losing Momentum Is Not Being Lazy

It is tempting to think that, when we aren't moving towards our goal, we are being lazy. In reality, we may have just lost momentum. There is a difference. Let me give you an example.

I set aside one summer of my life to write the current book. I had spent years accumulating the material for it and now I just needed to put it all down on paper. After I finished up my teaching in the spring, I started working on it. Since I was just focusing on this book, I gained some great momentum. I was writing every day and so I was making incredible progress. Then I didn't write for a few days. When I got back to the book, I found it extremely difficult to get the words flowing again. Now here is the irony. The chapter I couldn't write was the current chapter.

I was writing a chapter on momentum and I couldn't gain enough momentum to write it. I had plenty of material to put into this chapter. I could probably write a whole book on just this one topic. I wanted to write the chapter. I spent many hard hours at the computer trying to get the words flowing again. I wasn't going anywhere, not because I was lazy but because I had lost momentum. I knew that I would not return to my previous levels of productivity until I regained momentum.

In the middle of this fight to regain momentum, I was eating lunch with my family. I told them that I had lost momentum and it was right when I was writing the chapter on momentum. They thought this was funny. The guy who wants to tell the world all about momentum can't seem to get the momentum needed to do so.

"It's easy to lose momentum," I told them. "We all do it from time to time." Then I turned to my kids and asked each of them how their summer was going. Each one of them had specific things they wanted to accomplish this summer. I asked one kid, "How is studying for that graduate school admissions test going?" To another, I asked "How about that extra studying you were doing for the difficult class you have coming up next semester?" I went around the table and showed each of them how they too had made great progress on their summer projects only to see their momentum dwindle in recent days.

Please note, I wasn't accusing my kids of being lazy. They aren't lazy. They are some of the hardest working students I know. The two who had lost their studying momentum are both straight-A students. Yet this summer their studying seemed to fizzle out. There is a huge difference between being lazy and losing momentum. If we aren't moving, it doesn't mean we are lazy. It means we don't have momentum and we need to discover how to gain it. If we have momentum, it seems like nothing can stop us. If we don't have it, we can barely get going. Very few people appreciate just how important momentum is to their daily schedule.

The Power of Momentum

Momentum is one of the most powerful forces in the universe. When Newton studied motion, he started with his very first law being, "A body in motion tends to stay in motion and a body at rest tends to stay at rest unless acted upon by an unbalanced force." If you want to understand how things move around in this universe, you have to understand momentum. It is momentum that keeps everything moving. This is a foundational law of physics but it doesn't just apply to the physical world.

Athletic teams need momentum to win. Coaches are always trying to figure out what they can do to swing momentum in their teams favor. Salespeople need momentum. At times, a salesperson might have such momentum that he could walk in, say "Hickory, dickory, dock..." and buyers will purchase by the truck-loads at full price. Yet the very same salesperson might have other times when he has lost momentum and he can't give his product away for free. Leaders need momentum. When John Maxwell laid out the laws of leadership, he said that momentum is a leader's best friend. Politicians need momentum. Many political campaigns have been won because of momentum or lost because of the lack of momentum.

So whether we are studying physics, coaching football, selling widgets, or running for office, momentum is of crucial importance to us. When we are trying to be as productive as possible with a limited amount of time, momentum is crucially important.

The Paradox of the Busy Schedule

That's why there is an apparent paradox of a busy schedule. It seems like the less time you have, the more you get done. There is an age-old expression that says that, "If you want to get something done, give it to a busy person." It seems like having less time somehow increases our productivity. I once thought that this was simply because busy people were ambitious and people who were not busy were lazy. So I thought that this is like saying, "If you want something done, give it to an ambitious person and not a lazy one." However, I am not so sure that this is the real reason that busy people can do a better job taking on tasks than people who have a lot of time on their hands.

Most college students will tell you that, when their life gets busier, their grades get better. For example, I have heard so many students say that their grades dramatically improved when they got a part time job or when they took on a leadership role in some campus organization. They didn't suddenly become more ambitious when they got the job. They just had less time to study. With less time to study, their grades went up.

What is it about having less time that makes us accomplish more? It is the Law of Momentum in action. If I woke up one morning and I just had a few small things to accomplish that day, I might not even get those few things done. Why? Because I would piddle rather than work. I would never get going and so nothing would get done. On the other hand, if I were to wake up with several important things to accomplish, I might zoom right through them. I would hit the ground running and quickly gain momentum. It would be the momentum that would take me through the day. I would get a lot done all day long because I started the day getting some things done quickly.

If you have forever to do something, it takes forever to do it because you never gain momentum. However, if you gain momentum, it is amazing how fast you can get things done. It took me days to write this chapter on momentum because I couldn't ever get momentum. However, just a couple weeks earlier, I had momentum and I wrote the rough draft of a different chapter in an amazing three hours. The difference between taking hours and taking days to accomplish basically the same thing is the difference between having momentum and not having momentum.

Four Forces of Momentum

This is how the momentum principle works. Speed creates momentum and momentum sustains motion. When we attack something with speed, power, and a sense of urgency, the momentum we create will move us to accomplish a lot in a very short time. When we half-heartedly work on a project, we never get the speed we need to make much progress. The key to really accomplishing something is to understand how to gain and keep momentum. We need to understand the four forces of momentum.

Momentum Makers

Momentum makers are the things in our lives that create momentum. Probably the best momentum maker is a tight deadline. When we have to move fast, we do. When we start moving fast, we seem to keep moving even after the project is done. That is what happened with the chapter that took me only three hours to write. I had not even planned on working on that chapter that particular day. I had been working on a different chapter and my goal for the day was simply to finish that one. I had no intentions of starting a new chapter because there was something else I was doing that day. I only had a two-hour window in the morning to write. I spent those two hours writing with a vengeance and I reached my goal right at the deadline. Just as I was finishing the chapter, the other thing that I needed to do that day got pushed back three hours. I had momentum and so I kept on writing. That momentum carried me through the next three hours and, when my new deadline arrived, I had completed another whole chapter. The tight deadline that I thought I had helped me gain momentum that carried me right along to accomplish even more.

Another thing that helps us gain momentum is good planning and organization. One of the best things we can do for our day is plan it out the evening before. That way, when we hit the office, plant, or sales route in the morning, we don't have to take one second trying to figure out what we need to do. As our day starts, that is likely how our whole day will go. In a similar way, Monday morning is the most important part of most people's work week. Hopefully, Monday arrives after a restful weekend where we were able to take our minds off of our work. Then, as we start moving fast on Monday morning, we can carry that throughout the whole week. As our week starts, that is how our week goes.

There was a high school athlete who set the state record for the high jump. When a reporter asked him how he did it, he answered, "I just threw my heart over the bar and my body followed." That is what we need to do anytime we have a challenging job. Get it started. Throw our whole heart and mind into it for a short time. The momentum we create will carry us through the whole job. Never give a half-hearted attempt to start a difficult job. It won't work. We won't gain momentum and we will struggle through the whole thing.

Momentum Takers

Momentum takers are those events or people that drain the momentum we have. Doesn't it seem like the minute we start to get momentum, someone will walk into our office and strike up some meaningless conversation? Why is it that people who have nothing to do seem to want to do it with us just when we get momentum? It is hard not to be rude but we do need to know how to get back to work.

Any interruption makes it hard to maintain momentum. Phone calls can strip our momentum. If we are supervising a group of people and we have certain reports we need to get done, we probably will have a hard time maintaining momentum with the reports. Every time one of the people we are supervising has a question or a random thought, our momentum will be at risk. We could finish the report with thirty minutes of uninterrupted time. However, with the constant barrage of interruptions, the thirty minute report might end up taking us all day.

The worst momentum takers are the ones we create for ourselves through poor organization. If we have to constantly stop and find something when we are working on a task, then it is very difficult to ever gain or keep our momentum. How many times have we been in the middle of a project and then something like this happens. We need to see something in a memo we received and so we grab for the memo but it is not there. "Where is that memo from the boss? It was here a minute ago? I know I had it..." By the time we find the memo and get back to work, our momentum has taken a serious hit. The more we can keep organized as we work on a project, the less the chances are that we will kill our momentum.

Momentum Breakers

One interruption here and there won't kill our momentum. However, there may be events that will totally stop us and redirect us in another way. One time I was writing in my home office. I was clicking along at top speed when I heard some commotion in the back yard. I rushed out there to find that my daughter's swing had broken and thrown her across the yard. From the swelling that was already occurring, I knew that she had broken her arm. Any momentum that I might have had in writing was gone. I couldn't say, "Honey, hold that arm still while I write a few more pages." I dropped what I was doing and rushed her to the emergency room.

Genuine crises will strip us of our momentum and there is nothing we can do about them. Priorities dictate that we leave what we are doing regardless of how well it is going. My daughter's safety and health is a lot more important to me than anything I might write. So that crisis killed my momentum as it should. We can't avoid momentum breakers. They are just part of life.

What we have to watch out for though are pseudo-crises. These are things that look like crises but which are not. For example, sometimes people try to dump their crises into our laps. I am sure you have seen the sign that says, "Poor planning on your part does not constitute an emergency on my part." Usually those signs are on the desks of government employees and not people who actually have to be nice to their customers to keep them paying their paychecks. Usually a crisis for a customer is a crisis for me. On the other hand, poor planning by a coworker or classmate does not have to be a crisis for me. Usually our momentum is more important than their crisis.

Momentum Fakers

Some of the hardest things to conquer in our battle to gain and maintain momentum are momentum fakers. These are things that make us think we are gaining momentum when we are not. As we discuss extensively elsewhere, just because we are moving fast, we aren't necessarily moving far. If we are spending our time on busyness, low priority tasks, or urgent tasks that aren't that important, then we won't gain the traction we need to develop momentum. It may feel like we have momentum but we do not. We only have momentum when we are moving fast towards an important goal or objective. Where we are going is just as important in determining our momentum as how fast we are getting there.

Momentum is a powerful force in the universe but it is not the only one. Next time you see the moon, think of the incredible momentum that keeps that gigantic rock circling the Earth day after day, month after month, year after year, century after century. Even with all of its momentum, the moon just goes around and around in circles. Now, that's OK for a moon. In fact, that's what makes it a moon. Moons are supposed to orbit around in circles. But that's not what we want our momentum to be like. We don't want to get this incredible momentum just to go around in circles. If we find ourselves always back where we started, we are falling victim to momentum fakers.

The key to identifying momentum fakers can be found in our definition of time management. Remember, our time is being managed to the extent to which my activities are in alignment with where I want to be at some point in the future. We want our momentum to be moving us towards our goals in life, not just taking us around in circles. Momentum fakers take us around in circles. Real momentum moves us forward.

Momentum Blocks

Momentum tends to come when we are able to focus all of our energy on a specific task for an extended time. It is like pushing a car that is stalled. You give it a push and start it moving. That takes a lot of work but it also creates momentum. With momentum, it is easy to keep the car moving. The longer you can keep the momentum going, the easier it will be to get the car to where you want it to be. That is letting the power of momentum work for you.

What would happen if, instead of keeping the momentum going, you stopped to catch your breath every time you got the car moving? You push to get the car going. It starts to move. You stop to take a breath. The car stops. You push to get the car going again. It starts to move. You stop to take a breath. The car stops... That would be a much harder way to move the car. That is often how our days go. We push to get going which takes a lot of effort. Once we are going, something stops us. Then we have to push again to get going. We often have momentum working against us rather than for us.

To overcome this problem, we can create "momentum blocks." Here is how a momentum block works. We set aside a period of time to either work on a specific project or work through a group of related items. For example, we could work on a report, call all of our customers in an area of the state, work clearing things out of our inbox, figure out training schedules for the office, etc. The more we can shield ourselves from interruptions during that time the better. We start out with a clear picture of where we are going with the block of time. We want to write down what specific outcome we desire from this block of time.

Next we figure out the first one or two things we need to do to reach that outcome. We write these down too. We don't need to write everything down that needs to be done in the whole block of time. The first one or two things will suffice. That's all we need to get the momentum started. Now we have what we need to gain momentum (the tasks) and to sustain momentum (the block of time). Then we give the project a shove. We start the first task. We keep working towards our outcome until we either achieve our goal or we run out of time. We only need to get momentum going once and it will sustain us through the whole block of time. That is much better than starting and stopping over and over again.

Becoming Unstoppable

If a train is going down a track at 70 miles per hour, it has momentum. We could put a thick concrete barrier in front of it and we couldn't stop it. On the other hand, if that same train was stopped, we could put a small piece of concrete under each of its drive wheels and it couldn't get going. That is the power of momentum. When we are going, it is hard for us to stop. When we are stopped, it is hard to get going. That is why one of the biggest time challenges is to get going and not stop.

The Momentum Challenge:
Resolve to start strong and fight
everything that says "stop."

15
Clarity

The Clarity Principle:
Clarity Speeds Things Up.
Confusion Slows Things Down.

We need momentum because it gets us going. We also need clarity because it speeds things up. We need to gain momentum to do things. We also need to have clarity if we want to do big things. Mahatma Gandhi accomplished very big things because he had both momentum and clarity.

He Changed the World

Have you ever wanted to change the world? Mahatma Gandhi did. Gandhi led India to independence and inspired movements for civil rights and freedom around the globe. That is not exactly what you would have expected from someone who was described in school as "good at English, fair in Arithmetic and weak in Geography; conduct very good, bad handwriting." He married very young and just kind of wandered through the early years of his life. Since English was his strong suit, he moved to England for his education. Returning to India, he tried to get a law practice started but he just didn't have the heart to viciously cross-examine witnesses. He piddled around in low level law positions in South Africa. Gandhi was like so many people who are just drifting through life with only a vague picture of where he might want to go and no idea whatsoever how to get there. Then came the night that changed his life.

Gandhi was on a business trip. Despite having purchased a first-class ticket, he was relegated to a lower class in favor of a white man. Gandhi protested and he was thrown off the train. He spent a long, cold night in a lonely railroad station. As he sat there that night, he had a decision to make. Would he return to India or would he stay in South Africa and fight injustice? By dawn he had made his decision and, as the saying goes, the rest is history.

In one night, Gandhi went from plodding along to changing the world. It was the moment Gandhi developed clarity. In his lifetime he would lead more nonviolent change than the world had ever seen. Gandhi was able to accomplish so much in such a short time because he had three types of clarity. He had clarity of purpose in that he knew what he wanted to do. He had clarity of process in that he knew how he wanted to do it. Then there was a third type of clarity he needed. He didn't want to fight the horrors of injustice with the terrors of war. He needed to get others to clearly see his purpose and process. He spent years developing what we will call team clarity.

To move fast, these are the three types of clarity we need. Whether we are changing the world, running a business, raising children, trying to teach a Sunday school class, or doing anything else, we can never get much traction if we don't have clarity. We need clarity of purpose, clarity of process, and team clarity. Let's explore each of these types of clarity in greater depth.

Clarity of Purpose

There was a famed violinist who was once told by an admirer, "I would give my life to be able to play the violin like you did tonight."

The violinist replied, "I did."

This violinist had a clarity of purpose that guided his schedule every day. In the mornings, he would practice the violin for four to five hours. Then he would eat lunch. Then he would spend his afternoon practicing the violin for another four to five hours. It wasn't that the violin took over his whole life. On the other hand, he didn't have a hard time deciding what he should do with his mornings and afternoons. Nothing could rob him of his quality time with his violin.

Our schedules should be purpose driven. Here I am not talking using purpose in the same way Rick Warren did in his book *The Purpose Driven Life*. He focused on our spiritual purpose for being here. I agree with Rick Warren that our faith should be a crucial part of our life. However, here I use the word "purpose" in a much more modest way. When I talk about clarity of purpose, I am focusing on the goals that our activities are targeted towards.

Clarity of purpose starts when we clearly understand what few things are most important to us. That's a starting point but it is not enough. Most people will say about the same thing when asked what the most important things in life are. I recently heard a pastor explain how difficult it is to give the eulogy at a funeral of someone who you don't really know that well. Let's say Uncle Fred dies and he really wasn't active in any church. So his nieces and nephews ask their pastor to speak at Uncle Fred's funeral. That's fine, the pastor is thinking, but you have to give me some material to work with.

This pastor is going to have to speak for fifteen minutes about someone he never even knew. So he asks the family what Uncle Fred was like. He always gets the exact same answer. The names change but the descriptions remain the same. They start off by saying, "Uncle Fred was a good man." Then they say that Uncle Fred loved his family. Next in the official liturgy to the deceased is that Uncle Fred worked hard. Finally, they pick out Uncle Fred's favorite sports team and say how much Uncle Fred loved that team. This pastor said that those are the only four things the family ever gives him to work with.

When I heard that, I told my wife Lisa that I knew why that's all the family can think to say about Uncle Fred. It is because Fred is a guy and guys are very simple creatures. Women can be complicated but guys are quite simple. If you look into our brains, we only have four moving parts. We want to be considered "good." We love our families. We like to think that we work hard. And we each have some team that we are crazy about. That's it. That's all there is to a guy.

Saying that we want to love our family and do a good job in our work is not enough to have clarity of purpose. That's because these could mean so many different things. What does it mean to "love your family"? For me it meant being extremely active in my children's education. On the other hand, I never once considered coaching a team that they were on. As a family man, I was much more into academics than athletics. Sometimes I felt it was a chore to go to their ball games but I never felt burdened helping them with their school work. That was me. I know other fathers who love their family just as much as I love mine and they felt like they could leave the academic stuff for the schools to handle. At the same time, they coached every sporting team their kid was on.

We all love our families but we do so in quite different ways. If you were to ask a bunch of guys what their "purpose" in life is, most of them would put being a good father right up there at the top. But if you asked them what that means, they might come up with dramatically different answers. I grew up being into sports. As an adult I look back on those years and I feel as though I spent too much time playing and not enough time studying. I felt my life really began to take off when I started taking my school work more seriously and my sports less seriously. So when I became a father, I saw my purpose much more as preparing my kids for life through academics and less through sports. Somebody else who lived a different life might think that his purpose as a father is the exact opposite of this. My vision of being a good father does not need to be the same vision that others may hold. It just needs to be clear to me.

135

That relates to all the key areas of our lives. What does it mean to say that we want to be successful at work? I am a professor. Do you know how many different directions you can take a career as a professor? For me, it is all about teaching and the activities that will allow me to do that to the best of my ability. Even what being a good teacher means can be taken in so many different ways. I am a business professor and so it has always been important for me to have one foot in the business world. I also think that it is important to keep up with the latest developments in my field and so I want to stay active in my research.

That vision leaves me very little time for other aspects of my job. Though I have been asked to be the Department Chair on multiple occasions, I have always declined. I have avoided administrative responsibilities like the plague. I try to stay away from serving on committees and going to meetings. I see people on my campus who love the very things I avoid. Their vision of what being a professor means is quite different than what it means for me.

So gaining clarity of purpose is much more than just having some vague notion of what is important to me. It is coming to a very clear understanding of what that means to me. Alvin Toffler said, "You've got to think about big things while you're doing small things, so that all the small things go in the right direction." If we are struggling trying to decide what to put into our schedule and what to drop out, it may be because we lack clarity of purpose. I know I need to put my family in there but what does that mean? I know I need to put my work in there but where should I focus in my career? Saying that my purpose is to balance family and career is an important first step in gaining clarity of purpose but we need to be much more specific about each.

When our purpose is clear, our decisions become a lot easier. Remember that night Gandhi spent in the railroad station. The decision he was trying to make was whether to stay in South Africa or go back to India. That was a tough decision to make with so many things to consider. But once he decided he would fight injustice, the decision was made for him. He had to stay and fight.

If we find we aren't moving as fast as we would like to be in some area of our lives, it might be because we need to gain clarity of purpose in that area. When I have been asked to coach one of my kid's teams or take over as Department Chair, I never needed to agonize over those decisions. I knew they would fit quite well in someone else's vision of their life but they didn't at all fit with my vision of mine. Decisions like that are made easy in areas of our life where we have clarity of purpose.

Clarity of Process

If we have clarity of purpose, we will only go fast if we also have clarity of process. Clarity of process means we know how to get where we are going. Once we have a destination, then things slow down unless we also know how to get there. Imagine that you are in your car and you are going somewhere that you have only been once or twice before. You glance over at your new GPS unit and it isn't working. You try to get it up and running without success. Now, you are trying to get where you need to go based on some vague recollection of how you got there before. You are looking for a familiar landmark or street sign that will tell you where you need to turn. You have great clarity about where you want to go but you don't have much clarity about how to get there. That is like having clarity of purpose without having clarity of process. You know where you want to go but your confusion about how to get there is what is slowing you down.

When your GPS went out, you slowed down. Let's say that you suddenly remembered that you have GPS on your cell phone. You pull into a parking lot and enter your destination. In no time, you have street by street directions showing you exactly how to get where you want to go. Now with this clarity of process, you can speed up again.

Confusion will always slow you down. Clarity will always speed things up. We need clarity of purpose. Even the best GPS unit on the planet can't help us if we don't know where we are going. We also need clarity of process. We can't possibly make good time until we know the best route to take. But once we have both clarity of purpose and clarity of process, we can make great time.

That is why we spent so much time in the middle chapters of this book emphasizing planning, processes, systems, and habits. That is what gives us clarity of process. I hate taking time out of an already busy life to plan my day, week, month, and year. However, I know I have to do that or else things will slow down. It is like when I am taking a trip. The part I hate the worst is everything that happens before I get in the car. I have to think through where I need to go and put all the addresses in my GPS unit. Once I get them in there, the trip becomes a lot more fun and a lot faster because I just need to follow the GPS unit's directions. The time management process we develop can be like a GPS for our life. It can guide us to exactly where we want to go. But it takes us time, thought, and discipline to get the process up and going. Still, nothing meaningful happens until we have a very clear picture of where we want to go.

Team Clarity

There is one other type of clarity that is extremely important. What applies to individuals applies many times over to teams. If you want to slow your team down to a crawl, enter a bunch of confusion into the organization. If you want your team to accomplish great things, make sure everyone is crystal clear about where you are going and what the next step is to get there.

Leaders Must Develop Clarity

How does a team gain this clarity? Everything starts at the top. As John Maxwell says, "Everything rises and falls on leadership. Everything!" If a leader doesn't have clarity, it is very likely the team will be confused. In the business school, we teach the importance of having a mission statement. That is a nice exercise but companies can't assume that, just because they have a mission statement on some plaque somewhere, they have clarity of purpose. There is only one place that clarity of purpose can reside and that is in the heads of the leaders. You can have plaques on all the walls with the greatest mission statement in the world, but if it isn't in the heads of the key leaders, it isn't the real mission of the organization.

When a leader stays up late at night trying to figure out what an organization should do next, he had better have clarity of purpose. When the key leaders of an organization get together for their daily or weekly staff meetings, the common vision that they share is the real mission of the organization. What happens if the leaders of the organization don't have a shared vision? The weekly staff meetings will become nothing but a bunch of people engaged in turf wars jockeying for position. The organization will slow to a crawl. That is when we can throw all of our past accomplishments out the door. Our team may have had a long series of victories but we are about to experience defeat at the hands of the first team that comes along where everyone has a shared purpose. When clarity is gone, the end is in sight.

Even with clarity of purpose, gaining clarity of process for a whole team is a huge challenge and here is why. People are committed to what they own. If I give someone on my team a process, they won't be nearly as committed to it as they will be to a process they come up with themselves. They won't understand it as well either. So I don't want to be the one who is doing all the thinking. I want people on the team to have an active role in developing their own clarity of process. As a leader, I need to provide a framework and an environment for creating clarity of process. Within that framework, I want to empower the team members to fill in the blanks. As anyone who has ever been in leadership knows, this is a very difficult balancing act. We know that we must insist on clarity of process and we also know that people on the team need to be all working in the same direction. However, we also know that we must remain a bit flexible in what that eventual process becomes as individuals develop their own clarity of process.

Make Sure You Have Clear Communication

There is one thing that will always make team clarity disappear and that is poor communications. Team clarity cannot exist in an environment where communication is not clear. Here are four warning signs of poor communication:

- *Constantly being blindsided:* If we are constantly being blindsided, we probably need to work on our communication skills. We aren't in the communication loop enough to know what is going on.
- *Composing when we should be listening:* When someone is talking to us, if we are thinking about what we want to say, then we need to work on our communication skills. When the other person is talking, we should be listening and not composing our answer.
- *Not connecting with key people:* If we aren't touching base with every key member of our team on a regular basis, our commitment to clear communication is lacking. We quickly get out of touch with the people we don't talk with regularly.
- *Misunderstanding and confusion:* If misunderstandings are common on our team, then we have a problem. Just because words are coming out of my mouth, that doesn't mean the other person understands what I am saying.

To have clarity and not confusion, it is so important that we keep clear lines of communication open with our team.

Keeping Our Clarity

Once we have clarity, how can we make sure we keep it? Let's look at four things that helped Gandhi maintain his clarity. They can help us keep our clarity too.

Events: Remember the night Gandhi spent in the railroad station. Every step of that trip gave Gandhi greater clarity of purpose. Simply because of his color, he was forced to ride on the outside of a stagecoach, he was refused a hotel room, he was told he must travel third-class, he was forced to wander a city looking for a place to stay, and he was told he could not eat with the other guests in a dining room. Gandhi never forgot that humiliating journey. If he ever found himself losing clarity of purpose, he would only need to go back in his mind to all that injustice and his clarity would return.

People: Gandhi's approach of nonviolence had varied roots. Part of it came from Leo Tolstoy. Gandhi never met Tolstoy and he only communicated with him for a year before Tolstoy's death. However, Tolstoy's correspondence with Gandhi along with a story Tolstoy wrote stayed with Gandhi for his whole life. It helped Gandhi keep his clarity of process.

Values: As a child, Gandhi concluded that the ultimate virtues were truth and love. It would have been inconceivable to him to have pursued a means of hate to achieve an end of love. He spent his life trying to develop a stronger sense of what mattered most to him.

Necessity: Gandhi was not the type of person who would ever seek fame. He didn't take the spotlight so he could bask in its glow. He knew that he couldn't fight injustice by himself. If he would have gone to the British by himself and said "get out of my country" they would have said "get out of my face." But when millions practiced non-cooperation, there was little the British could do. When 60,000 people were so connected to Gandhi's purpose and process that they went with him to jail, the British were shaken to their core. Independence was still a long way off but this was the beginning of the end of British rule.

Changing Our Own World

Few of us will ever take on something as massive as freeing a people from the rule of an outside force. Obviously Gandhi's clarity needed to be immense to accomplish what he did. But the principles of clarity still apply, even when it comes to changing our own worlds. Whether it is from events, people, values, or necessity, we need to hold on to clarity of our purpose, clarity of our process, and clarity among members of our team. Clarity is a very important time basic because without clarity, everything slows down.

The Clarity Challenge:
Resolve to gain clarity to gain speed.

16
Andretti

The Andretti Principle:
If Everything Seems Under Control,
You Just Aren't Going Fast Enough

What does it feel like when you really get good at managing your time? Imagine this. You have momentum so you are moving. You gain clarity so you are moving fast. Things start really clicking. That's what you wanted to happen. You are finally a time manager par excellence. You are managing all the priorities in your life. You are moving to where you want to be and not wasting time getting there. How does it feel?

It probably feels like you are on the verge of losing control. If you want to feel totally in control, go back to moving slow. If you are going fast, you probably aren't going to have a nice, warm, fuzzy feeling like everything is just right. That's a time management principle most people don't understand. The better you manage your time, the more things you are able to do. The more things you are doing, the faster things are moving. The faster things are moving, the less we feel in control.

Why We Manage Our Time

I live in a small Southern city. Things move slowly here in Valdosta. That's how I like it. Two of my children live in Atlanta. To get to where they live from Valdosta, we have to take the interstate straight through the middle of Atlanta. On the Atlanta freeways, you aren't sure what you will get. You may be stopped, you may be crawling, or you may be going eighty miles an hour just to keep from getting run over in bumper-to-bumper traffic. When I am slowly puttering around through the streets of Valdosta, I feel perfectly in control. When I am going eighty miles per hour in bumper-to-bumper traffic in Atlanta, I never feel like things are totally under control.

We always feel more under control when we are moving slow than when we are moving fast. Part of managing our time is making sure we don't waste any of it. That means speeding things up. When we do, the feeling of complete control starts to slip away. We don't manage our time so that we can get this nice feeling like everything is under control. Getting back to our definition of time management, we manage our time to make sure that our daily activities are aligned with our long term goals. If that means bringing more order to our life, then that is what we should do. But control is not our time management goal. Managing our time may actually push us to places where we really don't feel like everything is under control.

I remember hosting a very successful businessperson once while he was giving some lectures on campus. He had accomplished some very impressive things. It seemed like he was so much in control of everything. In my office, he confided that nothing could be further from the truth. I remember him telling me, "I always feel like I am on the verge of getting everything under control but I never quite get there." Did he accomplish what he wanted to accomplish? Yes. Was he successful in his career? Extremely successful. Judging by results, he was much better at managing his time than most people are. After all, he did a lot more with his twenty-four hours than almost anyone else I know. However, managing his time pushed him to places where he never felt in control. Sure, he could have done what he needed to do to get everything under control. But that would have meant slowing down and getting less done. Getting everything under control would be a big step in the wrong direction.

We have a large penitentiary in the town where I live. One of my friends is the recreation director there. He has told me of several people who were released from prison and then got into trouble just to get sent back. They became accustomed to the orderly environment of the prison and they couldn't handle the lack of control that freedom brings. If our only goal is to live in a nice, neat, controlled environment, then we don't need a time management system. We need a jail cell. We just need to get arrested for something. Then everything in our little world will be completely controlled. If our goal is to go far and to go fast in life, then we need to manage our time. In doing so, there will be times when things seem totally out of control.

Mario Andretti

That's the Andretti principle. The faster you go, the less you feel in control. The current principle is named in honor of the famed racecar driver Mario Andretti. If there ever was a name synonymous with going fast, it was Andretti. His illustrious career spanned four decades. If it had four wheels, he raced it and he probably won a championship in it. He was known for his steady personality. He very rarely lost his cool, which is quite amazing for someone who spent his life driving around in cars going 180+ miles per hour. He always looked like he was in complete control.

However, at least on the race track, it didn't always feel that way to him. He once said, "If everything seems under control, you just aren't going fast enough." I remember seeing that quote and realizing that I had just found one of the most valuable pieces of wisdom about time management I had ever seen. We spend our lives trying to get everything under control. Unfortunately, we do it by slowing down.

Here is what Mario Andretti's business manager said about that quote:

> To Mario, it distills his belief that triumph is milked from the edges of chaos. Yet it's not necessarily brute speed to which he is referring, the kind unleashed by a relentless right foot. For Mario, comfort is the enemy of victory. If you're not hyperventilating, if you're not straining under the mental and physical pressures of pushing a racecar on the slithering edge of havoc, you're not going fast enough. When you're at the limit, you exert everything. If you're under the limit, it means you're giving something away; you're leaving something on the table. That's basically racing in a nutshell.

When I saw that, I thought "that's hard core." Comfort is the enemy of victory. Wow! You have to be hyperventilating. Really? If you are under the limit, you're giving something away.

We don't need to be that hard core with our time. Maybe we can afford to back off because we aren't racing cars. But we might need to ask ourselves some serious questions. I see Mario Andretti and I ask myself if I have become so soft that I am backing off for a feeling of comfort? After all, what happens if my life gets out of control for a while? I lose a day's productivity. What could have happened in Andretti's world if things got out of control for one second? When you are in a crowd going 180 miles per hour, it's not something you even want to consider. If Andretti could handle things seeming out of control doing what he did, then perhaps my world being a little crazy isn't really that big of a deal. When I talk about things at the workplace crashing into a ball of flames, I am just speaking figuratively.

So here is the challenge. We need to be going so fast that, at least at times, we lose the feeling of total control. At the same time, we don't want to actually lose control and crash. We need to live with the feeling of being out of control. We also need to avoid losing control.

Why We Feel Out of Control

How do we balance these two? To answer that, we need to look at why we get that out of control feeling.

Sometimes We Really Are Not in Control

Admiral Robert Peary is known for his expeditions trying to be the first person to make it to the North Poll. He had the best equipment. He was an absolutely brilliant navigator. His trips were planned out right down to the smallest detail. However, even with all of this, there were still times when he was definitely out of control. On one of his expeditions, he got up early and traveled north as fast as he could all day long. Still, when evening came and he confirmed his location, he was seven miles further south than he was when he started out that morning. How did that happen? Did he make a navigational error?

No, actually he was on a piece of ice that was drifting south faster than he was traveling north. Despite his best efforts, he was not really in control of his travels. Something much bigger than him--in this case, the ice under his feet--had a greater control over his journey than he did. Still, Peary didn't give up. He didn't say, "Well boys, we are heading south. Let's just ride this chunk of ice to Hawaii." The next morning, he started out again with a new appreciation for the fact that he was not in total control.

I like this story because I can relate to it. There have been days when I have started early, worked hard, and finished late just to find out that I was further behind than when I started. On days like that, it is difficult not to get discouraged. However we shouldn't let them get to us because there are a lot of things that come and go into our busy lives that we have no control over. We will have days when these things that are bigger than us will grab our time and take it in the opposite direction from where we are trying to go.

In fact, as we have discussed in the Chaos Principle and the NYCNO Principle, a big part of time management is simply learning how to respond when things do get out of control. As the Chaos Principle explains, we must diligently fight back against the chaos which is constantly making its way into our lives. As the NYCNO Principle explains, our plans will not always turn out as we expect and yet we must still be diligent at planning. Things will get out of control but we shouldn't let that keep us from managing our time. Actually it should make us even more determined to control what we can.

Sometimes We Do Not Take Control

We must resist thinking, "Since I can't control everything, I won't control anything." I think the best example we could follow is that of basketball legend John Wooden. He gets my vote for the best college basketball coach that ever lived. Here was his philosophy. Control everything you can and don't worry about the rest. If he could control it, he would. If it was something he couldn't control, he wouldn't spend much time thinking about it.

For example, he always started out his first practice of each season the same way. He showed his players how he expected them to put their socks on. That's hardly the way I would expect a coach to begin a national championship run. But here was his reasoning. He said that there are so many things that he couldn't control between that first workout and the championship game. However, athletes getting blisters on their feet because of how they put on their socks was something he could control. So he controlled what he could and that was amazing preparation for dealing with what he couldn't control.

The Andretti principle isn't a license to become sloppy and let everything around us tumble into a big mess. Quite the opposite. Because things will get out of control when we are accomplishing great things, we need to be careful to control what we can. I am sure Andretti and his crew spent every moment they could making sure his car was in top condition. When he was out of control, it was because he was going at top speed on race day and not because his team only went half-speed preparing for the race.

Sometimes We Are Still Learning How to Control

I am sure that, every year Andretti raced his car, he gained more and more control. He could go faster and faster before he got that out of control feeling. That's because we learn to handle out of control situations by handling out of control situations. Do you remember the first time you drove a car? I am sure your mother or father does. Do you remember how hard you had to concentrate and focus on everything that was involved in keeping the car on the road without hitting something? If you are like most people, you probably felt a bit out of control.

When we drive a car, there are actually a lot of things we need to think about. We need to be conscious of our speed. We need to be aware of the position of all the other cars on the road–who is behind us, who is in front of us, and who is coming at us. We need to think about the traffic signals and signs. We need to calculate in our head the proper rate of slowing down so that we don't hit the car in front of us while also making sure we don't stop too far back. We need to monitor how much we are turning the steering wheel so that we don't end up in the ditch or the wrong lane. We need to remember the speed limit. We need to remember where we are going and what route we are taking to get there. And we need to remember all these things at the same time. No wonder we feel out of control when we are just learning to do all those things simultaneously.

Here is what often gives us that out of control feeling. Our conscious mind can only think about a limited number of things at one time. The closer we get to that limit, the more out of control we feel. When we are first driving, all the things we mentioned must be handled by our conscious mind. However, the more we do things, the more we are able to shift the mental activity associated with it from our conscious mind to our preconscious or even subconscious mind.

Remember the last time you drove the car? You still had to think about all the things I just mentioned but I bet you barely even noticed you were thinking about them. Your conscious mind probably wasn't thinking about steering, braking, dodging the other cars, etc. That was all going on way deep inside your brain at the subconscious level. That freed your mind to think of other things like what was on the radio, the appointment you just had, or what you were going to have for dinner. You were thinking about the same things but because they weren't overfilling your conscious mind, you didn't feel the slightest bit out of control.

How did we get rid of that out of control feeling? We did so by doing the very thing that made us feel out of control. We continued to drive even though we didn't feel comfortable doing so. Then, after a while, we got to the point where we no longer felt out of control.

Andretti didn't start out at the Indianapolis 500. He started out in stock cars. From there, he wanted to get into the single-seater open wheel cars so he moved up to midget cars. In one year, he raced in over one hundred events. He then went to sprint cars. Finally, he made it to Indy Car racing. If Andretti had not learned to handle out of control situations on the half mile dirt track in Nazareth, Pennsylvania, there is no way he could have handled the out of control situations in the Indianapolis 500. That's what we want to do. By handling out of control situations, we learn to be out of control at a higher level.

A word of caution is in order here lest I be misunderstood. There are good reasons to feel like things are not under control and there are bad reasons. For example, we could drink a couple of six-packs, grab our cell phone, hit the interstate, and text all the way to Miami. That is not a good way to be out of control. That is a good way to get somebody killed and that is not what I am talking about.

Costs of Comfortable Inaction

What I am talking about is more in the spirit of what John F. Kennedy said. Kennedy understood that nobody enjoys the risks associated with being out of control. But he also understood that the real risk is in always being in control. Here is what Kennedy said:

> There are risks and costs to a program of action. But they are far less than the long-range risks and costs of comfortable inaction.

There is a danger in being out of control. But there is also a danger in always being in control. What we want to avoid is the "long-range risks and costs of comfortable inaction."

What are the risks of comfortable inaction? Probably the biggest risk is that we will keep shooting at a target that is no longer there. Things move and change so rapidly that, if we spend too much time getting things together, we won't have a place to put them. In economics there is a concept called, "creative destruction." What it says is that everything has to be shaken up for things to move forward. Whatever industry we are in, the changes are coming at an astounding rate. No wonder we always feel out of balance. The target is always moving.

Another reason why we must be willing to feel out of control is that, at times, it takes a shake-up to make us wake-up. We could be driving along with our minds a million miles away and not particularly paying attention to the road. If we suddenly noticed the person beside us drifting into our lane, we would quickly exit la la land and check back into the present. Nothing is as engaging as the effort to try to gain control of an out of control situation. In that way, if we are drifting along, suddenly being a little out of control might just be what we need to engage our mind and body into the here and now.

The other risk of comfortable inaction is that we never have the breakthroughs that chaos brings. Remember Andretti's philosophy. "Triumph is milked from the edges of chaos." The best classes I ever teach are the ones where I feel out of control at times. Here is a formula for a great class. Take a group of students who are very diverse. Throw in a couple of live-wires that will say whatever comes to their mind. Mix things up with some interesting and potentially controversial discussion topics. Then hold on for dear life. If you are the teacher, you are in for a wild ride. I have seen moments so out of control that I wasn't sure the safety net of tenure would protect me. In the end though, I have had student after student tell me that one of these out of control classes was the best class they ever took.

When we are out of control, the journey may be quite difficult but the eventual destination can be phenomenal. Do I feel uncomfortable when one of these classes is going off in some real strange direction that I didn't anticipate? Absolutely. Could I pull the class back into line? Yes, if that is what I wanted to do. But, in terms of education, the price of control would be way too high. My need for control would rob the students of an incredible educational experience. If we are always demanding to be in control of every situation, we need to take a minute to consider what that control is costing us. The price of control may be way too high. We need to feel OK with the fact that our most productive times are often the times when we feel the least in control.

Time Management Versus Stress Management

When I speak on the Andretti Principle, some people who hear me are always surprised or even disappointed. They believe that, if they could just manage their time, things would suddenly become peaceful and relaxed. That's why they want to learn time management. They want to live in a world that isn't so stressful. I tell them that they don't need a class in time management. They need a class in stress management. Managing your time effectively can sometimes be stressful. They really have one of two choices. If they can't handle the stress of being a bit out of control, they need to slow down. If they can't slow down, they need to learn to handle the stress of being a bit out of control. There is no middle ground. When you start to move fast, you start feeling a little out of control. Now obviously you don't want to lose control and crash. Andretti didn't go so fast that it sent him spinning into the wall. But he did push himself fast enough to win. That's what we need to do if we want the most life can offer. We need to move fast even if it means feeling a bit out of control.

The Andretti Challenge:
Resolve to keep moving fast even when it
makes you feel a little out of control.

17
Discernment

The Discernment Principle:
Activity Does Not Mean Progress and
Urgent Does Not Mean Important

We have spent the last two chapters discussing what we can do to get more done in less time. For the next two chapters we are going to discuss a couple of things that can slow us down. If our efforts are misdirected or misguided, it doesn't make any difference how fast we are going. We are not going to reach our destination.

Be Careful Where You Build

One of my lifelong friends is a lawyer. I remember visiting his brand new dream house that he had just built. It was beautiful. After telling me how much time, work, and effort it is to custom build a house, he shared with me that all his time and money could have ended up being totally wasted. After the house was built, the only thing my friend needed to do before moving in was go down to the courthouse and file some papers. While he was filling out the paperwork, he discovered something that literally made him sick. He had built the house on the wrong lot. His lot was actually the one next to the one his house was sitting on. He had built his dream house on someone else's property.

He said that he quickly looked up who owned the "vacant" lot that his dream house was on and made them a very good offer to buy it. Fortunately, the owners of the property didn't know there was a house sitting on their "vacant" lot and my lawyer friend wasn't going to tell them. It puts you at a disadvantage in negotiating when you are trying to buy a lot because you accidently built a house on it. They took my friends offer and now his dream house is on a double lot.

I learned two lessons from my lawyer friend's painful experience. The first lesson I learned was that, if I ever own a vacant lot and somebody seems really motivated to buy it, I need to go check out the lot. You never know what might be sitting on your "vacant" lot. A more important lesson I learned was that, before you build, make sure you're building in the right spot. If my lawyer friend had not been able to pull off his purchase of the lot, all of the money and expense of building his dream house wouldn't have benefited him at all. It doesn't do you any good to build if you do so in the wrong place.

That lesson doesn't just apply to building a house. It applies to anything you might do with your time. If you are building in the wrong place, you are wasting your time. We may work really hard. We may build exactly what we set out to build. We may love the end product. Still, if we misdirect our efforts, we may not be able to enjoy the product of all our work.

Seldom does someone build a house on the wrong lot. We've figured out ways to check and see where to put a house. However, it takes greater discernment to make sure we aren't wasting our time. There are two areas where we are in particular need of discernment in managing our time. Sometimes it can be easy to mistake activity for progress. It is also particularly difficult to discern urgent from important. So let's look at these two places where we need discernment so as to not waste our time building in the wrong place.

Activity and Progress

To my friend, it never once felt like he was building on the wrong lot. To him, it felt like he was building his dream house and, in a sense he was. He was just building it in a place where he might not be able to enjoy the benefits of all his hard work. We have to understand that it doesn't always feel like we are wasting our time when we are wasting our time. At times, we are very busy working hard but we aren't building anything that will benefit us. We are settling for activity rather than insisting on progress.

One time I was using busyness to avoid progress and I ended up with some fish in my office. For years I had said that I wanted a fish tank. Actions speak louder than words. It had never been worth my time and effort to actually turn that wish into reality and so I probably didn't really want a fish tank. I guess I liked the idea of a fish tank more than the work of a fish tank. Then one day I had a pile of exams on my desk. I hate grading exams but I was dutifully plodding away at them. As I sat there grading, my daughter walked in the door and told me that she had just seen a fully equipped fish tank on sale for $100. I immediately put those exams aside and headed off to buy it. I spent all afternoon putting together that fish tank. In my mind, I was doing so because it was a golden opportunity to do something I had always wanted to do. In actuality it wasn't about the fish tank. It was about the exams. I know that, if I had not been grading those exams, I would have never bought the fish tank. I wasn't working on the fish tank because I really wanted a fish tank. If I really wanted a fish tank, I would have bought one long ago. I was working on the fish tank because it was a way of avoiding grading those blasted exams.

Being busy is not the key to success. The bee is praised for being busy. Why? Because he is making sweet honey. But the fly is busy too. And what does he get? Swatted. If you are going to be busy, make sure that you are doing something useful. You don't want life to swat you.

Two Types of Busyness

Busyness can trap us in two different ways. Let's look at each.

The Trivia Trap

If we are busy doing a bunch of unimportant meaningless activities while we could be doing much more important things, we are caught in the trivia trap. To borrow from Jim Collins and his incredible book *Good to Great*, we cannot afford to let good be the enemy of great. We have important things we could be doing where we could really make an impact. But instead, we spend our time working hard at trivial things. Some people have six-figure income potential and they spend time working at minimum wage jobs.

We may have big responsibilities but we get distracted by small jobs. It is like me putting together a fish tank when I should be grading an exam. It isn't that there is anything wrong with me putting together a fish tank. The problem was that I was using the busyness of putting together a fish tank as a means to avoid doing what I really should be doing. Fish tanks are great but not when they take us away from the more important things we need to be doing with our time.

The Dawdle Trap

Then there is the dawdle trap. Here, we are actually doing the things we need to be doing but we aren't doing them in an efficient way. We don't want to be like the guy who was hired to paint stripes down the middle of the road. When he shows up for work the first day, the boss sets a can of paint down in front of him and hands him a brush. Not wanting to disappoint his boss, he starts painting with all his heart. The boss was delighted the first time he came by to check on his progress. He had painted more lines in the first couple hours than the boss had ever seen anyone paint. But, as the day progressed, every time the boss came by, the guy had painted fewer and fewer lines. By midafternoon, this fellow was hardly painting any lines at all. The boss asked him why he had slowed down so much. The guy replied, "Because I keep getting further and further away from the paint can."

You certainly couldn't fault this line painter for being lazy. He was the hardest working painter you could find. Neither could you fault him for not doing what he was supposed to do. He was hired to paint lines in the road and he worked at it with all his heart. But you could fault him for the way he did it. That's what happens with the dawdle trap. We are working. We are kind of doing what we should be doing. But much of our effort is wasted because of the way we are doing it. The guy was busy going back for paint when, if he had carried his can with him, he could have spent that time painting. All that walking was unnecessary and so it was busyness.

The Dangers of Busyness

If we are not careful, our lives can be like sitting in a rocking chair-- lots of activity but no progress. If there isn't adequate progress, then we need to change how we are doing things. A big danger in busyness is that we can let the activity fool us. We tend to think that, since we are working hard every day, we are actually doing something with our lives. The measure of how well we spend our time isn't based on how hard we work but rather on how much we accomplish.

A bigger danger of busyness is that we will start using activity to justify not doing what we know we should do. If I have a pile of exams sitting on my desk, I know what I should be doing. I should be grading. I remember how bad I hated it when I was a student and my professors did not get my exams back to me in a timely manner. There is no way I could plop myself down on the couch and just chill if I had exams to grade. My conscience wouldn't let me. I would feel too guilty to enjoy the couch. So doing nothing or even doing something fun isn't an option when it is time to grade. But what if I am working hard putting together a fish tank? That's a lot of work. I don't feel guilty when I am working hard. I used the fish tank that day as a way to make me feel good about not doing what I really needed to be doing.

That's why busyness is the worst form of laziness. It is a lot worse than just lying around the house and being lazy. If I am not doing much, at least my conscience can talk me into getting to work. But if I am working hard, my conscience usually feels just fine, even if I am working on the wrong thing. Being busy allows me to ignore what I am supposed to be doing without feeling guilty at all.

So that is the real danger. We settle for easy activity rather than hard progress. Our mind is at ease because we are working. But we should never let that be the measure of what we are doing. We must measure our activity, not by how busy we are, but by how much progress we are making towards our goals.

Urgent and Important

The other way that we build in the wrong place happens when we mistake urgent for important. This was pointed out so clearly by Stephen Covey in his book on the habits of highly effective people. Covey said that there are things that are important and there are things that are urgent. However, he pointed out that, just because something is urgent, it isn't necessarily important.

The Perception Problem

Here is where urgent things can fool us. Things that are urgent always seem important. In fact, one way to make something seem important is to make it urgent. Salespeople do that all the time. They tell you that it is the last product in stock or that the sale is about to end. They want to make the purchase of their product seem important and they know that urgency creates the perception of importance. So they use urgency to turn an unimportant purchase into an important one.

This perception problem works the other way too. Very important things may seem unimportant if they never become urgent. Take exercise for example. How important is it to get adequate exercise? It is extremely important. There are few things that we can do that will have as much of a direct impact on our quality of life as staying healthy and in good shape. But on any given day, how urgent is it that we exercise? It is not urgent at all. If we only respond to the urgent, then we will forfeit all the benefits exercise will give us.

The Motivation Problem

If we are not careful, urgent can quickly crowd out important and here is why. Urgent is more motivating than important. We have all experienced the phone ringing at dinner time. What makes it seem so important? Is it that most of the calls we get are important? No. We all know that a lot more important things happen when we spend time with our families than when we spend time on the phone. Yet the bump in perceived importance that our phone call gets from being urgent makes us leave the family to answer the phone.

How motivating something is relates very strongly to how long I have to do it. Remember back to school. Six weeks before the end of the term, the term paper is not that motivating. It is so hard to actually pull myself away from the TV, video game, web site, or whatever to work on the project. On the other hand, that very same term project is extremely motivating the night before it is due. TVs, video games, social networking sites suddenly lose their pull and all my motivation comes from the term project. The only thing that changed between being an unmotivated college student and a totally focused student is the amount of time I have to do the paper.

Here is the problem. How long we have to do something has almost nothing to do with how important it is. The paper was just as important six weeks before the end of the term as it was the night before. In fact, it may have been more important to do it then because the prospect of doing A-quality work then is much greater. About the best you can hope for when throwing something like that together at the last moment is a C. If making an A on the project is important, then the paper is even more important to do before it becomes urgent.

The Last Minute Train Wreck

We don't want to hold off doing important things until they become urgent. Going back to the college example, all my students can relate to the problem this creates. They only need to think back to the end of the previous semester. There was so much to do and everything was urgent. None of these urgent things were thrust on them at the last minute. The semester projects were assigned many weeks prior. They were just as important then as they are the night before they are due. There is no rule that says that these projects cannot be done until they become urgent. The final exam schedule is published before the semester even starts. For weeks before the end of the semester, the students knew all the important things they would need to do. The problem is that we aren't motivated by important. We are motivated by urgent. Unfortunately, all the important things collide in one huge urgent mess at the end of the semester.

We are indeed more motivated at the last minute but the habit of waiting until then creates two problems. The first is that urgency can be incredibly stressful. Stress is OK if it is temporary. One benefit my students have is that eventually the urgent will end, grades will be turned in, and then there will be Christmas or summer break. The stress is just temporary. But what happens if you live in a world where everything you do is urgent? That type of stress is unhealthy. You need to find a way to get out from underneath the tyranny of the urgent. That tyrant will make our lives miserable and might even kill us.

The other problem with urgent is that it is a train wreck waiting to happen. See, here is the way the universe works. If we wait until the last minute to print the report, the printer won't work. If we wait until the last minute to send the email, our connection to the Internet will go down. If we wait until the last minute to call someone, they will be on vacation. It is the curse of the last minute. Whatever we do at the last minute will be more involved than we expected and waiting until then creates the distinct possibility that we will miss important deadlines.

Creating Urgency

As pointed out by Covey, the best way to avoid these two problems is to deal with important things before they become urgent. That's nice unless you are among the 90% of the world's population who cannot seem to get motivated until something is urgent. You may be the person who says, "If it weren't for the last minute, I wouldn't get anything done." What do you do? You make the motivating power of the urgent work for you. You do that by making things seem urgent before they really are.

Let me give you an example. I love to spend time in the car with my kids. One of my sons needs to be at the library by 10:30 AM. I have been trying to finish the first draft of this chapter since 6:00 AM. Right now it is 8:50 AM. I actually still have several weeks to finish the draft of this chapter. However, what I told myself is that, if I don't finish the chapter before 10:15, he can take my car. That gave me some urgency. I have both a carrot and a stick. I will either get to spend some quality time with my son or I will see him drive off in my car.

There will come a time when this task will become urgent. I do have an external deadline. However, I am not there yet. I can still make the deadline even if I don't finish the rough draft this morning. However, setting this deadline with consequences keeps me working and helps me avoid distractions. I increased my motivation to write by making the writing of this chapter a lot more urgent than it really is.

Now here are the two keys to making this work. First, the deadline has to be tied to something external. I didn't set my son's schedule. He has to be at the library at 10:30. Second, missing the deadline also has to have consequences. These can be positive consequences like getting to spend time with my son or they can be negative consequences like seeing my son drive off in the car. Neither of these are huge consequences. I already get to spend a lot of time with my son and he is a very good driver so I'm not really worried about my car. Still, even small consequences can create a sense of urgency that can have a dramatic effect on our motivation.

Never Settle for Thrills or Comfort

For my lawyer friend, it was a close call when he built his dream house on the wrong lot. He was able to recover but he did have to pay a premium for the lot where he had built his home. Sometimes, when we build in the wrong place, we cannot recover so easily. If we waste our time staying busy and responding to the urgent, we will never get that time back. That is why we need the discernment to diligently guard against wasting our time building in the wrong spot.

We must reach a point in our lives where we won't settle for the comfort of activity or live by the thrill of the urgent. Settling for activity is a lot easier than demanding progress. For example, it is a lot easier for a salesperson to alphabetize business cards than to call the numbers on them. But the real payoff comes from making the sales calls, not from having a nice, neat deck of business cards. The most organized business cards on the planet won't bring in one single cent of revenue. So if we want to live more than a settle-for life, we cannot settle for activity. We must demand progress of ourselves, even if it is a much harder road to take.

In a similar way, sometimes important is tedious and boring. Urgent is thrilling and exciting. However, living by urgent rather than important is like taking a ride on a roller coaster. The ride may be fun but, in the end, you are right back where you started. Look around and you will notice that the most successful people are the ones who find a way to get just as motivated by important as the average person is motivated by urgent.

So if we are driven by the ease of activity or the thrill of the urgent, we run the risk of building in the wrong spot. We must make sure that our efforts are not wasted. We must focus on progress and not activity. We must focus on important and not urgent.

The Discernment Challenge:
Resolve to never settle for the ease of activity
or the thrill of the urgent.

18
Useless Perfection

The Principle of Useless Perfection:
Nothing Is as Useless As Doing Well That
Which Should Not Be Done at All

If I could throw one of the Time Basics away and not teach it, it would be this one. I hate to talk about it because I always get dirty looks from certain people in the audience. They have ingrained into their brains, "If a job is worth doing, it is worth doing well." I can't argue with them on that point. That is one of those sayings that falls in the "trite but true" category. If we are going to take our time and invest it in something, then we might as well make that investment count. Everything worth doing should be done well. Unfortunately, here is what life in the real world is like. We are often stuck doing things that aren't worth doing at all but we have to do them anyway. What do we do then? Well, if a job isn't worth doing at all, then it certainly isn't worth doing to perfection. That will only slow us down and keep us away from doing things that really matter.

Useless Tasks We Must Do

Every one of us, from time to time, finds ourselves being saddled with some task that serves no useful purpose. In my profession, they usually take the form of some useless report that must be done. Some bureaucrat working for the state or an accrediting body decides that the worth of his position can be measured by the number of reports he can force others to write. I am convinced that most of these reports are never read. In terms of significance, their impact on the quality of education is about as small as the impact of one drop of rain on the Pacific Ocean. Unfortunately, I cannot say "no" to this endless flow of mindless reports. I do my part to make sure that these report mavens have their never ending supply of unread reports in hopes that they will leave me alone to actually do my job of educating students.

I remember one time being in a meeting where we were working on a set of these reports. The person heading the meeting asked, "What is the best way to do these reports?"

"As quickly as possible" I replied. Everyone chuckled. I asked around the room to see if anyone saw any way these reports would actually benefit our students. Everyone drew a blank. It was obvious to everyone in the room that the only benefit of doing the reports would be that we could say that they were done. We all seriously doubted if anyone would even actually read them. But the choice of not doing them was out of the question. If our accrediting body told us that the faculty had to spend their weekends guarding the flagpole, that is what we would have to do. So there we were, eight highly educated and well paid professionals spending hours doing something which should not be done at all.

Is there something wrong with us spending hours upon hours writing these useless reports that no one would read? The reports themselves were harmless. They aren't bad, just useless. However, when we remember the Principle of the Excluded Alternative, we can see the problem they create. To say "yes" to something means to say "no" to something else. Here was the problem. What important things would not get done as we worked on these useless reports? What would we have to take time away from to write them? Would it be the time we spent improving our lectures? Would it come from our time advising students? Would it come from the research we were doing that might help society? What useful things would we have to say "no" to so that we could say "yes" to these reports?

We shouldn't say "yes" to unimportant things because, when we do, we say "no" to important things. But it is not always possible to say "no" to every unimportant thing that is thrown our way. Sometimes we cannot dodge these trivial tasks we are saddled with and so we just have to deal with them. This raises an important time basic we must consider. If we are stuck doing some useless, unimportant task, how well should we do it? Should we throw everything we have into some trivial task that won't really matter five minutes from now?

A Time for Perfection

There is a time to be a perfectionist. There are times when nothing but the best will do. For example, when I board an airplane, I hope that my pilot is a perfectionist. I don't want him to have a "good enough is good enough" attitude. The same has been true the few times in my life when I have had to have surgery. I wanted my surgeon to be obsessed with getting everything exactly right. There are certainly times when perfectionism is a virtue. If my life is in your hands, please take all the time you need to do the job exactly right.

On the other hand, there is a problem with a mindless addiction to perfection. This can be one of our biggest time wasters. We can have things drop in our lap where any time spent on them is a waste. So certainly the extra time spent getting them done perfectly is totally wasted. What a waste of time it is for eight Ph.D.'s to take hours away from their students and their research to make sure some file drawer has a wonderful report to enjoy.

Here is the challenge. We must be sure to let the nature of the task determine when to require perfection and when to settle for good enough. But that's not the way we tend to operate. Instead, we follow our natural tendencies. Some of us tend towards perfection in everything we do. Such people are called "perfectionists." On the other hand, there are also some of us who always seem to have the "good enough" attitude. These people could be described as "perfectionless." It is a challenge for both the perfectionist and the perfectionless to manage their time but for different reasons.

The Struggle of the Perfectionist

Most of the people I work with are perfectionists. They are all highly educated. They got that way by being at the top of their academic class through making sure their school work was done to perfection. They feel terrible if anything they do isn't flawless. Remember back to the meeting where I told my colleagues that we needed to do those meaningless reports as quickly as possible. They all understood my point but they could not stomach the idea of turning in a report that might not be "A+" work. So, in the end, those file cabinets got some wonderful reports. It is a shame that nobody will ever read them because they were really done well.

If we lean towards perfection, then regardless of the situation or the task, we will take the time to make things perfect. And that's the problem—we *take* the time. While we are taking the time to dot every i and cross every t, we are taking that time away from something. Now again, I don't mind my surgeon taking time away from his golf game to make sure he sews everything up just right. On the other hand, it doesn't make sense for professors to take time away from class preparation and important research to make sure meaningless reports are written to perfection.

In some ways, perfectionists have the biggest challenge. To get everything done that needs to be done, they must tame their perfectionism. They will never get to the point where they can feel good about imperfection. They will always see flaws in their work and cringe. However, to manage their time, they must develop the ability to look beyond these flaws to the more important things that must be done within the limited amount of time they have. Their focus must turn from the ugliness of imperfection to the beauty of importance.

The Struggle of the Perfectionless

Sometimes good enough really isn't good enough. If the job requires perfection, then it really is a waste of time to settle for anything less. For example, when I am writing a research article for publication in an academic journal, I know that it will be reviewed by other professors. Their job will be to determine whether it is worthy of publication. If they don't like it, then my research will never see the light of day. Remember, I said that professors tend to be perfectionists and so, for them, good enough is not good enough. If they see flaws, then they will reject the paper and it will never be published. If that happens, all of the time I spent doing the research and all of the time I spent writing it up is wasted. I get zero reward for research that is not published. My only reward for doing research comes when I publish it. There is no sense in even doing my research if my attitude is "that's good enough."

That is the problem faced by those whose life could be described as "perfectionless." They won't have the problem of useless perfection. They won't waste a lot of time doing well that which should not be done at all. On the other hand, there will be times when they will not take important jobs as seriously as they should. They will waste their time doing tasks at such low quality that they might as well have never done them at all.

Follow the Task Not the Tendency

That's why we shouldn't let our natural tendencies determine whether to settle for "good enough" or go for "nothing but the best." We should let the job itself dictate that for us. The challenge is to never settle for less than the best when the best is required. At the same time, we must be willing to live with good enough when it is indeed good enough.

Either way, there will be times when we won't enjoy the quality of our work. If you are a perfectionist, there should be times when you look at the job you have done and hate that you didn't give it your best. If you must do something that isn't worth doing, you must resist the temptation to take the extra time to do it just right. You must somehow find it in your heart to say "good enough." If your life could better be described as perfectionless, there are times when you must keep going even when you feel OK about the job you have done. There are things in your life that should be done to the best of your ability even if it means pushing yourself beyond the point where you are satisfied.

Dealing With Useless Tasks

We must understand that some jobs require our best and some jobs do not deserve our time. Some of the stuff in our lives is really quite trivial. Let's not be so vain as to think that the world will suffer dire consequences if we don't do everything just right. We must know how to do things to perfection but we must also know how to best deal with the trivial stuff that comes our way. Let's look at three ways to deal with useless tasks.

Delete It

Many years ago when I purchased my first computer, I realized something. I often needed to save a file for a very short time and then I would never need it again. I might need it as a step in converting some information to a different format. I may need it as a place to store information I am accumulating to copy somewhere else. I may just need it long enough to print it. So I started naming all these computer files with a usefulness of less than five minutes "Zap Me." I chose "Zap Me" so they would always end up together at the bottom of the alphabetized list of file names. On my computer, any time I see a file name that starts with "Zap Me" I know I am totally free to delete it even if I don't know anything about its content. If it were important for me to keep, I would not have tagged it with the name "Zap Me."

Wouldn't it be nice if we could deal with our useless tasks the same way I deal with these useless files? What if I could just tag useless tasks "Zap Me" and then come back in a few minutes and delete them. Actually, we can. We don't have to say no to something. We just need to be careful not to say yes too quickly. If we don't say yes to some meaningless task, it may fade into insignificance in five minutes and we won't even need to say no to it. The less important the task, the more likely it will just fade away. We saw how this works when we covered the Procrastination Principle. We put stuff at the bottom of the pile knowing that no one ever gets all the way to the bottom of the pile.

Give It Away

It is said that when John Steinbeck finished an early draft of *East of Eden*, he gave it to another writer to read. Ignoring the content, this other writer told Steinbeck that, "The spelling is bad and the grammar is terrible."

Steinbeck, who would go on to win the Nobel Prize for Literature despite the fact that he never graduated from college, was not fazed by the critics comment. He said, "My publisher has rooms full of bright college educated men and women who know all about grammar and spelling. They can take care of that. But not one of those college educated men or women could have written *Grapes of Wrath*."

Some jobs may be important for somebody to do, just not us. Before Steinbeck's books were published, they were cleaned up by people who were good at that stuff. But why would Steinbeck want to waste his important mental powers making sure everything is said in proper English? There may be a time and place for perfection but you may not be the person on whom the perfecting process needs to fall. At times, we should leave the job of perfecting to someone who really cares about the outcome.

Zip Through It

Throughout our day, we will likely have a bunch of small, insignificant things that we need to get out of the way. There are a couple of ways to zip through them. One is to bunch them together. I notice that a lot of the trivia comes to me in my email account. I just leave it there until one time in my day when I zip through all the trivia. I can get it all done at once and I don't have to let it constantly interrupt me while I am working on more important things.

The other way to zip through a small task is to do the exact opposite. We can do it as soon as we get it. Don't touch it twice. I just took a call from a business associate who needed me to do something for him. Notice, it was for him, not for me. The job had no value to me. However, I may need him to return the favor some day and so I agreed to do what he asked me to do. Before I even sat back down in my chair, I finished the task and was done with it. It took two minutes. I just zipped through it and got on with the things that were important to me.

If we are zipping through something, we need to think in terms of minimal acceptable quality. When I was an undergraduate, the university I attended allowed us to take three classes "pass/fail." We could only make a grade of pass or a grade of fail and nothing else. The grade didn't affect our GPA. The reason for the pass/fail option was to encourage us to try classes we might not take if we were worried about a grade. It worked for me. For my foreign language, rather than taking Spanish like everyone else, I signed up for four semesters of ancient Greek. I guess I thought it would be useful should I ever run into Socrates. The first semester, I worked very hard because it was for a grade. However, for the other semesters, I used my three pass/fail options on Greek. I did well enough to pass. That is all I needed to do. That freed up time for me to study for my other classes. Since I have never run into Socrates, this was a case where good enough was good enough.

For many things we do, there is a minimal acceptable quality. In the pass/fail classes it was a 60 average. If I were taking the class for a grade, that would not be acceptable. I was fortunate in my Ph.D. program in that I was able to take my marketing theory class from the greatest scholar in marketing theory that has ever lived. I certainly didn't approach that class with a "good enough" attitude. Nothing but a high A was acceptable. I could approach Ancient Greek with a pass/fail mentality but I certainly didn't look at marketing theory that way.

If a task is not worth doing at all and yet we must do it anyway, then we should think about what the minimal acceptable quality would be. We don't need to feel obligated to give much more. We can save time by only reaching that minimal acceptable quality. That time can then be invested in things where the quality requirements are higher. If it is in our major, shoot for the A. If it is a pass/fail elective, just worry about passing. Don't take time from the major classes to make a high grade in a pass/fail elective.

We Need to Know Both

There is the joke told around colleges that really isn't much of a joke. It says that the A students go to work for the C students and the B students go to work for the government. Say that around campus and you will get either chuckles or sneers. We all know that there is a lot of truth to it. Why is that?

Our A students don't know how to do a job any other way than perfect. Our C students are always looking for easier and simpler ways to get what they want. Our C students have figured out that they don't have to be perfect. When they graduate, they learn to hire perfection when it is needed. They hire the A students. The A students cannot be the boss because they don't know when to be perfect and when not to be perfect. They are just perfect all the time. That wastes scarce financial resources on perfection when perfection isn't really needed.

The advantage of hiring A students is that you know that, whatever you give them to do, they will do perfectly. The disadvantage of hiring an A student is that they don't know when to be perfect and when to be good enough. An A student needs a C student to direct their perfectionism to where it is required. The A students know how to be perfect but they don't know when. The C students know when to be perfect but they don't know how. So the C students subcontract out perfection.

The challenge is to know both. We need to know how to achieve perfection and we need to be wise enough to know when to be perfect. To get the most out of our time, we cannot afford to waste our time doing well that which should not be done at all.

As I wrote this chapter, my mind kept drifting back to a prayer that most of us have heard. It was the Serenity Prayer written by Reinhold Niebuhr. It says,

> God, grant me the serenity
> to accept the things I cannot change,
> courage to change the things I can,
> and wisdom to know the difference.

I can think of no wiser way for us to live our lives. If there was a prayer for managing the tasks that come our way, perhaps it might look like Niebuhr's Serenity Prayer.

> Grant me the patience to do exceptionally well
> those things that matter the most.
> Grant me a willingness to do quickly or not at all
> those things that matter the least.
> And as these two are competing for my time,
> grant me the wisdom to know which is which.

That is the spirit of the challenge of useless perfection. At times, we cannot keep from doing some useless task but we can keep it from robbing our time from those things which are far more important.

The Challenge of Useless Perfection:
Resolve to let the nature of the task decide if good
enough is good enough or if only the best will do.

Power

The Mastery Principle:

The Surest Way to Save Time Is to Get Better At What You Do

The Aristotle Principle:

Excellence Is Not an Act but a Habit

The Discipline Principle:

It Is Impossible to Enjoy a Good Life Without Self-Discipline

---

The Team Principle:

To Go Fast, Go Alone.
To Go Far, Build A Team.

The Balance Principle:

Balance Comes From Quality Time at Work and Quantity Time at Home

---

The Reality Principle:

The Future Is More Real Than It Appears

Part 4

Power

Speed can be fragile. I often experience this when I am driving on the Atlanta freeways. We can be driving along at a nice clip and then suddenly everything stops. We are not going anywhere and we are totally powerless to do anything about it. The same can be true as we manage our time. We can be zipping through the day getting all the important things done. Suddenly, something happens and we are in a time management traffic jam. We had speed but now we are powerless to do what we would really like to be doing. In the current section, we will look beyond speed to the things that can add power to how we manage our time. Such power comes from four sources.

First, time power comes from within. So often, we seem to be limping through the day from self-inflicted wounds. We need to look no further than the mirror to find the solutions to many of our time management problems. We will spend the first three chapters of Part 4 looking at what that person in the mirror can do to help us better manage our time. We will discuss the Mastery Principle. By getting better at whatever we are doing, we will be able to dramatically cut down the amount of time it takes to do it. Next we will discuss the Aristotle Principle. This principle focuses on the time management habits we create. Vince Lombardi said "Winning is a habit. Unfortunately, so is losing." Good time management is a habit. Unfortunately, so is bad time management. Then we will discuss self-discipline. To-do lists are great, especially when we have the discipline to actually do what is on them. But a to-do list without self-discipline is nothing more than a wish-list.

Second, time power comes from the synergy that a team brings. We may not always want to be part of a team but there is only so much we can accomplish by ourselves. Teams can really frustrate us, especially when we are trying to get something done. They just seem to slow things down. Through looking at the Team Principle, we will explore when to build a team and when to go it alone.

Third, time power comes from balance. How many flat tires does it take to slow down our trip? Well, if you have four tires that aren't that good, then one flat tire can stop you all together. But what if you have three really good tires and one flat tire? How far can you go? That one flat tire can still stop you. In managing our time, we may try to replace our three good tires with even better ones. We hope that, if the other three tires are good enough, we won't have to worry about the one that is flat. If we really want to put power into our time management system, we may need to quit focusing as much on our good tires and go to work on our flat tire. We will discuss the Balance Principle. Our discussion will mostly look at the balance between our careers and our families. We do so because that is the biggest time management balancing challenge we have. However, the principle applies to other areas where we need to keep things in balance—areas such as our spiritual walk and our health.

Finally, time power comes when we actually connect with our future. As we have said so many times in this book, our time is managed to the extent to which our current activities are consistent with where we want to be at some point in the future. Obviously that implies that we are thinking about the future. Whatever we are doing today is creating whatever reality we will experience in the future. Unfortunately, the future we want can be so abstract and unclear. In discussing the Reality Principle, we will explore the power we gain over our time when we turn our vision of the future from an abstract dream into something we can actually feel today.

By the time you finish this last part of the book, you should have more than just speed when you manage your time. You should have the power that will propel you to whatever future you want with the limited time you have to get there.

19
Mastery

The Mastery Principle:
The Surest Way to Save Time Is to
Get Better At What You Do

There is a limit to how fast most time management techniques will help you go. There is only so many ways you can rearrange your schedule. There is only so much you can throw out. Momentum will only propel you so fast. There is a limit to how much clarity we can gain. We can only go a certain speed before we go from feeling out of control to actually being out of control. You can reach a limit on how fast you can go through traditional time management. You don't need to just get faster. You also need to get better. I saw the power of getting better one night as I watched my daughter develop an animation on her computer.

My home used to be arranged with two computers such that, when I was working on one computer, I could view what was happening on the other one. That night as I worked, I enjoyed watching my daughter slowly develop this really neat little animated movie. I was really impressed at what she was learning to do. Suddenly, I heard her cry out in agony. The program had crashed and she lost everything she had been working on for the last three hours. Three hours of work went down the drain. About ten minutes later, I glanced over there again and she was right where she was when the program had crashed. I asked her how she had recovered the file. She said that she had not. She had learned so much in the first time through that it only took her ten minutes to recreate what had originally took her three hours to create.

Imagine that. Before she mastered the program, it took her three hours to create an animation. After she mastered the program, she was able to do the exact same job in ten minutes. She took a three hour job and turned it into a ten minute job. Now it is hard to find any time management system that can beat that. I could manage to-do lists and calendar pages all day long and I doubt if I would figure out anything that would save that much time. Get better and time is saved. That is the Mastery Principle. The surest way to save time is to get better at what you do. There are two things we need to do to get better. We need to learn the rules that relate to what we do. Then we need to develop the tools that will help us be more efficient. Let's look at how this works.

Learning the Rules

Everything has its rules. For example, the area of a library in which most of the books are shelved is called "the stacks." When libraries have thousands upon thousands of books in the stacks, it is important that they are arranged in a specific way following a well laid out set of rules. If our job is to find books in the library, we don't need to learn the best time management techniques. We need to learn the rules of the stacks.

When I was teaching at the University of Oklahoma, one of my advisees worked at the library. Her job was to find stuff in the library and deliver it to people on campus. She told me about this one guy who worked with her. She said it took him forever to do his job. She said that he would be given a list of books and articles to pull from the stacks. Off he would go. A long time would go by and he would still be gone. She told me that the other workers would begin to wonder if he was off in some study carrel fast asleep. She would run off to the stacks to find him. There he would be, working harder than anyone else in the library. Still, he was the least productive library worker. He didn't have a time management problem. He had a knowledge problem.

Now how could we make this guy a more productive library worker? Would it be to buy him a day planner and teach him how to use it? Would it be to show him how to set goals every day, monitor them, and then align his behavior with the goals? Would it be to teach him how to set priorities, evaluate alternatives, and eliminate distractions? No. For this worker, the problem wasn't that he didn't know how to manage his time. The problem was that he didn't know how to find things. He didn't need a better time management system. He needed to learn the rules of the stacks.

Think about your job. What are the stacks in your job? What are those few things that you have to do over and over again? What are the rules of the stacks? Do you know the stacks better than anyone else? If not, then we have found your time challenge. Get better at what you do. That will free up so much time to do other things. The two biggest time management breakthroughs in my career came when I learned how to prepare my classes and when I learned how to write journal articles that editors wanted to publish. Once I could prep my classes faster and write articles that editors wanted, I could move on to do other things with my time. Eventually, I could get done in a few hours what it once took me weeks to do.

Remember the story of the two lumberjacks who had the five hour wood cutting contest? One was a big, strong guy. The other was little and skinny. The big strong guy worked hard for the full five hours. The little guy worked some and rested some and worked some and rested some. When the contest was over and the wood was weighed, the little guy had won. The losing lumberjack couldn't believe it. He was bigger. He was stronger. He had worked harder. In fact, he never stopped to rest and the other guy probably chopped less than forty-five minutes every hour. How did this happen?

The problem was that the big lumberjack didn't understand one of the rules of cutting wood. The little lumberjack explained that he never rested. He just took time off to sharpen his axe. This guy knew that it wasn't the biggest, the strongest, or even the hardest worker who chops the most wood. It is the one with the sharpest axe. There is a place in the woods for big, strong guys who work hard. There isn't a place in the woods for a dull axe. Many people think they don't have time to stop and sharpen their axe. Consider this. What if these two lumberjacks were being paid by the pound for the wood they cut? The little lumberjack was making more money when he was sharpening his axe than the big lumber jack was making while he was chopping his hardest.

Jim Rohn was an author and speaker who has had a huge impact on my life. His signature line was that, "Your life gets better when you get better." Here is how he learned that lesson. Long before Jim Rohn was a successful businessperson and speaker, he was a broke twenty-five year old man who couldn't even pay the bills. It was then that he had the good fortune to meet a man named Earl Shoaff. Rohn complained to Mr. Shoaff that things cost too much. Mr. Shoaff said, "That's not the problem. The problem is that you can't afford them."

"Of course I can't afford them. Just look," Rohn replied pointing to his paycheck. "This is all the company pays."

With a questioning look on his face, Mr. Shoaff asked Jim Rohn. "Is that all the company pays or is that all the company pays you?"

"Actually there are people who the company pays a lot more than this" Rohn answered.

"Why?"

"I don't know," said Rohn scratching his head.

Mr. Shoaff started to nod. "Now I think we are beginning to find the real problem. They know something you don't. I think there is something you need to learn." Jim Rohn started looking at his life and work and he realized that indeed, there was a lot he could learn. He learned it and six years from the day he met Mr. Shoaff, Jim Rohn was a millionaire.

Everything we do takes time. Could we make it take less time? Think of the one thing that you did today that took up the most of your time. If I were to ask you why you spent that much time on it, you might reply, "Because that's how long it takes." Ask yourself, is that true? Is that how long it takes or is that how long it takes you? Are there other people who get more accomplished than you do in less time? If so, then you need to ask, "Why?" Do they know something you don't know?

Developing the Tools

Just like everything has its rules, everything also has its tools. No matter what you do, there are tools available that can help you do it faster. A tool is anything that will save us time. The three tools I would like to briefly discuss are technology, networks of relationships, and our work environment.

Technology

Most people use only a fraction of the technology that could make them more productive. We just need to learn to use this technology. It is like we have a nice new car sitting in our driveway and yet we walk ten miles to work every day because we don't want to learn how to drive it. There is no need for technology to be that intimidating. For example if you are not using all the power of your computer because you don't know how to use the software, there are many ways to learn. Every dummy has a book for their needs. There are internet sites that will walk you through exactly how to use almost any piece of computer software you can imagine. My favorite one is the subscription site Lynda.com. For a very reasonable monthly fee, you can quickly master any of hundreds of different software packages. If your technology axe is dull, it needs to be sharpened.

Networks of Relationships

Another resource that most people under-utilize is the network of people around us. We can't be good at everything. The wisest people in business are the ones that staff their weaknesses. We need a network of people who will help us. We don't want to manipulate people into doing our work for us because we are lazy. What we need to do is develop a network of mutually beneficial relationships that will enable us to do things faster.

For example, when I am working on a research project, I know that there are things that I can do very well and I know that there are things that others can do much better than me. My strengths are in designing the project, positioning the research, developing the theoretical base, and writing the final report. On the other hand, I am not always up on the latest methodological innovations or statistical techniques. Rather than trying to master them all, I simply team up with people who know more than me. Working together, we can turn out more than twice the research that we could do individually. I am not using them and they are not using me. We are working together to maximize our own unique strengths. We have one of two choices. We can either try to be good at everything or we can find a few things that we are good at and team up with others who can do the rest.

A Well Planned Work Environment

Another tool at our disposal is our work environment. Is our workplace organized so that we have immediate access to everything we need? I have some tools but, since I don't do much work around the house, they are just all thrown together in a tub in a closet. Every time I need to hammer a nail, drill a hole, or tighten a bolt, I have to drag out the tub and dig through every tool I have to find the one I need. It wastes a lot of time. But that's OK because I don't have to do it much. My usual approach to fixing something around the house is to call someone who knows what he is doing. I let the professionals do the jobs for me.

You know what I notice about these professionals? They don't keep their tools all randomly thrown together in some tub. When they need something, they don't have to dig through every tool they have to find the one they want. They have everything well laid out and organized. That's what professionals do. My tool tub is a mess because I am an amateur.

My professional life is quite different. Recently, a film crew came by my office to interview me. They commented that I must have cleaned up my office for the video shoot. "No," I said. "It is always this way. I didn't do anything to prepare for you." They said that they seldom find offices as neat and organized as mine. Because I have so much to do, I can't afford a disorganized office. I need to know where everything is and I need to have easy and immediate access to it. I cannot afford to take the time to search through all my drawers and bookshelves for an article when I am writing or preparing a lecture. Amateurs can afford to have a messy work environment. Professionals cannot.

Learning What Will Make Us Better

OK, so we understand the need to find the rules and develop the tools. Where do we start? Here is what I have discovered about successful people. They are always trying to figure out ways to improve their skills. For them, life is almost like a game where the goal is to see how good they can get at what they do. How do they do that? There are two things any person who wants to get better in an area will always do.

Learn From Others

Brian Tracy said that, "We have to learn from other people. Life is too short to learn it all from scratch." We must find people who are further along than we are in an area and learn everything we can from them. Where do we find these people?

For starters, we just take a look around us. Ask ourselves, "Who really knows what he or she is doing?" My experience has been that people love to share what they are doing with people who are eager to learn. I have an exercise in one of my classes where my students find a successful person and interview him or her. I have seen them interview some of the most successful people in our state. My students are amazed at how willing these people are to share their knowledge. Even the most successful people are usually flattered when someone recognizes what they have accomplished and asks them about how they did it. A highly successful person may go for years and years with no one asking for the wisdom they have accumulated. When a person achieves great financial success, quite often old friends will show up. Usually, they are looking for a job. Occasionally they are looking for a handout. Almost never do they show up looking for the knowledge that would help them achieve the same thing. Which is more useful, the job, the handout, or the wisdom?

One time, a sales trainer went in to teach a group of salespeople how to get better at generating sales. There were about fifty salespeople in the room and they all worked for the same company. He asked them who the best salesperson in the room was. They all pointed to a man named Ken sitting on the front row.

The trainer looked at Ken and asked, "Is that true? Are you the best salesperson here?"

"I don't know about that," Ken answered. "I wouldn't say I am the best salesperson here but I have been blessed to have some good years."

"Well," the trainer went on, "obviously you have done very well or else everyone in this room wouldn't think you are the best. Let me ask you another question. Everyone here wants to be able to do what you have done. How many of them have come to you and asked you how you have done it?" The star salesperson said that he had never had someone ask him that question. The sales trainer looked at the salespeople and asked them, "So why am I here? You know who is the best and you haven't even asked him how he does it."

Another place to find successful people is in the bookstores. No, I don't mean that they all congregate there waiting to give someone advice. Many highly successful people have written books. Many other books are written about what makes people highly successful. Within the pages of books are ideas that can give us anything we want and yet few people care enough to read them.

Let's say I was interested in getting wealthy. Chances are I couldn't just walk up to a billionaire and ask him how he made his money. But I wouldn't have to. I could find out exactly how a lot of billionaires and even more millionaires made their money. I would just need to read the many books written by wealthy people or about wealthy people. For example, if Sam Walton were alive and I had the opportunity to have an afternoon of his time, would I take it? Absolutely. He became the wealthiest person in the world and I know that I would learn something if I could spend some time with him. I could do something just as valuable as spending an afternoon with Sam Walton. In the last two years of his life, Sam Walton wrote the book *Made in America*. For the price of the book and the time it took to read it, I can learn exactly what he did to become so incredibly successful.

Learn By Doing

I heard a speaker say that mastering anything is simply a three step process: try, fail, adjust. The more times we go through the process, the better we get. Our life should be a process of try, fail, adjust, try, fail, adjust, try, fail, adjust... I have heard several successful businesspeople say that this is the exact process they went through to become wealthy. Often, they would spend their evenings reading and studying what other successful people were doing. Every day, they would commit to taking at least one new idea they learned and seeing if it worked. Most of what they tried did not work. But through trial and error, they would end up bringing two or three new things that did work into their business every week. Imagine what would happen in your job or in your business if, over the next year, you found 100 things that would help you improve. You can. You just need to find about 1,000 new things and see how they work. Don't expect them to work the first time. Give them ten tries or so and see how they work.

Saving Years of Time

I assume you have some things that you want to accomplish over the next ten years. I know I do. If so, I absolutely guarantee that there are things that could save you two to five years getting there. That applies to me too. They are either rules we don't know or tools we don't use. Imagine learning something that could save you years of hard work. That's not just good time management. That is powerful time management. There is the need to plan, organize, categorize, align, etc. But none of that can possibly replace the time we save when we get better at what we do.

The Mastery Challenge:
Resolve to take some time away from doing
and invest it into learning.

20
Aristotle

The Aristotle Principle:
Excellence Is Not an Act but a Habit

Most time management books focus on what we do. Even in this book, for the most part, we take that approach. However, in order to have power in our time management system, we need to look at who we are. There is a place in athletics for trying harder. Every coach wants a player who will "leave it all on the field." However, coaches also want players who will bring more with them to the field when they arrive. Trying harder will only let us push so much weight. We can reach a point where all the effort in the world won't lift another ounce. Then the only way to push harder is to get stronger. When you are giving it your all, it is no longer about what you do. It is about who you are. To become more powerful, you have to get better.

In the previous chapter, we began to look at becoming better. Learning the rules and developing the tools will definitely help us get better. In this and the next chapter we will dig deeper towards the core of who we are. In this chapter we will explore habits. According to Aristotle, our habits make us who we are. In the next chapter we will explore self-discipline. The real power in managing our time comes from living a disciplined life.

You Can't Photoshop Life

People are always looking for a quick and easy way to get that fit and trim body they want. The only quick and simple way to dramatically improve the way we look is with Photoshop. That works right up to the point where people meet us in person. Then the Photoshop approach isn't the best one to take. The next best approach is to develop good habits. It takes much longer but it also helps us actually look like our profile picture. If we really want to improve our physique, we must do the right thing over and over day after day. That applies to almost every area of our life. If we want to get rich, we can. It will take time and good money habits but we can do it. On the other hand, one of the surest ways to go broke is to try to get rich too fast or with too little effort.

The point is this. We don't get health, wealth, and happiness in one quick move. We get it little by little, one day at a time. If we want to find the real source for getting the things we seek in life, we can find it in the habits we follow. When we form good habits they give us what we want. When we develop bad habits they steal from us on a daily basis. They steal our health. They steal our money. They steal the joy we can find in life. There is another thing bad habits steal from us. They steal our time. If we will patiently work at it, we can break bad time management habits and develop good ones. Every step we make doing so will increase the control we have over our time.

New Habits Are Fragile

A crucial time basic that we must understand if we want to manage our time was best articulated by Aristotle twenty-five hundred years ago. He said, "We are what we repeatedly do. Excellence then is not an act but a habit." Habits hold the key to managing our schedule and making the most of our time. The problem is that it is easy to develop bad habits and difficult to develop good ones. To develop bad habits, all we have to do is live life. By default, we will develop all kinds of bad habits. We don't even think about developing these bad habits. It just happens and we don't even know it is happening until it is too late. As Warren Buffett said, "Chains of habit are too light to be felt until they are too heavy to be broken." On the other hand, good habits don't come naturally. We have to work to develop them.

Good habits are particularly hard to develop when we don't understand the process for doing so. We tend to have unrealistic expectations when we start forming habits. Habits are fragile when they are new. Nothing can kill these fragile habits quicker than treating them like they are strong and robust from the start. Once we understand how habits are formed—that they start out weak and grow stronger as time progresses—then we will be able to develop the ones that will last.

We don't develop habits perfectly from the start. We don't decide to change a pattern of behavior and then successfully do so overnight. We develop habits over time as we slowly get better and better at not messing up. Let's use nutrition as an example. Getting the most from our time requires energy. To have energy, we need to live a healthy lifestyle. That healthy lifestyle requires good nutrition. We cannot get all of the nutrients that our bodies need from the stuff most of us eat. By far the easiest thing we can do to improve our health is to get into the habit of taking a quality multivitamin every day. If we aren't going to get the nutrients from the food we eat, we need to get them somewhere and taking a multivitamin every day is a great place to start. If you aren't already doing so, let me challenge you to start.

You need to form a habit for taking a multivitamin. Every day, you take a pill, stick it in your mouth, throw in some water, and quickly swallow. How difficult is that? I cannot imagine an easier habit to develop. It may be harder than you think. Why? Because you are forming a new habit and new habits are fragile. If you aren't already in the habit of taking a vitamin every day, I would say that your chances of doing it every day for the next month are about the same as the chances of a snow-storm hitting Phoenix, Arizona this August. You aren't going to start out going 31 for 31 that first month. My guess is that remembering to take the vitamin 25 times would be a great first try.

For something as simple as taking a vitamin every day, you probably won't start out perfectly. It will probably be hit or miss for a while until you get into the swing of things. This simple habit only takes seconds and it is as easy as taking a gulp of water. Still you had better be prepared to have some failures while you are working on developing it.

If getting into the habit of taking a vitamin every day is that hard, imagine the success rate if you are starting something really hard like planning out every day. If you haven't been in the habit of doing that, I think a first month where you succeed 50% of the time would be outstanding. How about getting into a workout routine? Some of us quit if we miss two workouts in a row because we take that to mean we really weren't serious in the first place. We must quit thinking we can form superhuman habits in the first week. Everyone is going to miss some workouts when they start. I have been faithfully working out for decades and I missed my workout this morning. We can't start with the expectation of perfection.

Aim for Progress

The problem with expecting perfection is that we beat ourselves up when we fail. Instead we should be proud that we are even trying. Let's say I haven't been taking a multivitamin and I decide to start this month. I fail miserably. I only take it three times in my first month. How did I do? A lot better than I did the previous month. I am sure my body appreciates the nutrients I got those three days. It was certainly a lot better than never giving my body anything other than the stuff I have been eating. If we are developing a good habit, it is like the system principle. Any success is better than doing nothing at all.

Let's say the next month comes and this time I still fail but not quite so miserably. This time I take the multivitamin five times in a month. How did I do in Month 2? We might be tempted to think that we are really messing up because we have only taken eight vitamins in sixty-one days. Or we could celebrate because we did so much better this month than we did last month. We are making progress. That is worth celebrating. Not only have we given our bodies more good nutrients in the last two months than we may have in the previous year, we have set ourselves on the path of progress. If we continue to make progress we will eventually be taking vitamins almost every day. We need to think in terms of progress, not perfection. When I am speaking, I like to illustrate this point in two ways.

First, I ask if there is anyone in the audience who would like to learn to juggle. I find a volunteer and invite her to the stage for a demonstration of the first step in learning to juggle. I have three bean bags I put in her hand. I then tell her to drop them. Then I tell her to pick them up off the floor. As she picks them up, I tell her that she is now learning the very first thing about juggling. You need to learn to pick the bean bags up off the floor because you will be doing that a lot. In learning to juggle, you don't start with the goal of always perfectly keeping all the bean bags in the air. That won't happen any time soon. For the foreseeable future, a realistic goal is to make it longer and longer before they hit the ground. The longer you can go without them hitting the floor, the more progress you have made in learning to juggle. But be certain of this. They will hit the floor. Over and over, you will fail at keeping all three of them in the air. That's just how it is when you are learning to juggle. That's also how it is when you are forming habits. If you want to form a habit, don't think you are going to avoid failing. Just try to make it longer and longer between the times when you do fail.

My second demonstration also starts with a volunteer from the audience. I ask him to hold his palms together with his two index fingers extended pointing towards the ceiling. I then pull out a spool of thread. I wrap it once or twice around the two index fingers. I tell him to pull these two fingers apart. He does so very easily. I then do the same thing but this time I wrap the thread five or six times around the fingers. It is harder but he can still pull them apart. I then start wrapping and wrapping. I go around his fingers thirty or forty times. Now, he can't pull his fingers apart.

I explain that this is how it works with habits. The string is like a habit which binds us to some action. Let's say we are trying to develop the habit of planning our day. Every time we start our day with a plan, it is like wrapping the thread around our finger one time. However, when we miss a day, it is like unwrapping the thread once. The more times we succeed, the tighter we become bound to the action of planning our day. On the other hand, the more days we miss, the less we are bound to the planning process. How tightly we are bound to the habit of planning our day is determined by how many times we start our days with a plan and how many days we don't.

Missing one day of planning isn't a big deal except that it does make it easier to miss the next day. That missed day can build momentum for missing another day. If we change that momentum by planning the next day, we are back to binding ourselves to the habit. The only thing that will kill our habit development process is if we take a small failure and let it make the whole thing start to unwind.

Over time, the strength of our habits becomes stronger and stronger until they are unbreakable. About thirty years ago, I decided to start every day with a private devotional. I would read a little out of the Bible and pray. My first year, I probably didn't have over eighty of these devotionals. That was a far cry from the 365 I envisioned when I committed to the devotionals but it was a lot better than the zero I had the previous year. The next year, I did better. I probably still just barely broke 100 devotionals. After a few years, I reached the point where I was having a spiritual devotional almost every morning. Now, I have been doing this so long that I just about can't start my day without my spiritual devotional. I don't even think about having it. I just naturally start every day that way. I am tied very tightly to this habit. But it didn't start that way. It took years to develop such a strong habit.

Good Time Management Habits

So what does all this have to do with managing our time? Well, to borrow again from Aristotle, good time management is not an act. It is a habit. How do we follow a process? We develop a habit. How do we implement a system? We develop a habit. We are successful in having a time management system to the extent to which we habitually follow our system. It becomes a habit. The hardest part of implementing a time management system is getting into the habit of following it. Studying processes can be interesting. Designing a system can be fun. But these two things are useless unless we get into the habit of following our system.

So what are some good time management habits worth developing? Here are five habits I find essential to do on a daily basis to manage my time. Your list may be different but this will get you thinking about the habits you need to develop to manage your time.

Define Tasks: I have a running list of the tasks I need to do. When something pops up, I don't just drop what I am doing and switch tasks. I make myself a note and I add it to my master list. Then, I am in the habit of making a list of the most important things I need to accomplish every day. Whenever I add something to my master list, I estimate how long it will take me to accomplish it. That way, I can easily see how many tasks I can tackle on any given day. I don't put any more tasks on my list for the day than I can reasonably complete in that day.

Set Priorities: Once I decide which tasks I want to tackle on any given day, I prioritize them. This habit helps me make sure that, if something gets thrown out of my day, it won't be something I really needed to get done that day. Most days, at least some chaos occurs. Before I even made it into the office this morning, forty-five minutes worth of chaos had hit my life. NYCNO struck and it wasn't even 8:00 AM. It was clear that I wouldn't get everything done that I had placed on my to-do list. Something had to drop off. I didn't panic. I knew what to drop off the list. If I don't get to something, I want it to be the lowest priority task for that day and not the most important one.

Spend Time With People: Here is what I have discovered about life. Success comes more from the people you work with than it comes from the tasks you complete. You can achieve a certain level of success by yourself. However, to really make an impact, you need to team up with others. We will actually discuss this in greater detail when we get to the Team Principle. In the process of handling tasks, it is very easy to overlook the people we need to work with. For that reason, every day I am in the habit of looking at the people who I need to work with and setting aside specific times to meet with them or give them a call. It is also during that time that I return any calls that I have missed or that I was unable to take. I also have certain habits in my life that make sure that I spend time with my family every day.

Managing Contacts: Not only is it a good idea to make time for people. It is also important to spend some time keeping records on the contacts we make. Perhaps the best author in this area is Harvey Mackay. Over and over, he says, "Pale ink is better than the sharpest memory." There are so many advantages to making notes about our meetings and phone calls while they are still fresh in our minds. So I am in the habit of making myself notes every time I talk with someone. I actually do that on the computer. I also have a habit of setting the date to get back with people. When that date rolls around, I make sure that I build the time to contact them into my schedule. Managing the people in our lives is a crucial part of managing our time. Few people do this important time management activity in any systematic way. The only way to make sure that we do keep up with the people who are important in our lives is to develop the habits needed to do so.

Assess the Day: It is also good to take a few minutes each day to reflect on how we spent our time. I like to write down on my calendar page what I actually accomplished every day. Then I can go back and see if I am really spending my time in a way that is helping me achieve my goals. The future may be deceptive but the past never lies. It is good to honestly assess what we are actually accomplishing with our time. That is a lot easier to do if we get into the habit of taking a few minutes each day to write down what we actually accomplished that day.

These are habits I have found that are effective in helping me manage my time. Your life and your activities may be totally different. However, here is a way that we are alike. I will never manage my time effectively unless I develop a few key habits for doing so. Neither will you.

The Benefits Will Come

Many times I have heard it said that we form our habits and then our habits form us. We struggle to form good habits or break bad ones. As they form, little by little, they form our lives into what we want them to be. The problem is that the work of forming habits comes at the front end when we are just getting started but the benefits come in the back end after we have changed our patterns of behavior. Since new habits are fragile, the earlier we are in the process of forming them, the harder it is to keep them alive. If we have a strong habit, it isn't much work to keep it going. It is getting a good habit going that's the hard part.

Unfortunately, while we are struggling to keep these fragile habits alive, it can be hard to see the benefits we are receiving from doing so. Think about what it is like when you first start a new workout routine. Do you feel better? Not after the first few workouts. All those muscles you haven't used in years are reintroducing themselves to you. You actually feel worse. Do you look better? Not much. You started this workout routine so you would look and feel better. In actuality, you feel worse and look about the same. You are struggling to keep this fragile new habit from dying. It is so tempting to quit. Don't!

When we get to the Reality Principle, we will discuss why it is so hard to do something today that will benefit us tomorrow. It is hard to see ourselves in the future benefiting from struggling through the process of forming good habits. But, to get the most out of our time, that is what we need to do. We need to keep telling ourselves that the benefits will come.

We also need to see that we actually are making progress. In the Living the Basics workbook, I present a simple tool that can help us develop good habits or break bad ones. It is the Habits Checkerboard. With this tool, we can watch good habits slowly form before our very eyes. I always have a few good habits I am trying to form and a few bad habits I am trying to break. Forming good habits can be tough but not as tough as living with bad ones.

The Aristotle Challenge:
Resolve to develop the habit of
developing good habits.

21
Discipline

The Discipline Principle:
It Is Impossible to Enjoy a Good Life Without
Self-Discipline

When Hollywood and Madison Avenue try to portray the good life, what do they show? They show wealth, fame, position in society, sensual pleasure, travel, talent, accomplishments, and influence. Those are the colors that are so often blended together to paint a picture of the good life. Very few people get to experience all of these in their time here on Earth.

One person who had them all was famed Russian novelist Leo Tolstoy. He was born into the Russian aristocracy. His family was granted a position among the elite of society by Peter the Great. He was possibly the most talented writer of his whole generation. He traveled the world and enjoyed all the good pleasures, and many of the bad pleasures, that he could find. In his lifetime, his fame spread far and wide. Even after he died, his influence continued. Mahatma Gandhi and Martin Luther King ascribed much of their philosophy of nonviolence to Tolstoy. But it wasn't in fame, fortune, or pleasure that Tolstoy found the good life. It was in self-discipline. Tolstoy said, "It never has been, nor will it ever be possible to enjoy the good life without self-discipline." Tolstoy discovered that you can take all the pleasure, fame, and fortune together and they won't give you nearly what self-discipline will.

In the early years of his life, Tolstoy had it all. In the latter years of his life, Tolstoy gave everything up. He threw aside his wealth and lived the life of a pauper. He gave up all the pleasures life had bestowed upon him. Looking at Tolstoy's life, it is easy to understand why he did what he did. Through much of his life, he didn't handle either his wealth or his position in society very well. They were just tools of selfish indulgence to him. Eventually, he saw the vanity of it all and so he just walked away from everything.

What is Self-Discipline?

I don't think Tolstoy's later life was a picture of self-discipline any more than his younger years were a picture of the good life. He sacrificed but sacrifice by itself is not self-discipline. We are self-disciplined because we want something and we are willing to sacrifice to get it. Though it is true that self-discipline involves sacrifice, we don't give up something just to get rid of it. We sacrifice to get something in return. We sacrifice for a reason and a season.

Self-discipline is not like taking a $100 bill, putting a match to it, and burning it up. It is like taking a $100 bill and investing it somewhere where it will earn a great return. Then, when we do spend it, we get to enjoy much more than $100. We put our money aside not because the money is evil but because we can have so much more of it if we are willing to sacrifice for a season and for a reason. The problem isn't that we seek to enjoy the good things that life has to offer. The problem is that we look for them where they cannot be found. We spend all of our lives trying to find a path to the good life that doesn't go through self-discipline. That path doesn't exist. We can't get to the good life without going through self-discipline.

Tolstoy finally realized that the undisciplined life isn't a primrose path. If we want to struggle, we can do what Tolstoy did early in his life. Never sacrifice. Grab everything we can with no thought of tomorrow. The hardest life to live is one with no self-discipline. But, if we want to live a good life, we probably shouldn't take Tolstoy's approach to sacrifice that he followed later in life. We don't sacrifice with no thought of tomorrow. It is precisely because we want a great tomorrow that we sacrifice today. We live a disciplined life because we want to live the good life.

Managing Our Time Requires Discipline

Brian Tracy wrote the most comprehensive book on self-discipline that has ever been published. In it he said, "There is perhaps no area of your life in which self-discipline is more important than in the way you manage your time." Why is that so? Let's look at some basic reasons why self-discipline is so important to time management.

We Need to Develop Good Habits

As we have seen, good time management involves discovering a process and then developing a system to make that process work. We then develop the habit of following the system. The more we get into the habit of following the system, the more we enjoy the results of the process. It takes both discipline and patience to develop that habit. Planning out my day isn't something I enjoy doing. But I do enjoy looking back and seeing what I have accomplished because I have started my days with a plan. Sure, it may be more fun to just rush into the day with no planning whatsoever. But, if I have disciplined myself over time to develop the habit of planning every day, I will accomplish so much more with my life.

We Need to Do the Boring and Unpleasant Things on Our Plan

The other day, I was speaking to a group about how we must make sure we do the unpleasant things on our to-do list. I brought out my cell phone and pulled up my to-do list. I looked at it and told the group what I saw as I went from item to item. I told them my feelings about each item on the list. "That's no fun, that's boring, that's no fun, I hate doing that one, that's hard, that one's very fun, that's no fun, and I don't like doing that." I only placed one thing on my list in the "fun" category. Most items were neither enjoyable nor unenjoyable. There were a few items I really wish I didn't need to do. I am not whining because my guess is that your typical day isn't that much different from mine. I actually love my job. Still, not everything on my to-do list is fun.

When we plan our day, chances are that we will see some things on our plan that need to be done but which are boring or unpleasant. Everyone's plan is a mixture of things that are fun and things that are not so fun. Here is the interesting thing though. The people who are disciplined to do the things that are not fun end up having fewer and fewer of these unpleasant and boring things to do. How does this happen? Success comes when we do what others won't do. With success comes options. With success, we have more career choices. We are in a position to choose a job that lets us do more of what we want to do. With success comes money. We can then hire people to do the things we don't want to do.

We Need to Stay On Task

I know that one of my biggest time management challenges is to stay on task. Even as I write this sentence, I can think of ten things that are trying to entice me away from my keyboard. However, if I am arranging the bookshelf in my kid's study room, this chapter is not getting written. If I am checking my email for the fifteenth time today, this chapter isn't being written. If I do any of the other things that can so easily catch my attention, this chapter won't get written. The only way this chapter will get written is if I keep my promise to myself and spend this time writing it. That takes discipline.

We Need Energy to Keep Up the Pace

Here is what I have noticed. So often, when someone says, "I don't have the time" he is really saying, "I don't have the energy." His schedule would permit him to do a lot more but he is just too tired. One reason why we need to live a disciplined life is so that we can have the energy needed for a demanding schedule. If we eat right, exercise, and get adequate rest, we can go at a much faster pace without getting tired. That's where discipline comes in.

I was speaking at a conference once. Another one of the speakers said we should eat six different fruits and vegetables every day. I thought, "I'll try that." I discovered a few things. I discovered that I don't like fruits and vegetables nearly as much as I like pizza and ice cream. However, I also discovered that, when I ate fruits and vegetables rather than pizza and ice cream, I have a lot more energy. I discovered one other thing. This one really surprised me. Over time, the fruits and vegetables started tasting better and pizza and ice cream lost much of their appeal. Eventually I started to get all the benefits of eating right and my taste buds quit complaining so much.

We Need to Say "No"

As we have already said, we need to say "no" to a lot of good things if we want to have enough time to say "yes" to the best. But sometimes "no" is such a hard word to say. We don't want to hurt people's feelings. We don't want to say "no" to something that seems fun or interesting. We don't want to say "no" to an opportunity because we are afraid we will never see it again. Elton John wrote a song that said that "Sorry seems to be the hardest word." Not for most people. For most people, "no" is the hardest word to say. It takes a lot of discipline to say it.

Four Keys to Self-Discipline

So how do we live a disciplined life? Part of it comes down to pure willpower. However, we don't want to make things harder on ourselves than they need to be. There are four keys to living a disciplined life. They will help us make the most of the willpower we have.

Resist the Temptation to Be Tempted

When my daughter went off to college, it became so much easier for me to eat right. For twenty years, I spent most of my life working in my home office that was on the other side of the kitchen. Any time I wanted to go into the house, I had to go through the kitchen. I couldn't even go to the bathroom or get a drink of water without walking through the kitchen. Whether or not I am hungry, just being around food makes me want to eat it. I hate to think of how much food I stuffed in my mouth during those journeys through our kitchen. When my daughter moved out, I took over her room as my office. Now I am all the way across the house from the kitchen. Problem solved. I rarely find myself just walking through the kitchen. All those temptations to stuff food in my mouth are gone.

A big key to being self-disciplined is temptation management. Leonardo da Vinci put it this way, "It is easier to resist at the beginning than at the end." Benjamin Franklin said, "It is much easier to suppress a first desire than to satisfy those that follow." When we give into temptation, it usually started long before we think it did. We can be like the kid who got into a fight at school. The school principal asked what happened and he said, "It all started when he hit me back." Actually, it started before then. It is the same way with us when we have a lapse in our self-discipline. It can usually be traced back to something we did before we actually gave into the temptation.

For example, let's say we have decided not to eat dessert until we lose a few pounds. We go out to dinner with some friends. We go to this buffet with a great dessert bar. Is it easier to stick to our commitment from the table or from the dessert bar? If we will resist the temptation to go to the dessert bar, it will be very easy to resist the temptation to get a dessert. But what happens if we decide to go over there "just to see what they have"? Once we get there, the beautifully delicious once-on-the-lips-always-on-the-hips special chocolate delight starts screaming at us. A little chocolate this one time won't hurt anyway. Three bowls later, we haven't done a very good job of being disciplined. The easiest way to overcome temptation is to quiet it while it is still just a whisper.

Decide and Quit Deciding

Good decisions are easier to make the further away we are from having to implement them. The closer we get to actually having to do what we've decided to do, the less attractive the right choice becomes. "I don't want to" starts to crowd out "I should." "I don't want to" wins out and we throw out the good decision and replace it with a bad one. We need to fight to hold on to our good decisions.

The closer we get to implementing our decision, the greater the chances are that we will change our minds. This is how it often goes.

We look to the future. We decide what we should do. Our decision is based on an objective look at what needs to be done. Then the future arrives. Now it is time to implement our decision. We decide to revisit our decision given new information. I am not against changing our decisions based on new information. However, in many cases, the only new information we have is that we really don't want to do what we decided to do. That isn't a good reason to change our mind.

Let's look at a time management example. In the evening, we decide what time we need to get up in the morning. We calculate where we need to be and when we need to be there. We consider the time it will take us to shower, get dressed, eat breakfast, etc. We take into consideration travel time and traffic. Based on all this information, we set the alarm to wake us up at 6:30 AM. That was our decision. It was a good decision. Precisely at 6:30 the next morning our alarm tells us it is time to follow through on the decision we made last night.

Now we can either decide or we can implement. We can either follow through with the decision we made last night or we can start the decision process over again. If we choose to implement rather than to decide, the morning will start out well. However, if we choose to decide what we should do, we will not make nearly as good of a decision as we made the night before. We will decide that 6:30 AM wasn't such a good idea after all. We will hit the snooze button a few times. At the last moment we possibly can, we will jump out of bed and run through the shower barely getting wet. We will skip breakfast. We will run out to the car half-dressed planning to finish the job at red lights along the way. We will risk several moving violations and yet we will still arrive late to our destination. In this case, the time for deciding was the night before. When 6:30 AM comes, it was time for implementing. We needed to decide and then quit deciding.

Use Guilt to Navigate not to Motivate

A key part of living a disciplined life is to know how to deal with failure. None of us will live a perfectly disciplined life. It just isn't possible. New Year's resolutions will fall by the wayside. Days will go unplanned. Chocolate delights will end up enticing us away from our diet. The snooze button will make us revisit earlier decisions. When we fail, we must be careful not to let these failures send us on a guilt trip.

Guilt is great for navigation but terrible for motivation. Though we can't use guilt as the perfect measure of right and wrong, it can often tell us when we need to change our behavior. I recently saw a movie where there was a dialog between two fathers. One was committed to his responsibilities and the other was a deadbeat dad who had never even seen his four year old daughter. The deadbeat dad asked his friend why he felt so guilty. The good father answered, "Because you are guilty." What he was saying to the deadbeat dad is that he needed to listen to his conscience. It was telling him that he needed to man-up to his responsibilities as a father. The guilt here was telling the deadbeat dad what he needed to do. That is useful. Guilt is one thing that helps us navigate through the moral issues we face. It can certainly tell us when we are off-course.

However, once we have decided to change directions and get on the right road, we must not try to use guilt as the force that will keep us on that road. Guilt is a terrible motivator and here is why. Guilt is negative meditation. We think about our failures over and over again. That can be devastating to our self-image. We always act in a way that is consistent with our self-image. We may try to use the pain of guilt to punish ourselves for our failures. We think that if the psychological pain of failure is great enough then we won't fail again. Unfortunately, it doesn't work that way. Guilt does not increase our resolve. It decreases our self-image. A lower self-image will cause us to fail again and again.

So, guilt can help us know when we are not living the disciplined life but it cannot provide the motivation to actually be self-disciplined. That comes from a positive desire for what we will gain from being disciplined.

Practice, Practice, Practice

Carnegie Hall is one of the finest places in the world for a musician to play. There is a joke about Carnegie Hall that is almost as old as the concert hall itself. A tourist looking for directions stops a random stranger and asks, "How do you get to Carnegie Hall?" The stranger happens to be a master violinist. He replies, "Practice, practice, practice." That's also how you get to a disciplined life. You practice discipline. I have recently spent a lot of time studying the neurophysiology of success. One of the most astounding things I have found is that the part of the brain that is responsible for self-discipline actually acts like a muscle. The more we use it, the stronger it gets.

Of course the opposite is true too. The more we live an undisciplined life, the harder it is to be disciplined when we really need to be. If we don't practice discipline, the centers of our brain responsible for discipline begin to atrophy. As we contemplate human travel to other planets, one of the big challenges will be to deal with the effect that weightless years in space have on the body. Because astronauts aren't using their muscles as much, they begin to waste away. That's the way it is with the person who doesn't practice self-discipline. We won't stay disciplined unless we practice discipline on a regular basis.

One of the biggest off-season stories in the NBA one year was how LeBron James lost a lot of weight over the summer. All the pundits were trying to figure out why he did it. Was it because he didn't have enough energy to make it through the previous season? Was it so that he could play more years before he retired? Was he trying to get a quicker step to the basket? Finally, at the first news conference of the year he told them why he lost the weight. He said it had nothing whatsoever to do with his game. He said that every summer, he does something that requires self-discipline. That summer it just happened to be sticking to a diet that caused him to lose the weight. He believed that, if he could stay disciplined in the summer when there are few pressures to do so, he could show up at camp a more disciplined person. Just like LeBron didn't want to lose his physical toughness over the summer, he didn't want to lose his mental toughness either.

If we practice the disciplines of exercising, eating right, keeping our commitments, getting to bed on time, etc., it will be much easier to practice the discipline we need for all the challenging things that go along with managing our time. We need to practice self-discipline so we will be able to practice self-discipline.

The Easy Road

Many times, I have heard it said that the easy road gets harder and the hard road gets easier. That is so true. Just look at people who decide to throw off all discipline and live a "good life." Watch them for a few years and see if their life gets better over time or worse. Also, watch someone who is willing to sacrifice for a reason and for a season. See how their life changes. The real question is whether we want a few drops of enjoyment today or gallons upon gallons of enjoyment for years to come. Which one seems more like a good life?

The Discipline Challenge:
Resolve to develop the discipline to live the
good life.

22
Team

The Team Principle:
To Go Fast, Go Alone. To Go Far, Build A Team.

The story of David and Goliath has fascinated Western civilization for centuries. Often, when an underdog defeats a much stronger opponent in business, sports, or politics, the image of the David and Goliath story is invoked. Little David defeated the Giant Goliath. I recently read that story and I concluded that David wasn't really an underdog. David was actually the one you would have expected to win the battle.

Now bear with me here as I explain. When I recently read the story, here is what I noticed. David was very careful not to let Goliath draw him into close combat. David wanted to stay nimble so he didn't wear any armor or even take a sword into battle. Goliath had all this incredible armor weighing him down. Goliath wasn't just carrying a sword but he was also carrying a spear and a javelin. When Goliath ran towards David, David ran the other way. As long as David used his speed and quickness to stay a safe distance from Goliath, all Goliath's strength and power meant nothing. Had David let Goliath get close enough to use his great size, that would have been the end of little David. Eventually, David used his speed and a long distance weapon, a sling shot, to defeat Goliath.

You may not agree with this assessment and I don't want to change any spiritual significance you may attach to the story. But here is why I bring that up. Under some circumstances, strength wins. Under other circumstances, speed wins. Goliath's size and weapons were made for close-up battles. David's speed and weapons were made for distance battles. David kept the battle at a distance and he won with his speed. In a different set of circumstances, David wouldn't have had a chance against Goliath's size. If you are David, I hope it is in a realm where speed is more important than size. If you are a Goliath, I hope the opposite is the case.

This point is important. People working alone are quick but weak. People working together as a team are slow but powerful. Now which is better? Refer back to David and Goliath. Which is better in battle, to have speed or to have power? It depends on the battle. Is it better to have the power of a team or the speed of working alone? It depends on what you are doing. If you want to go far, go as a team. If you want to go fast, go it alone. Just don't expect to go fast as a team or far by yourself. That is the Team Principle. To go fast, go alone. To go far, build a team. Big teams don't move fast. Lone Rangers don't go far. The number of people you take with you is based on how far and how fast you want to go.

What Do We Want, Power or Speed?

Here is why the Team Principle works. Teams come with two big advantages: diversity and strength. Every person has things they do well and things they don't do well. If we get the right people on our team, the strengths of others can make up for our weaknesses. Also, there is strength in the synergy of a team. Draft horses are powerful horses that were uniquely bred to have great strength for pulling things. Despite popular opinion, the huge Clydesdale horses weren't bred to sell beer. They are draft horses bred to pull things. What is interesting is that one Clydesdale horse can pull about 8,500 lbs. but two Clydesdale horses working together can pull about 20,000 lbs. Do the math. Adding a second Clydesdale more than doubles the amount they can pull. That is synergy and that is why we want to work with a team. Teams can do more than the sum of what all of the individual team members can do by themselves.

However, teams also come with a big overhead. There are two major costs that must be paid when working together with a team: communication and coordination. Any leader will tell you that one of the biggest challenges in leadership is communication. It is such a challenge to see that everyone on the team knows and understands what is going on. The other big challenge is to make sure that the team is working together as a unit rather than as a bunch of individual parts. The best teams are the ones where a lot of different individuals are perfectly melding their unique abilities to operate like one big unit. The worst teams are the ones where the atmosphere is filled with personal agendas and turf wars. The coordination of a team takes a lot of work on the part of the leaders.

So, teams can tackle big jobs but they cannot react and move as quickly as individuals. Teams have a greater diversity of skills and they have more resources to throw at whatever problems come their way. On the other hand, they must also use their precious time and resources to communicate and coordinate. Individuals don't have to do that and so they can move fast. Still there is only so much someone can do by himself or herself.

Four Approaches to Taking a Journey

Knowing that, we can see that there are four approaches to taking the journey. Two of these approaches are made for success. Two of them are wrought with problems.

Going Fast Alone

If we have something small that we want to do, there is no need to engage a whole team. We can just go it alone. Here is where time management skills pay really big dividends. We can get a clear picture of what we need to do and we can head right into action. If we stay focused, we can finish what we need to do quickly.

We must be careful though. Because we can move so fast alone, it is easy to fall in love with speed. When we are accustomed to going fast, slowing down can be a painful experience. It is like moving from a fast computer to a slower one. If we've been working on a slow computer and we move to a faster one, we barely notice the difference. If we've been working on a fast computer and we move to a slower one, the difference is painful. Moving from fast to slow is a hard thing to do. However, we must not get so comfortable with the speed of working alone that we aren't willing to slow down when we need the power of a team.

Going Far With a Team

Teams lumber along at a slow pace. But, think of how much more you can accomplish as a team. If you want to climb a hill, you can do that by yourself. If you are going to climb a big mountain like Everest, you don't go it alone. It takes a whole team. Individuals go on hikes. Teams go on expeditions. If you wanted to climb Mount Everest, it might take years just to pull the team and the resources together to do so. Building a team is slow but we can go so much further with a team.

Trying to Move Fast With a Team

We can't go fast with a team. Stephen Covey said you cannot be efficient with people. You can be effective with people but not efficient. If you try to move fast with a team, it can really be frustrating. Teams slow us down. When we don't have far to go, we don't build a team if speed is our main consideration. On the other hand, there are many times when we may want to take the whole team along even when we don't have far to go. If that is the case, we must not try to go too fast. It will ruin the trip.

When our family gets together, we like to eat a dessert. Who doesn't? Sometimes, my wife Lisa just grabs something from the store. Other times we all go to the store together to get the dessert. Which one do you think is quicker? If Lisa goes and buys the dessert, we have it in no time. When we all go to the store together, it takes forever. Just getting everyone to the car takes time. That is the first major task. In the time it takes to get all of us out to the car, one of us could have gone, purchased the dessert, and been halfway back home. When we get to the store, we cannot decide until everyone is at the dessert section. Once everyone is finally there together, it takes some time finding a dessert that all of us agree on. Then we have to get everyone back to the car.

Sending one person to the store is fast. Taking the whole family to the store is slow. So why do we ever go together? We do so because there are times when it is important to take the team on the trip even if it isn't the most efficient way to get there. Our goal isn't to see how efficiently we can get through the dessert process. Our whole reason for being together is so that we can enjoy each other's company. Going to the store gives us something to do as a family.

Let me give you another example. I am part of a huge committee at my church. There are thirty of us doing the job that could be done by one or two people. But we want as many people as possible to buy into the results, and so we are getting a lot of people involved in the process. It isn't about getting there as fast as we can. It is about getting a lot of people to take the trip.

If we need to move fast, if speed is our utmost consideration, if there is someplace we need to be in a hurry, then don't take the whole team. When speed isn't that important, then taking the team may be alright. Just remember that, when you bring the whole team along, you won't go as fast. Don't try to push a team too fast. You will be frustrated and the team will be annoyed.

Trying to Go Far Alone

There is one major problem with trying to do big things all by ourselves. We will fail. As John Maxwell says, "One is too small of a number for significance." The bigger our dream, the more we need a team. We must not let the fact that we are going fast fool us into thinking that we are going far. If we want to go far, we need a team.

The reason people don't like to go with a team is that all teams have problems. No team will always do things exactly the way we think it should. I remember my pastor saying that he finds it humorous when people say that there are things down at the church that they don't like. He said that there are things down at the church that he doesn't like and he is in charge of running the thing. He says that, at times he doesn't always like the decisions the pastor makes. And he is the pastor. He said that there are times when he will do something and later realize that he should have done something else. He is just like the rest of us. Don't we all look back and, in retrospect, realize we maybe should have done things differently. So why do we expect perfection from our teams which are run by people just like us.

No team is perfect even if we're the ones leading it. Teams are made up of imperfect people like you and me. Still, here is what happens. We join the team giving no thought to the fact that all teams have problems. We start with this idealized view of the team. Inevitably, we start seeing things we don't like. We start thinking less and less about the reasons we joined the team in the first place and we start thinking more and more about the things we don't like about the team.

Eventually, these things we don't like bother us so much that we quit. Just when we could start to make a big impact by being part of a team, we decide to either go it alone or join another team. Well, if we go it alone, we aren't going to do much. Remember, we can't go very far alone. If we join another team, we are going to eventually find problems there too. Either way, if we want to go far, we just have to resign ourselves to the fact that we are going to have to take the trip with people who aren't perfect. Not being able to go far is a high price to pay for not being willing to go along with imperfect people.

Fitting Our Personality Into the Mix

How should we choose whether to build a team or go solo? We should do so based on whether we need to go fast or far. How do we actually make that decision? Too often, it has a lot more to do with whether we prefer working with others or we prefer working alone. Roughly two-thirds of us are people oriented. We don't mind going slow. We just like doing things with other people. About one-third of us are task oriented. We don't care if anyone else is working with us. In fact, we often think others just slow us down and get in the way. We don't want to work with people. We just want to get the job done quickly.

Guess who wants to be part of a team? It's not usually the people who have a long way to go. It is the two-thirds of us who are people oriented. Guess who wants to go it alone? It's not usually those who need to go a short distance quickly. It is the one-third of us who are task oriented. We need to quit making our decision to either go it alone or go with a team based on whether we are task oriented or people oriented. We need to choose based on how far and how fast we need to go. If we are people oriented, at times, we need to pick up the pace by working alone. If we are task oriented, at times we need to just slow down and put up with the pace of a team.

Making Teamwork Actually Work

Sometimes the truth makes you laugh and sometimes it makes you groan. There is a set of charts I show my students that makes them groan. If you were part of group projects in college, you may have seen it too and groaned. It is two pie charts. One says, "What group projects are supposed to teach you." The slices are divided between things such as teamwork, communication skills, and collaboration. The other pie chart is titled "What group projects taught me." Around 95% of that pie chart is one big slice labeled "Trust no one."

As our students painfully discover, working in a group can be tough. Still, we subject our business students to them throughout their whole college experience because they will be working in groups throughout their whole business careers. We give them teamwork because they need to learn how to make teams work. Nowhere is the need to understand teamwork more important than when we are running a meeting, heading up a committee, chairing a board, etc. Meetings can be one big waste of time. On the other hand, seldom can we build a team without meeting together. Meetings have the potential to bring a diversity of ideas and skills together in one place. They are often the most efficient way to coordinate and facilitate communication. When done right, meeting together as a group can gain buy-in from the members of the group. So how can we make sure that the time we spend together as a group is valuable? There are four keys for making group work actually work.

Key #1: Work Outside the Meetings

Some people are under the mistaken impression that a meeting is where work gets done. No, the real work starts when the meeting adjourns. The purpose of the meeting is to communicate what has happened since the last meeting, coordinate what should happen before the next meeting, and gain clarity about the direction the team should be going. If you are running the meeting, make sure people have specific tasks to accomplish between meetings. Then don't feel compelled to call another meeting every time some little thing needs to be done. Meet with members individually or in small groups in place of meeting with the whole group. The smaller the number of people you involve at any moment, the faster the team will move towards its goal. Nothing is worse than being at a meeting where you are not involved in anything that is being discussed.

Key #2: Beware of Hijackers

Do not let anyone hijack the meeting. Beware of the person who might push their agenda forward or monopolize the meeting time. Some people love to talk at meetings. Usually their contribution to the meeting does not justify everyone else's time. On the other hand, some people really don't like to say that much. These people could contribute a lot more but they just sit there saying very little. A good leader knows how to quiet down some people to keep them from taking over the meeting while bringing other members into the conversation. A great leader can do this while not offending anyone.

Key #3: Get Members to Take Ownership

There is an old saying that, "Everyone's business is nobody's business." One of the biggest challenges in teambuilding is to get everyone to take ownership. Ownership is the most powerful behavioral force in the universe. When people take ownership, they are working on their own personal project and they won't let it fail. On the other hand, when people don't take ownership, they do their job and nothing more. If you cannot get people to take ownership of the whole project, at least get them to take ownership of part of the project. But beware. The larger the number of people who are involved, the less people take ownership. That brings us to the last key to making your team work.

Key #4: Keep the Team Size to a Minimum

As the team size grows, whatever we are doing slows down. So we should try to keep the team as small as possible for what needs to be done. The larger the team, the more you will waste people's valuable time and resources. One of the most important concepts in economics is that of opportunity costs. Using a resource for one thing means not using it for something else. The cost of using a resource should be seen in terms of what I am taking it away from. If I have five people on my team and their average hourly wage is $25 per hour, then the cost of the meeting is at least $125 per hour. I say "at least" because we don't pay people $25 to get $25 worth of work. There wouldn't be any profit in that. So the actual cost of the meeting is the sum of what these people could be accomplishing if they weren't sitting in that room for an hour. Meetings can get very expensive very quickly. I am convinced that most meetings do not justify their cost.

We also need to remember that every time we add someone to our team, we add to its complexity. The coordination becomes more difficult. The communication becomes more complex. Just setting up a time where everyone can meet becomes a bigger challenge.

There are two things we can do to help keep our team small. First, do not duplicate skills. We want to bring a diversity of skills to the team. Don't bring in two people from the accounting department if one will do. Don't have two sales managers if they just duplicate each other's skills. Second, choose members rather than ask for volunteers. Then use your selling skills to get them to join you.

Who Would You Choose?

Imagine this. There you are facing a battle. Who do you want fighting for you? Do you want the speed of David or do you want the power of Goliath? Written into the folklore of our culture, we have always assumed that David's are the underdogs and that, if they ever beat Goliath, it is a fluke. What we don't take into consideration is that, even though Goliath's are strong, David's are fast. Do you need the speed to go quickly or do you need the strength to go far? Let that be what determines whether you decide to go with the little David of going it alone or the huge Goliath of building a team.

The Team Challenge:
Resolve to go it alone when speed is needed
and build teams when power is needed.

23
Balance

The Balance Principle:
Balance Comes From Quality Time at Work
and Quantity Time at Home

Powerfully managing our time doesn't just mean doing more. It means doing more of what matters. Achieving significance is more than significant achievements. That happens when we live a life of balance. In the current chapter, we will look at the most challenging balance to achieve in managing our time. That is the balance between family and work. If you have both a career and a family, these are probably the two parts of your life that take up the vast majority of your time. However, the Balance Principle does not just apply to these two parts of life. In almost everything we do, power comes when we maintain balance. Problems come when we don't.

The Need for Balance Is Everywhere

Yesterday, I was eating lunch with the head baseball coach from our university. We were talking about how hard it is for coaches at his level to deal with injuries, especially to pitchers. If a pitcher throws a ball 90 mph., that means some part of his body accelerates to 90 mph. very quickly and then decelerates back down to nothing. This all happens in the time it takes to throw a baseball. He explained to me how trainers deal with this very challenge. They are spending a lot of time working on the muscles that control the slowing down of the arm after the pitch is thrown. Most pitching injuries seem to happen during deceleration. The trick is to train a pitching arm to accelerate to get the ball going and to also train the arm to decelerate after the pitch is thrown. If there isn't a balance between the muscles that accelerate the arm and the ones that decelerate it, then injuries occur.

Later in the evening, I was explaining a bit about photography to a couple of my children. We were talking about how photography is one big balancing act. For a given level of light, the photographer must decide how to balance shutter speed, "film" speed (ISO), and aperture. If you want depth of field, you need a smaller aperture. But that lets in less light so you need either a larger ISO or a slower shutter speed. Unfortunately, with a slower shutter speed, any movement causes the image to blur and the higher the ISO, the more grainy the picture begins to look. To master photography, you have to learn to balance these three so as to get the best depth of field, least grainy look, and least distortion due to blurring.

After these two conversations, I was thinking about how everything always seems to come back to balance. Everywhere we look in life, we see a need for balance. If we are throwing a baseball, we need balance. If we are taking a picture, we need balance. Since balance is everywhere, how could we expect to have power in managing our time if we don't keep things in balance?

As we try to figure out this thing called "life," there is no doubt that one of the biggest challenges we face is to learn how to maintain balance. Nowhere is that more important than in balancing our time between work and our other commitments. We want to achieve as much as we can at work but we don't want to sacrifice the family time along the way. The key is to spend quality time at work and quantity time at home. The workplace spells love "R E S U L T S." Our families spell love "T I M E." Powerful time management is able to both get results and give time. Let's explore how to do both.

Getting Results at Work

At work, if we aren't getting the job done, we have one of three choices. We can redirect our careers, we can spend more time at work, or we can get more done at work with the time we have. There really isn't another alternative.

We Can Redirect Our Careers

There was a boy who hardly ever saw his workaholic father. One day, the boy asked his mother why his father was never home. She explained that he had more work to do at the office than he could get done during the day and so he needed to stay late and finish everything. The boy was trying to understand this from his perspective as a schoolboy. He asked his mother, "Why don't they just put him in a slower class?" There are times when we may need to put ourselves in a slower class. That doesn't mean that we place our career totally on the back burner for the family. We don't want to set this up as an either/or situation. We may just need to pursue our career aspirations at a slower pace so as to fulfill our obligations at home. This can be for a reason and for a season. Slowing down the pace today doesn't mean I cannot speed it back up when the kids get older and the demands at home get fewer.

We Can Spend More Time at Work

Sometimes we really do need to take time away from the family to make sure our economic future is bright. This gets back to that phrase we have seen so often in this book. We may need to make this sacrifice if it is for a reason and for a season.

Just today I had a conversation with a student who was determined to get his education over as soon as possible. He said that he remembered when he was young, his father went to graduate school. The time he was able to spend with his father almost disappeared. Fortunately, the father graduated, moved on to a better job, and the time they spent together came back. My student understood that the need for an education is just a reality of today's work world. He also understood that if he didn't finish his education before he started his family, it was very likely that the family would have to make sacrifices. So he didn't want to go there.

Others have no choice. They have hit the ceiling in their careers for the level of education they have. If the family can just sacrifice for a short time, they will benefit in many ways for years to come. This is one of those examples where it is worth the sacrifice if the sacrifice is for a reason and for a season.

There are many times in our careers when we just need to spend more time at work. While we are in the learning or growing stages of our career, we need to invest more hours. For some, that may mean working long hours at something that will increase our value to the marketplace as we get better. For some, that may mean starting a part-time business or taking a second job if either of these can eventually replace the current source of income.

We may also work in a profession that has a "harvest time." For our careers, this is the high value time we spoke about earlier in the book. How much time do farmers spend in the fields during harvest time? They spend however much time it takes to get the crops in. It would be silly for them to "clock out" at 5:00 and let the fruits of their labor die in the field. They know that there is a season when they will just need to work harder and longer. That doesn't just apply to farmers. Many professions have greater requirements at certain times of the year. Accountants call it tax season. Retailers call it Christmas shopping. For me and what I do, it happens around final exams. But remember, eventually the harvest is in the barn, the tax forms are filed, the Christmas buying season is over, and final grades are turned in. If we take time away from our families during the harvest, we need to be sure to give it back when things slow down.

Just as there are many good reasons to sacrifice family time for work, there are also a few terrible reasons to do so. Some people cannot control their spending habits and so they simply add more hours to the work week. At the end of the month, the money is gone, the kids have been ignored, and the person is no closer to being able to get their life in balance than they were a month earlier. We should avoid working long hours and ignoring the family if it is just to feed a never-ending craving for more and more stuff.

We also don't want to ignore the family because we enjoy being at work more than we like being at home. Jack Welch was a very shrewd businessman. He said that, when he was a plant manager, he wanted to make the factory a place where his managers wanted to spend their Saturdays. His goal was to make it more fun than their homes. If he succeeded, he could easily get six days of work from his managers rather than five.

What I am about to say can be quite sensitive so I want to be careful. But it still needs to be said. What I am about to say is only true sometimes so take it or leave it at your own discretion. Still, this is the undeniable truth. Many people who are supposed "workaholics" are no such things. They are just choosing the more enjoyable of two alternatives. Work is more fun than home and so they expand the time they spend at work so they have to spend less time at home. If you have a "workaholic" spouse, make it hard on him or her but don't do it through nagging or by making him or her feel guilty. Do so by making home more fun than work. If they need to work on Saturday, make them feel like it is a sacrifice not an escape. Don't make them say, "I need to work this Saturday" so they won't have to say, "I really don't want to paint the den."

So, if we have a thriving career, it is totally unrealistic to think that we should never let work take time away from our family. It can and it should if it is for a season and for a reason. We just need to make sure that it doesn't turn into a permanent lifestyle. We also need to make sure that we aren't using work as an excuse to escape our family obligations.

We Can Do More With the Same Amount of Time

This brings me to the third option for getting greater results at work. We can focus on spending the same amount of time at work but getting more done. We do that by focusing on quality time at work. Time standing around the water fountain telling jokes is not quality time. Time spent surfing the net is not quality time. Time spent alphabetizing your business cards is not quality time. Time spent with any of the thousands of distractions that show up every day at every office, shop, and factory on the planet is not quality time.

So what is quality time? *Quality time is any time we spend relentlessly focused on the results for which the marketplace is paying us.* If you are a salesperson, quality time is the time you spend selling. If you are a manager, quality time is the time you spend managing. If you are a leader, quality time is the time you spend leading. Nothing else counts.

Unless the marketplace values our jokes, then standing around the water fountain telling them does not qualify as quality time. Unless the marketplace greatly values our knowledge of last night's box scores, then quality time is not reading the sports section at work or rehashing last night's game in the hall. Unless the marketplace values our social networking, then time spent on Facebook at work does not count as quality time. Quality time is doing whatever the person or organization that buys our time values. Even then, it only counts if we are doing it in the most effective and efficient way possible. Here is the big challenge for work--to actually get work done at work. There are so many distractions in the workplace. We must ignore everything that would take ourselves away from what we are actually paid to do.

Spending Time at Home

It became popular a number of years ago to excuse time spent away from the family by saying, "Well, I don't have quantity time so I spend quality time." Here is the problem with that. Quality time at home only comes from quantity time. You cannot walk into your kids room, plop yourself down on the end of their bed and say, "I've got five minutes. How about some quality time?" It doesn't work that way. Quality time comes in special moments when two or more people happen to be together.

As I mentioned earlier, I like to teach my college students through country and western songs. The music video I always show to my students when I go over the Balance Principle is one by Trace Adkins. It is called *Just Fishin'* and it is about a father taking his daughter to the lake. The father talks about all the incredible ways they are building their relationship. The daughter thinks they are just fishing. The whole song is about all the things that happen on their fishing trip but it ends with the father saying, "This isn't about fishing."

Trace Adkins certainly got that right. When it comes to our families, quality time is quantity time spent doing something together. What we are doing is not nearly as important as the fact that we are together.

However, there are some things we can do to ensure that our families will get quality time.

Fight the Distractions

Just being under the same roof with other people doesn't mean we are spending time together. Some of the loneliest places I have ever been have been in the middle of a crowd. Here is the challenge. We need to structure our time at home so that we actually spend it with our family. That's a huge challenge because there are so many distractions at home that keep us from being together.

A few generations ago, if you were at home, there wasn't a lot to do but hang out with whoever happened to be there with you. The door through which others could enter our house was small. Then came the telephone and radio. People could join us at home and not even be there. The door to the house got larger. Then came television. The door got even larger. Now, the door of the house is huge. Hundreds or even thousands of people can come in through it every day. With today's technology, think of all the musicians who sing to us, actors who entertain us, reporters who inform us, virtual villains who fight us, e-friends who talk with us, advertisers who pitch to us, politicians who campaign to us... Also, think of all the ways they come into our house. There is the radio, television, gaming system, computer, internet...

If we fight hard to make sure we are spending quantity time at home, let's make sure we are spending a lot of it with our families. Don't be the father who knows all the important information that is happening in Washington, Afghanistan, and South Africa but doesn't know what is happening in his son's school room. Don't be the mother who can tell you all the things that are going on in her favorite TV series but cannot tell you what is going on in her daughter's life. Don't be so well connected to your virtual social network that you are unplugged from the person you pledged your life to.

Make Family Time Hard Time

Remember how hard time crowds out soft time. So what kind of time does our family get? Is it all soft time? If so, we may want to make some of the time we spend with our family substantially harder. Many families make dinner time sacred. Everyone gets together for dinner and no distractions are allowed. The TV and music go off. If the phone rings, it just rings. No person on the other end of the phone line is as important as the people at the table. Some families make some other time of the day or week hard time. For our family, it was our nightly spiritual devotion. No one went to bed until we all got together for it. Family vacations are great for creating hard time. Mini-vacations or weekly rituals like date night or family night work too. The key is to find some family time that is sacred and fight for it with everything we have.

Make the Most of Time in the Car

Cars are wonderful things. They are probably my favorite place to spend time with people. Why? As long as I turn off all the distractions like the radio, we don't have any choice but to be together. I always jump at the chance for taxi duty. There is no better time to get into my wife or kids' life than to go somewhere in the car together. It is amazing how quickly meaningful conversation fills the void created when two people are driving down the road in a car together with no distractions.

Key In On Others' Interests

A classic Dale Carnegie quote is, "To be interesting, be interested." He explained that, "You can make more friends in two months by becoming interested in other people than you can in two years by trying to get other people interested in you." Try that with your spouse or your kids. Don't try to get them excited about what interests you. Show a sincere interest in what they care about. Or, better yet, merge the two together. One husband loved watching sports. His wife didn't like seeing a bunch of sweaty guys running around bumping into each other. But she loved finding out interesting things about people. He started learning about the personal lives of the people on the field. When the wife came through the den, he wouldn't comment on touchdowns or field goals. He would start telling his wife interesting stories about the coaches and players. Suddenly, these sweaty guys became humans with interesting lives. She started spending a lot of time with him watching what all her new found friends were doing.

Create a Void and Then Let Your Family Fill It

The Principle of the Excluded Alternative says that if we say yes to something, we are saying no to something else. That works in reverse. If we say no to something, we will fill the void with something else. Many of the most tight-knit families have gotten there by saying no to a lot of the distractions. They limit television time. Everyone in the family doesn't have their own computer with internet connection. Video games aren't allowed to be played 24/7. They don't totally eliminate these from their lives. They just limit them. They don't take their kids back to 1850. Maybe just 1965.

Focus On the Home and Not the House

A perfect house comes at a very high price. It takes a lot of time and money. Unless we have an abundance of both, we need to count the costs and decide if it is really worth it. The way I have it figured, when I die, there probably will be dirty dishes in the sink and I bet they won't even be mentioned in my eulogy. Don't get me wrong. This too is about balance. We need to be good stewards over the material things we possess. But if we are spending all our time and energy keeping everything spotless and in perfect order, we will have a wonderful house but not a wonderful home. Clean as you must but don't let it rob the family of all your time with them. Don't think that your house needs to look like that picture-perfect one you see on TV.

What Really Matters

We don't focus on our family to the exclusion of everything else in the world. It is called the "Balance" Principle. Why is family such an important part of that balance? Because, in the end, that is all we have. One of these days, we will be saying goodbye to this world. It will be our last moments with everyone and everything here on Earth. The people attending to us won't say, "Bring in the video game so he can make it to one last level." They won't call in our boss or co-workers. They won't call for the television set so we can watch one final episode of our favorite program. They won't give us a final report on how our favorite team is doing. They won't bring us a newspaper so we can catch up on the latest news out of Washington.

What the people attending to us will do is they will call in our family. We all know that, at that moment, our family is what really matters. Doesn't it make sense that we would also see how much they really matter between now and then? Through my writing, speaking, and teaching, I have been given the opportunity to impact a lot of people. But here is what I know. In the end, I know that the real impact I make in this world will be the impact I make on my wonderful wife and my terrific four children. I can only succeed in having that impact if I apply the Balance Principle, making sure that I focus on quality time at work and quantity time at home.

The Balance Challenge:
Resolve to achieve significance through
maintaining balance.

24
Reality

The Reality Principle:
The Future Is More Real Than It Appears

The very first time basic was the Perception Principle, which states that it is later than you think. We must grasp just how precious time is or else we will treat time like a trinket and not a treasure. Without understanding the value of time, we will never get a vision for what we can do with it.

Now we come to the last of the time basics. Here too we look at something we must grasp. To have power over today, I must understand that the person in my future really is me. It is hard to grasp that the things I do today really will affect me, especially the further in the future the consequences are. Returning to our definition of time management, our time is managed to the extent to which what I am doing today is consistent with where I want to be in the future. That is why we really do need to clearly see and feel our future.

The most powerful thing we can do to manage our time is this. We need to so connect with the future that we treat our future self with the same concern as we treat ourselves in the present. The more we can experience the joys and feel the pains of our future self, the more power we will have to manage our time today. Unfortunately, we tend to feel very little compassion for our future self. At times, we will abuse our future self for the smallest of pleasures in the present.

Who Is That Future Self?

There is something about our brains that makes it difficult for us to connect with our future. An interesting study was done by a group of neurological psychologists. They wanted to see how the brain processes our vision of other people. They wired subjects up so they could measure which parts of the brain were most active when they were thinking about other people. Once they mapped out the part of the brain that we use to think about other people, they wondered if we use the same part of the brain when we thought about ourselves. What they found out is that we don't. We use a totally different part of our brain to think about ourselves than we do to think about others. So, there appears to be a "self" part of the brain and there appears to be an "others" part of the brain.

The psychologist then decided to look at one more thing. They decided to see which part of the brain we use when we think about ourselves in the future. That is when their research got very interesting. They found that when we think about ourselves in the future, our brain treats it as though we are thinking about someone else. It is that "others" part of the brain which we use to think about ourselves in the future. What this means is that I don't really see the future me as me. I see it as someone else.

When I heard about that study, it explained a lot of things for me. For example, have you ever been perplexed as to why young people start smoking knowing that it will kill them? I see a young person puffing on a cigarette and I just shake my head and wonder why. Do these people have a death wish? Not at all. If a criminal showed up with a gun and pointed it at them, they would do almost anything to keep him from pulling the trigger. But at the same time they will sit there and suck on a cigarette that they know is likely to kill them.

The problem is that the brain isn't thinking that it's going to kill them. Their brain is thinking that smoking is going to kill some "other" poor unfortunate soul who lives in the future. Their brains are not even using the same brain cells to think about themselves as they are to think about the person who is going to die from the smoking. If their brains would tell them that they were actually killing themselves, their survival instincts would likely kick in and the cigarettes would be thrown out. However since their brain thinks it is some "other" person in the future who is going to have to live and die with the consequences of their smoking, they aren't particularly concerned. They don't do anything to save themselves, because they see that future self as someone else.

Seeing Our Future Self

This unique way that our brain works creates a huge problem for those of us wishing to manage our time. Here is the problem that this creates for our brains. Managing our time is all about doing things today so that we will be where we want to be in the future. The problem is that seeing the future can be difficult. Still we must see ourselves in the future in order to know what we should be doing with our time today. The problem of seeing ourselves in the future was illustrated by something that happened to speaker and author Jack Canfield.

He was giving a speech on living our dreams and a woman came up to him afterwards. She said she wanted to become a nurse but it really wasn't practical. He asked her why not. She said that it takes five years to become the kind of nurse she would like to be. She told him that, since she was already 38 years old, she would be 43 years old in five years if she went to nursing school. He asked her, "How old will you be in five years if you don't go to nursing school?"

In five years, the woman was going to be 43 years old. In truth, that 43 year old woman actually was going to be her. If she managed the next five years right, she would be a 43 year old woman doing exactly what she loved every day. If not, she would be a 43 year old woman looking at many years of working at a job she didn't enjoy. She didn't have a choice about whether or not she would be that 43 year old person in the future. But she had a huge choice about what that 43 year old version of herself would be doing. That choice would be made based on what she did with the next five years of her life.

Where is There?

To properly manage today, we need to see tomorrow. To drive this point home one day, I went into class and asked my students a question. I told them that I was going to a wedding over the weekend and I needed to know the best way to get there. So I asked them for directions but I didn't tell them where the wedding was. A student then asked the logical question. "Where is the wedding going be?"

I told him to quit changing the subject. I just needed to know how to get to the wedding. The students gave me a perplexed look as I again asked for directions. I stood there silently waiting until someone spoke up. "Are you going to tell us where the wedding is?"

I responded, "There you go, changing the subject again. I just want to know how to get there."

Then a student said, "Dr. Muncy, we cannot tell you how to get there unless you tell us where there is."

"Exactly," I replied. "Nobody can tell you how to get to there unless you know where there is." We want to learn about time management. At its very nature, time management is about getting us to some place in the future. But if we don't know what that place is, then how can we know how to get there?

We are all on our way to somewhere. It is important that we gain a clear perspective of where the road we are on is taking us. At times that is very hard to get. We are so focused on the road that we can't see the destination.

The Right Question Is Easier to Answer

A little south of where I live is a town called Lake City, FL. That is where Interstates 10 and 75 intersect. Now if you are sitting in Lake City, it is difficult to say which of these two is a better Interstate. Interstate 75 may be better because it is three lanes each way. Interstate 10 is only two lanes. Also, because Interstate 10 runs east-west, you can sometimes have the sun in your eyes. On the other hand, Interstate 75 is the main pathway into Florida from the whole Midwest making it crowded with trucks and elderly drivers. Also, if you are not careful, Interstate 75 can dump you onto a toll road. Then there are the rest stops. I think Interstate 75 has better rest stops. So which is the better interstate? That is a difficult question to answer.

Actually, it is only a difficult question because I am looking at the wrong things when I am trying to answer it. We don't sit there looking at two interstates and decide which one to take based on the things I just listed. There is really only one question we need to ask to determine which interstate is better. Where do I want to go? If I want to go to Atlanta, then Interstate 75 is better. If I want to go to Jacksonville, then Interstate 10 is better. Forget looking at the number of lanes, trucks, or elderly drivers. Forget worrying about the direction of the sun or the number of rest stops. All of these things don't matter. I can enjoy Interstate 10 from the Atlantic to the Pacific Ocean, but if I want to go to Atlanta, I chose the wrong interstate.

If I am sitting in Lake City and I need to decide which interstate to take, it is a simple decision. I only need to ask one question. Where do I want to go? Until I answer that question, it is tough to figure out which one is better. As obvious as that seems when we are managing our trips, we often miss that point when we are managing our time. We are sitting there looking at all we have to do and trying to decide what we should do next. What do I want to do? What are people telling me I should do? What would I feel guilty if I didn't do? What seems to be the next logical thing to do? What do I typically do?

These are all interesting questions but they miss the key question. I am looking at various roads I could take. Where do they lead? Is that anywhere I would want to be? At some point in the future, I will be somewhere. It won't be some other guy sitting wherever the road leads. It will be me. Five years from now, will I be happy with the choices I have made with my time? Or will I be sitting there wondering why I always seem to end up arriving somewhere and wishing I were somewhere else?

Seeing a Little Further Ahead

Brian Tracy says that all good time management is based on what he calls "back from the future" thinking. We start by looking at where we want to be at some point in the future and we start working backwards to today. We decide what we have to do every step along the way to get from where we are to where we see ourselves in the future. Often the challenge is actually seeing the future. The better we see the future, the better we will be able to manage our time.

Back in my sophomore year in high school, I really enjoyed playing chess with some of my friends. The reason I enjoyed it was that I always won. I could always beat them because I would look at the chess board and I wouldn't just see it as it was. I could see it as it was about one move in the future. They could only see the board as it was. After the school year ended, I spent my whole summer working on my basketball game and they spent their whole summer working on their chess game. By the end of the summer I could still see one step ahead in chess but now my friends could see two steps ahead. I didn't enjoy chess nearly as much my junior year as I did my sophomore year. They could see further ahead than me and they could beat me every time. In chess, you need to be able to see the board as it can be not just as it is. Whoever can see the furthest ahead will win every time.

That doesn't just apply to chess. That applies to life. The further we can see ahead in life, the better our lives will be. This was so well illustrated by the classic marshmallow study in psychology. Stanford psychologist Walter Mischel took some young kids and put them in a room with a marshmallow sitting on the desk. They were told that they could eat that marshmallow now, or, if they would wait, they could have two marshmallows in just a few minutes. The researcher would step out of the room for a little bit. If the marshmallow was still sitting on the desk when he got back, then the kid would get a second marshmallow and he or she could eat both of them then.

Mischel found that there were two types of kids. One-marshmallow kids gobbled theirs down as soon as the researcher stepped out of the room. Two-marshmallow kids sat there patiently staring at this one delicious marshmallow waiting for the second one to arrive. So what? Who cares if kids eat one marshmallow or two? All Professor Mischel did was identify which kids settled for one and which kids waited for two.

The interesting part of his study didn't come until several years later. Mischel looked these kids up to see how they turned out. He wanted to know if there were any differences between the lives of the one-marshmallow kids who didn't wait and the two-marshmallow kids who did. What he discovered was astounding. There were huge differences between these two groups of kids. On almost every dimension he studied, the two-marshmallow kids achieve greater success than the one-marshmallow kids. They did better in school. They were healthier.

Over the next few decades, this experiment was tried over and over. Researchers used different things to entice the kids but they always got the same results. Whether they used cookies or pretzels, they would always find the same thing. The kids who were willing to give up a little in the present to receive a little more in the future were the ones who went on to accomplish the greater things in life.

The meaning of this classic marshmallow experiment has been debated for years. There are many different interpretations as to why the one-marshmallow kids never could quite do as well as the two-marshmallow kids. Let me give you the way I see it. Some people seem to do a better job of seeing that person in the future as themselves. So, in order to make themselves happy, they are willing to do certain things now knowing that sometime in the future they will be happier for doing so.

On the other hand, some people simply haven't made that connection. Their brains seem to be fooling them into thinking that sacrificing for the future means nothing. They never make the "what's in it for me" connection. Instead, they feel like the sacrifice is going to benefit some person that is rattling in that "other" side of the brain. It might be interesting to see what would happen if those neurological researchers handed out marshmallows before they wired people up to their equipment. They might find out that those who scarf down the first marshmallow have different brains than those who patiently wait for a second marshmallow to arrive.

Time Horizon

The concept we're talking about here is that of *time horizon*. Some people walk through life with a long time horizon. They have the ability to make decisions today based on what they want to happen tomorrow. It is just natural for them to think about themselves at some point in the future. For them, they really can see themselves doing certain things right now and, as a result, having exactly what they want in the future.

In a sense, they are willing to do things that will make that future self happy, fulfilled, and successful. They are the ones who get to eat two marshmallows rather than having to settle for one.

Then there are people who walk through life with a short time horizon. They aren't bad people. In fact, they may be some of the nicest people you'll ever meet. They just face a problem. When they look into the future, they don't see themselves. They see someone else. So they see the choice as being between happiness for me today and happiness for somebody I don't even know in the future. That's an easy choice to make. I'll go ahead and make myself happy today. Such people feel perfectly comfortable ignoring that person in the future. Unfortunately for them, when the future arrives (as it always does) they haven't done much to prepare for it. That person in their past has eaten their marshmallow and they are left wondering why so many people they know get to eat two marshmallows.

Fixing Our Eyes on the Future

Once we have developed this clear picture of the future, we have the basics of building our time management system. We will be managing our time to the extent to which our current activities are making that picture a reality. It may be easy for my brain to trick me into thinking that that person in the future isn't really me. I must keep convincing myself that it is.

I recently heard someone speak about what life was like growing up on a dairy farm in Pennsylvania. As an early teen, he was so excited when his dad finally gave him the keys to the tractor. The plan was for the son to drive the tractor cutting the hay while his father followed him in another tractor bailing it. One row across the field and the father was really frustrated. For this to work right, the son had to learn how to drive that tractor in a straight line. Instead, he was all over the field.

The father took this young man aside and gave him a quick lesson on how to drive a tractor in a straight line. He said that the problem that you have is that you're only looking at where you are and you're so distracted with everything that's going on around you. He gave his son the following instructions. When you start going across the field pick out some object that is at the other side of the field. It could be a fence post, a tree, a telephone pole, or even a distant building. The father then instructed the kid to drive straight towards his object until he made it across the field. As long as he kept that object in his sights, he would take the most direct path to it. That path would be a straight line.

That is exactly what we need to do in order to manage our time. We don't fix our eyes on some physical object. Rather we fix our eyes on a future vision of ourselves and we drive our lives straight towards it. In doing so, we will be taking the quickest and most direct path towards the future that we want. The quicker we have arrived at the future we want, the better we have managed our time.

The reason why so many people find it so difficult to manage their time is that they have never found anything to fix their eyes on. That is why they're drifting to the right and drifting to the left rather than moving straight ahead. Every trip to the right or left takes them off the path to the future they would want. For them, time management will begin when they finally figure out what they want to focus on and start moving in a straight line towards it.

Finding What Matters Most

Johann Wolfgang von Goethe said that "Things which matter most must never be at the mercy of things which matter least." The trick is trying to figure out what matters most and what matters least. If today is all we can see, then what matters most is what life is like today. We will waste much of our time on whatever seems best for the moment. If that means saying "yes" because I don't want to say "no" then I will do that. If that means spending endless hours on television, video games, or the internet, I will do that. When there is no tomorrow, what matters most is always what seems best today.

But we all know that there is a tomorrow. At least certain parts of our brains may know that. Other parts are not so sure. We must be able to develop a vision of what will matter most in the long run and not just what matters most today. What actually matters most today is that I realize that the future is on its way. It isn't some abstract idea to be faced by some unknown person. That person I see in the future really is me. The future is more real than I imagine it to be and it will come quicker than I think it will. What matters most is how I manage my time so I won't be disappointed when the future arrives.

The Reality Challenge:
Resolve to make the person I will be in the
future happy with the choices I make today.

Conclusion

Living the Basics

We started this book with the Perception Principle and ended it with the Reality Principle. We spent the pages in between making a journey from Perception to Reality. Our goal now is to apply what we have learned so as to make our perception of the life we want a reality.

You may have read many of these basics and thought, "I know that" or "that makes sense." I have read many personal development books. The ones that have impacted me the most were the ones that gave me that exact reaction. Either I already knew what they were saying or I found what they were saying easy to understand. Before you opened this book, you probably knew most of these basics at some level. The ones you didn't know, you probably had no problem understanding.

So if these basics are so easy to know and understand, why have we dedicated over two hundred pages to discussing them? We did so because life doesn't reward us for what we know. Life doesn't reward us for what we understand. Life rewards us for what we actually do. Life responds to our actions not our thoughts. Certainly our thoughts are extremely important. They guide what we do. Still, if we don't do the right things, it doesn't matter what we know.

The Ultimate Value of the Basics

So, in the end, the ultimate value you will receive from this book is not in how it makes you think about time. The ultimate value will be in what you do with these basics. How will they change what you actually do with your time?

Will you treat time as a treasure or a trinket? Will you start saying yes by decision rather than by default? Will different things make it into your twenty-four hour box? Will you spend your high value time doing high value things? Will you defeat the distractions that take you away from the right path? Will you fight back against chaos? Will you plan? Will you find a success process for managing your time and turn it into a time management system? Will you be careful about the hard time commitments you make? Will you keep your work hours at a reasonable level and focus on efficiency? Will you procrastinate on low value things and not on high value things? Will you gain momentum and fight things that drain momentum? Will you use clarity to gain speed? Will you not slow down to achieve a sense of order and comfort? Will you choose important activities over busyness? Will you respond to the important rather than react to the urgent? Will you settle for good enough when the job doesn't justify the time needed for perfection? Will you settle for nothing but the best when the job does require perfection? Will you work on developing your skills, habits, and self-discipline? Will you take the time to build a team when the job is big? Will you go it alone when you need to do something quickly? Will you spend quality time at work and quantity time at home? Will you make your choices such that, in a few years, you will be glad you made them?

On some days you probably will and on other days you probably won't. I certainly can't always answer yes to all these questions. But, to paraphrase the Apostle Paul, this is the one thing I do. I forget the mistakes that are behind me and I strive to the goal that is before me. I want to make the most of my time because I believe that one day, I will be held accountable for how I spent my time on this earth.

Mastering the Basics

How can we get better at following the basics? Here are a few ideas I have discovered from many years of teaching the Time Basics.

Read Them Again

When I read a book that impacts my life, I never just read it once. I read it over and over. There are a few books that I know almost every word in them by heart. Sometimes I read a book and I realize that I need to master what it presents. So I buy the audiobook. I put it in my car and I listen to it over and over. While I am driving around, I pound the ideas deeper and deeper into my brain. If you think the time basics can improve your life, don't let this be the last time you go through them. Read or listen to them over and over.

Commit Them To Memory

Another thing that you could do is commit the basics to memory. I have my students in my time management class memorize the basics. Five times during the semester, they must give them back to me verbatim on a quiz. They say that having these basics stuffed in their heads has often changed their behavior. For example, they may be about to procrastinate on something when a voice inside their head asks, "Will this I'll do it tomorrow attitude yield I should have done it yesterday results?" They may be wasting too much time on some no-value job when that voice says, "Nothing is as useless as doing well that which should not be done at all." They might be about to say yes because they don't want to say no when the voice in their head reminds them, "To say yes to something is to say no to something else." It can be very useful if you can take the twenty-four basics and move them out of this book and into your head. We have resources on our website *timebasics.com* that can help you do that.

Build on Them

These basics provide the foundation for managing our time. However, you don't want to build a foundation and never build the house. Nobody ever builds their dream foundation. They build their dream house. A huge part of building a dream house is to make sure it has a solid foundation. Without the right foundation, the house will never survive. But we wouldn't want to build a foundation for the house of our dreams and then spend our lives living on the concrete slab. How do you build on the basics? I would suggest that you continue studying time management. There are a lot of great books out there on time management. Different books will fill different rolls as you learn to get the most out of your twenty-four hours. Also, as mentioned earlier, we have a workbook that accompanies Time Basics. It is called Living the Basics and is available at timebasics.com. Don't fall victim to the Procrastination Principle. Hop on the internet now and order it. Then work through the exercises in the workbook. They will help you bring the basics down to where you live your life on a daily basis.

What the Basics Do for Us

Let me end this book with a story about a student I had named Tiffany. She graduated with her business degree and got a great paying job. That wasn't for her and so she started her own business. Her business was such a huge success that we brought her back to campus to give a special lecture to all our business students. She was asked which class had the biggest impact on her success as a businesswoman. Without hesitation she said it was my class on time management. Throughout her whole speech, she kept referring to how much my time management class helped her.

I know there were a lot of classes she took that were crucial to her success as a business person. She took accounting classes. Obviously she needed them to help her keep an eye on the numbers. She took finance courses, that I am sure helped her secure the capital for her company. Undoubtedly, she learned a lot about marketing without which she never would have gotten her company off the ground. And I am sure she learned some very useful things in her management classes that helped her run the company. Yet she kept mentioning the time management class over and over.

I couldn't imagine that my time management class was more valuable than any of these other classes. Then I realized what she was saying. All the other classes taught her the things she needed to do. My class is what made sure she actually did them. Knowing accounting only matters if you make time to look at the books. Knowing finance only matters if you make time to raise the money. Knowing marketing only matters if you make time to market and sell. Knowing management only matters if you actually take the time to manage. And when you are starting a business, it can be a real challenge to make time for all of these.

My class did nothing to teach her how to build her business. Here is what it did. It taught her how to make the time to do all the things she learned in her other classes. All of the knowledge in the world is useless if you never learn how to make the time to apply it. That relates to starting a business but it also relates to all of our lives. Whether we are managing a business, a family, our health, a charity, or just a fun trip to the mountains, we need to make time for the things that will allow us to do them right. That is why we need to know the time basics. They don't just help us manage our time. They give us the time to manage everything else.